THE SERMONS OF A
COUNTRY PREACHER

THE SERMONS OF A
COUNTRY
PREACHER

RAY HYDEN

XULON PRESS

Xulon Press
2301 Lucien Way #415
Maitland, FL 32751
407.339.4217
www.xulonpress.com

Unless otherwise indicated, Scripture quotations taken from the Contemporary English Version (CEV). Copyright © 1995 American Bible Society. Used by permission. All rights reserved.

Scripture quotations taken from the King James Version (KJV) – public domain.

Scripture quotations taken from the New American Standard Bible (NASB). Copyright © 1960, 1962, 1963, 1968, 1971, 1972, 1973, 1975, 1977, 1995 by The Lockman Foundation. Used by permission. All rights reserved.

Scripture quotations taken from the New King James Version (NKJV). Copyright © 1982 by Thomas Nelson, Inc. Used by permission. All rights reserved.

Printed in the United States of America.

ISBN-13: 978-1-49844-710-2

TABLE OF CONTENTS

DEDICATION

First, to my Lord and Savior Jesus Christ, who loves us so much that He voluntarily gave his life on a Roman cross for our sins, is this book sincerely dedicated. And then to Dr. Billy Graham, under whose preaching I first realized that there really is a God, that He really does love me, and that He has a wonderful purpose and plan for my life, I will always remain eternally grateful.

Over the past 48 years there have been so many wonderful churches and pastors who have given me opportunity to serve Christ that I would be amiss to try and name them all. To all the congregations, where I have been privileged to be their Pastor, I will always be thankful and appreciative of the opportunities you gave me to preach God's word.

To my loving and beautiful wife, Beverly, is this book sincerely dedicated. To all her wonderful years as a pastor's wife and the many areas she has served I will always be appreciative and thankful. I could not have done it without her love, help and support. To my Christian children, Toby and Tammy, of whom I not only love with all my heart but am extremely proud of, to their wonderful Christian spouses Amy & Steve, who love my children beyond measure, this book is also sincerely dedicated.

To my siblings, Montie, Sandi, and Sherry, who have gone through so much in life, I will always love and appreciate each one of you. Also, to their spouses who are all such wonderful people and to my wonderful nieces and nephews whom I love with all my heart is this book sincerely dedicated.

And last but certainly not least, to my wonderful, beautiful, adorable, granddaughter, Elliana Grace (Ellie), may this book be a source of strength and encouragement to you as you look back on your Papa's life of ministry and service. Live your life for Christ sweetheart and serve Him wherever this life takes you.

ACKNOWLEDGEMENTS

This book of sermons is made possible through the many years of wonderful Bible study which I have so diligently enjoyed, to the wonderful commentaries which I have studied, and to the Godly men which I have either listened to or read their works.

As I began my public ministry I had no intention or goal of writing a book. God gifted me with the ability to type 100 wpm many years ago and throughout my lifetime typing has given me so many wonderful opportunities. Typing, to me, has always been fun. Therefore, it just seemed natural to type all my sermons. Upon retiring and going back into teaching God's word, the Lord laid on my heart to put in print many of the sermons that I've preached. Albeit, there is no way to put years of sermons into one book. Therefore, you hold in your hands at least a years' worth of sermons that I have hand-picked in hopes they will be encouraging, challenging, and uplifting to my readers and will lead you into a closer walk with our Savior.

Some of the great men which I have listened to and studied their works are Dr. Billy Graham (who led not only me but millions of others to Christ), Dr. H.L. Willmington, founder and Dean of Willmington School of the Bible at Liberty University and author of Willmington's Guide to the Bible, New Zealand Christian Minister and Evangelist Ray Comfort, Dr. Ed Young, Senior Pastor Second Baptist church in Houston, TX., Dr. Robert Jeffers, Senior Pastor First Baptist Church in Dallas, TX., Dr. David Jeremiah, Senior Pastor Shadow Mountain Church in El Cajon, California, Dr. Tim LaHaye, Senior Pastor and co-author of the Left Behind series, Dr. Franklin Graham, President and CEO of the Billy Graham Evangelistic Association of whom I had the privilege of attending the Hanoi Vietnam festival with, in December 2017, and saw thousands come to Christ as their Lord and Savior, Christian Minister and author Randy Alcorn who has made Heaven very exciting and worth looking forward to through his book called "Heaven," and to Max Lucado who is one of the best Christian authors I have ever read. To all these men and to others, I will be forever grateful.

These sermons, by no means, are all inclusive of every book in the Bible, nor are they a complete and final list of all the sermons I have ever preached or will preach in the future. I have, in fact, preached every sermon that you'll find in this book but some of them originated from other great men of God that the Lord has allowed me to re-preach. I have diligently endeavored to put messages in this book of sermons that are relevant and will help all of us better understand the Bible, God's will for our lives, and help us walk through this life with more abundant living and purpose.

My hope is that you will read them and draw closer to Christ through the study of these messages. If you are seeking answers to many of life's questions, I hope these sermons will help answer those questions for you and that you will come to know Jesus Christ as the Lord and Savior of your life.

If you are a teacher or a pastor, please feel free to re-preach or re-teach these messages as God leads you. My hope and desire are that these messages will continue to be communicated to the world long after I have gone to Heaven.

FROM DESPAIR TO HOPE

1 Peter 1:3 – Praise be to the God and Father of our Lord Jesus Christ! In His great mercy He has given us new birth into a living hope through the resurrection of Jesus Christ from the dead.

I was born on November 14, 1949 in Houston, TX. and as a young child I lived with my family on the north side of Houston. We were a happy family of five, Mom, Dad, one brother and one sister, but a poor family as well. We had a two-bedroom home with no hallway and a very small living area and kitchen. The house was about 600 square feet. We did not have a bathroom inside the house but there was an outhouse in the back yard. My Dad worked very hard to get ahead and climb that corporate ladder and was gone a lot. I don't remember seeing much of him during my early years.

When I was around four years old we moved to Pasadena, TX where I grew up and lived until I graduated from Sam Rayburn High School in 1968. After living in a rent house for a short time; my Dad had a three-bedroom two bath house built for us; we even had two bathrooms in the house! It was there that our younger sister was born, when I was around five and a half years old.

My Dad was moving up in the world and now had a job in outside sales where he traveled from home a lot. My Mom loved to work in her rose garden, was a member of the garden club, and grew the most beautiful roses. I loved helping my Mom work in her flower bed and simply loved the ground she walked on. One day, as we were working in her flower bed, I asked her if she loved us. She was shocked! She said, "Of course I love each one of you, why do you ask?" I said, "Well you haven't spanked us in a long time." I don't know why, but I associated love with spanking. I guess it's because my brother and I got so many of them from our Dad. She lined each one of us up and gave us a good spanking. My siblings, years later, have never let me forget that.

I remember my Mom took us to church at the First Christian church in Pasadena, Texas where I first heard about Jesus. I was baptized when I was around twelve years old. About six months before my fourteenth birthday I began having dreams that my Mom was going to die. I don't know why that happened, but it frightened me! She wasn't even sick. When I was fourteen my Mom began having dizzy spells and thought she had an inner ear infection. After going to the doctor, she discovered that she was eaten up with cancer. I remember going to her hospital room, every day after school, where she stayed for the next six months. I loved her so much and could not believe that she was going to die.

One night, as I was leaving her room and headed home, I remember stopping at the door of her room and staring back at her for several minutes. This was a usual practice of mine and she would always say to me: "Goodnight son." However, this night was very different. She looked at me, ever so tenderly, and said: "Goodbye son." That was the last time I ever saw her alive. That image is forever engrained in my mind.

Coming home from the funeral, as I rode in the back seat of the family car, I remember just staring out the window and thinking to myself; IF there is a God, He sure doesn't love me for He just took the most important person in the world away from me. In my heart a great void began to develop as my sadness just overwhelmed me. My life began to go downhill from that point on and at only fourteen years of age I began skipping school, doing things that I shouldn't, and my grades really began to suffer. My brother and I shared a bedroom together and at the time of her death I was close to and looked up to him. Two weeks after my Mom died though he left for the Air Force and now even he was gone. My older sister worked after school, was a straight 'A' student, and was very busy with her grades and school work. It seemed like she was off to college before we knew it and our Dad then married a woman who drank very heavily. This was all new to us as we had never seen our Mother take a drink. And, just to get my younger sister and I out of the way, she wanted to put us in a boarding school, but our Dad refused. It was hard for my younger sister and I during that time as the fighting between our Dad and this woman got worse and worse.

One night, at the sound of a loud scream, we rushed into our Dad's bedroom to see what was going on. He had a gun pointed at her and when we came through the door he pointed it at us and screamed for us to sit down. We made it through that night, and many others as well, but emotionally we were a wreck. My little sister and I went out to the garage where I hugged her neck and told her that everything was going to be all right. But things were not all right! Our lives were falling apart!

After that marriage ended, my Dad married a woman who had four young children and I tried my best to be a good big brother to her children as well. During this time my Dad began to spend more time with me as he must have sensed the great void in my life. There were many times when we hunted and played golf together. I also worked very hard during my High School years throwing a paper route with 500 customers. I had to get up at 1 a.m., 7 days a week, leave for work and barely got back in time for school to start. Life still seemed so uncertain to me and I didn't seem to have much reason for living anymore. I just couldn't find any meaning and purpose to life!

The Vietnam war was going on during this time and after one semester in college I joined the Navy and volunteered for service in Vietnam. However, I didn't do it to avoid the draft. I saw people fighting for their freedom and I thought, "now there is a purpose and meaning that I can get behind." "I can go help them gain their freedom." After boot camp I was assigned to the USS Brinkley Bass, a U.S. Navy Destroyer (DD887) and was headed for Vietnam. We saw action up the Mekong Delta river where we gave support to our ground troops.

Before leaving for Vietnam, we were told we had two weeks before we pulled out. I took a one week leave, left the ship at midnight, and drove home from Los Angeles, CA. to Pasadena, TX. in just 24 hours. Needless-to-say, I was in a hurry to get home and spend time with my family before I left for Vietnam. At 10 a.m., the next morning, the phone rang, and it was my ship calling telling to come straight back as we were leaving early. After one night at home, my Dad drove me back to my ship where we had two days to visit while we drove down the road. I'll never forget waving goodbye to him as we pulled out and he stood on the pier. Tears were in both of our eyes. I turned to my buddies and said: "That's the last time I will ever see him." They asked, "Why, do you think we will not make it back from Vietnam." I said, "No, I believe we will make it back, but he will be dead before I return." I don't know why I felt that way, but it was just a deep feeling that came into my heart. It was just like those dreams that I had about my Mom dying.

We stopped at several ports before we reached Vietnam and I began drinking very heavily. Me and two of my buddies were known as the three ship drunks. That's saying a lot when everyone was drinking. When we were on land, you could find me drunk somewhere.

One night in Vietnam we were up the Mekong Delta river in a fierce gun battle. It looked like the fourth of July but instead of the flares going up in the sky, they were coming straight at us and over us as the ground troops were in a fierce battle. We gave gun support to our troops and it seemed like the battle lasted all night. The next morning, we pulled away from the river and back into the bay. Things were quiet that day, but the night was coming. It was even quiet the next night as we remained stationed in the bay. I'll never forget the sound over the loud speaker that summoned me to the Executive Officer's suite. My buddies looked at me and said, "What did you do this time?" I said, "I don't know." As I entered his office, which also served as his bedroom, he asked me to sit down, which I thought was unusual for an officer to ask an enlisted man to sit in his presence. He seemed to be such a kind and gentle man. I remember his tender voice as he looked at me and said, "I don't know how to tell you this, but your Dad is dead." He said that he didn't know how he died but he knew there was a gun involved somehow.

To attend my Dad's funeral, the Navy, working with the Red Cross, set up an escape mission to get me out of Vietnam. It was a day or two later, on a moonless night, when a speed boat pulled up next to our ship. I boarded the speed boat and we went full speed up the Mekong Delta being shot at all the way. I remember the pilot telling me that when we hit a bend in the river he was going to slow just a little and I was to dive out, swim the river, run through the jungle, several hundred yards, and there was supposed to be a plane waiting to get me out of Nam. Then, diving from the boat, swimming part of the river, running through the jungle for what seemed like a mile toward a plane that was waiting to take me out of Vietnam, diving into an open door of the taxying plane, I finally made it out of there.

When I finally arrived home, life was so different. My siblings met me at the airport and it was then that I found out that my Dad had put a pistol in his mouth and committed suicide. I felt utter despair! We went straight to the funeral home where I locked myself in his sitting room for over an hour. I sat by my Dad's casket and just rubbed his face and cried and cried. Why? Why? Why? Is life not worth living at all?

When I got out of the Navy I lived with my brother for a while as our house and all my Dad's possessions had to be sold to pay off his debts. Life didn't seem worth living anymore! I didn't understand the meaning of life at all. I saw my Mother, who loved God and tried to live right and bring her children up to know God, die at the age of forty. I saw my Dad climb the corporate ladder and move from a house with an outhouse in the back yard to a five-bedroom four bath house, drive a Cadillac, own his own business and a house on the bay. All those material things made him so happy and fulfilled that he put a gun in his mouth and pulled the trigger.

What was life really all about? You get sick, you die! You have all the money you need, and you end it all with a bullet! You get drunk and wake up feeling worse than you did the night before. I couldn't find any real meaning for even being alive. If all that happens, after we are born, is we do a few things while we are here and then die, then what was the reason for ever being born in the first place. I was lonely, and I was so depressed that I just couldn't find any point in living any longer. I was just shy of my 21st birthday at the time.

I went to the Pasadena police station, picked up the gun that my Dad had used to kill himself, and went to my brother's house with the intention of ending my life the same way my Dad had ended his. No one was home at his house and as I walked through the front door, the TV was just to my left. To muffle the sound of the gun shot, I turned the TV up as loud as it would go and went to the back bedroom and sat on the edge of the twin-bed. I slowly put the barrel of the gun into my mouth. I was very familiar with the gun as my Dad and I used to carry it with us when we went hunting. I knew that it had a hair trigger. If you just barely touched the trigger it would fire.

Just before I touched the trigger I heard a man on TV screaming at the top of his voice. The TV was blaring as this man said, "No matter what you are going through, right this second in your life, (then he repeated those words) I want you to know there is a God and He does love you and if you'll come to His Son Jesus Christ He will give your life meaning and purpose!" There it was, right before I took my own life, a message telling me I was loved and there was meaning and purpose to life. That was exactly what I was looking for. With trembling hands, I put the gun down and went into the living room. I was an emotional wreck! As a song was being sung I saw what looked like thousands of people walking toward this man. I didn't know, at the time, what it was that these people were experiencing but somehow I felt a love from God that I had never felt before. With tears in my eyes I went to my knees and sobbing aloud said, "Oh God, I don't know what it is that these people have but I need something. Please help me!"

My brother invited me to go with him to his church that week. They were having a revival and so on Friday night of that same week, we went together to a church revival at Lakeview Park Baptist Church. The preacher said almost the same words that I had heard on the TV just a few days before. I walked down the aisle to the front of that church and asked Jesus Christ to please forgive me of all my sins and come into my life and be my Lord and Savior. Something happened! Something changed inside of me! It was like a light had come on in my mind and in my soul. Suddenly, I knew there really was a God and I knew that He loved and cared for me. I knew that all the things I had heard as a child about Jesus dying for my sins and coming back to life was real! I can't really describe it but there was a peace that came over me that I had never felt before. It was the most wonderful experience I have ever had in my life!

I learned many things after that day. I began going to church and reading the Bible. I began to grow as a follower of Christ. I was so hungry to know more about Jesus that I read the entire New Testament the first week after I got saved. I began sharing Christ with everyone I met. I wanted everyone to know this same Jesus that I had come to know. I wanted them to have peace. I wanted them to be saved. I handed out gospel tracts to everyone. Some people began to call me 'The Preacher' or others just said I was a 'Jesus freak'. It didn't matter to me what they said. All I knew was that I loved Jesus with all my heart and He loved me.

For someone who didn't know Genesis from Revelation when they got saved, the church began to ask me to teach an adult Sunday school class the second week after my salvation. I was willing but studied for hours to prepare each week. It helped me know more about God and His word as well. I was also asked to teach boys in the Royal Ambassador program which I continued doing for the next 17 years. After Beverly and I got married in 1976, along with both of us teaching Sunday school and R.A.'s and G.A.'s, we began to work in the lay renewal ministry where we saw God do mighty works in people's lives. Doing lay renewals, we traveled to churches all over Texas and to one special event in California where we went to work with people in Los Angeles right in the middle of a riot torn part of town. We saw God do mighty works there as well as people were getting saved and turning their hearts and lives over the Christ.

When I was in my early 40's God called me to preach His word. Doors were opened for me and for the next 20 years I went on to pastor 5 different churches. I loved preaching and sharing God's message with others and leading them to faith in Christ. From there, God called me to be a Hospice Chaplain where I have been serving for the past 13 years. Life has had its challenges to say the least. In fact, there have been a lot more thorns than roses but through it all God has been there for me. He has never left me nor forsaken me. And years later I know that He lives and that He loves me. God had and still has a plan for my life.

Why do I tell you my story? Because I know that no matter what you are going through right this minute in your life, even if you are about to take your own life, that God loves you as well and He has a plan for your life too. For me, the plan was to share my story of how God saved me and how that He can save you too. That has always been His plan for my life and it has been a life of love and concern for others that has filled my heart with joy for many years now. Later on, I discovered that the man I heard on T.V. that day was Billy Graham. I have shared the story, of how I was saved that day, with hundreds of people over the years and I always had this burning desire to be on stage with Billy Graham and share my testimony with the world. I never felt worthy enough to even write to Billy Graham and ask if I could share my testimony with him.

On November 7, 2008, Billy Graham turned 90 years old. I wrote to tell him Happy Birthday and I sent my written testimony to him of how God intervened in my life, through his preaching, just at the time I was about to end it all. Nine years later I received a phone call from the senior producer of Billy Graham films telling me that he was reading the letter I sent to Billy Graham. To say the least, I was amazed. I said, you mean that letter I wrote 9 years ago? I couldn't believe, with the millions of people that have written to Billy Graham, that he was reading my letter.

He asked me if he could film me giving my testimony. That phone call led to a very humbling and honoring trip to Vietnam to hear Dr. Franklin Graham, Billy Graham's son, preach the gospel in Hanoi, Vietnam in December 2017. I will be forever grateful for the trip of a lifetime to return to Vietnam. On August 6, 2018, the Billy Graham Evangelistic Association released a powerful TV special called 'Vietnam Rising Hope' about the Hanoi, Vietnam Festival. It includes several Vietnam Veterans testimonies as well as mine. I encourage you to look for it as it will be online and also on 'You Tube'. You can also hear my story on podcast. Go online to God People Stories, a Billy Graham site, and scroll to 'Seconds from Death, Vietnam Vet Hears Life-Saving Words', July 3, 2018.

Was it a coincidence that I had a gun in my mouth, about the pull the trigger, when Billy Graham just happened to be on T.V. and just happened to say the exact words that I needed to hear? I don't think so! I think the chances of getting hit by lightning, about a hundred times, would be greater than that. God intervened in my life that day because He has a plan, because He loves me, and He loves you.

It begins by recognizing that we are all sinful people. The Bible says that all of us have sinned and that the wages of sin is death. When we agree with God on this matter and humble ourselves before Him, confess our sins to Him, and ask Him to forgive our sins and to come in and take control of our lives, He does just that. When we give our lives to him as our Lord and Savior then a brand-new life in Christ begins. And what a wonderful life it is! I pray that you will walk with Jesus and give Him your heart and life today. You'll never be sorry that you did. With all sincerity of heart, when you sense God drawing you to Him, pray a prayer, in your own words, something like this:

Lord Jesus I know I have sinned and done wrong in my life. I ask you to please forgive me and give me a new life. I believe you died for my sins and you rose again and are alive today. Lord I want to turn from my sins and live a new life, a life pleasing to you. I ask you, Jesus, to come into my life and save me. I give my heart and my life to you today and promise to follow you as my Lord and Savior for the rest of my life. Wherever you lead, I'll go. In your name, Jesus, I pray. Amen

And remember, above all else, there is a God, He does love you, and if you will give your heart and life to His Son Jesus Christ, He will give your life meaning and purpose and give you the gift of forgiveness and eternal life. You will never regret the decision you make for Christ.

> *John 3:16 – For God so loved the world that He gave His only begotten Son that whosoever believes in Him should not perish but shall have everlasting life.*

Ray Hyden

WHY THE CHILD OF GOD SHOULD STUDY THE WORD OF GOD

At first glance it would seem totally unnecessary to discuss reasons for studying God's Word. One might assume that, upon conversion, the most natural thing for a new believer to do would be to begin a lifelong study of the Book which originally brought them to Christ. But personal observation, as well as church history, proves the facts to be quite the opposite. The truth is, most Christians know very little about the Bible. Here then are some sound reasons for studying the Scriptures.

1. We should study God's word because of its Author.
   Often God is thought of as a Creator, a Redeemer, a Shepherd, a Judge, etc. But the wonderful role that is so often overlooked is that of Author! God has written a book, and that profound and priceless book is the Bible. As testified to by any human author, the nicest complement anyone can give an author is "Oh, yes, I've read your book." It is a tragic but true fact that many Christians who will one day stand before the Judgment Seat of Christ, never took the time to read His book! Thus, for no other reason, the Bible should be carefully read to allow the Christian to proclaim to Christ on that day: "Jesus, there were many things I did not do on earth that I should have done, as well as other things I did do that I should not have done, but one thing I did - "I read your Book!"

2. We should study God's word because we are commanded to study it!

3. We should study God's word because the Bible is God's message of His divine will. God speaks to us through His word.

4. We should study God's word because we grow and mature in our faith when we read and obey God's word.

5. We should study God's word because our enemy, the devil, has read it and will take its word's out of context and use it against us if we don't know the word ourselves.

6. We should study God's word because of the example of the apostle Paul.
   The Apostle Paul was probably the greatest Christian missionary that ever lived. He made the first four missionary journeys, founded and pastored the first dozen or more Christian churches, wrote over half the New Testament, and personally saw the resurrected Christ after His ascension. He was also arrested, condemned to death, and placed in prison for the crime of being a follower of Christ. At the point of death, he asked Timothy to bring him the Bible. He had read the Bible all throughout his entire lifetime and at the point of death Paul still felt He could benefit by reading the word of God.

7. We should study God's word because the Bible alone provides answers to life's three sixty-four-trillion-dollar questions.

   1. Where did I come from?

   Genesis 1:26,27 – And God said, let us make man in our image, after our likeness; and let them have dominion over the fish of the sea, and over the fowl of the air, and over the cattle, and over all the earth, and over every creeping thing that creeps upon the earth. So, God created man in His own image, in the image of God created He him; male and female created He them.

   Psalm 100:3 – Know you that the Lord He is God: it is He that has made us, and not we ourselves; we are His people, and the sheep of His pasture.

2. Why am I here?

Ecclesiastes 12:13 – Let us hear the conclusion of the whole matter: Fear God and keep His commandments; for this is the whole duty of man.

Revelation 4:11 – You are worthy, O Lord, to receive glory and honor and power; for you have created all things and for your pleasure they are and were created.

3. Where am I going?

John 3:16-18 – For God so loved the world, that He gave His only begotten Son, that whosoever believes in Him should not perish, but shall have everlasting life. For God sent not His Son into the world to condemn the world; but that the world through Him might be saved. He that believes on Him is not condemned; but he that believes not is condemned already, because he has not believed in the name of the only begotten Son of God.

John 3:3 – Jesus answered and said to him, "Most assuredly, I say to you, unless one is born again, he cannot see the kingdom of God."

John 1:12-13 – But as many as received Him to them He gave the right to become children of God, to those who believe in His name; who were born, not of blood, nor of the will of the flesh, nor of the will of man, but of God.

Romans 10:9 – That if you shall confess with your mouth that Jesus is Lord and shall believe in your heart that God has raised Him from the dead, you shall be saved.

Psalm 23:6 – Surely goodness and mercy shall follow me all the days of my life; and I will dwell in the house of the Lord forever.

Revelation 20:15 – And whosoever was not found written in the book of life was cast into the lake of fire.

CHAPTER 1

IN THE BEGINNING

T his morning we're going to look at the creation story. I've always believed in my heart that if you cannot get creation correct then you can have doubts about the rest of the Bible as well. If God did not create the universe, and all that it contains, then is the rest of the Bible true? So, let's take a closer look at the creation story.

> Genesis 1:1 – In the beginning God created the heavens and the earth.

And that's it! There is no explanation of how He did it and there is no explanation of where God came from. So, is this sentence true? Well let's take a closer look. There are three theories of how the universe came into being.

1. **Atheistic materialism (Evolution or the Big Bang)** This theory boldly assures us that everything that is, once came from nothing. In other words, if one gives nothing enough time, it will, all by itself, produce the music of Beethoven, the paintings of Raphael, the writings of Shakespeare, and the teachings of Christ. Or if one gives rocks enough time, after they collide, to just lay there and mutate they will eventually produce intelligent life; birds, animals, fish, trees, grass, rivers and lakes.

2. **The Second Theory of How Life began is Theistic Evolution.** This theory attempts to unify evolution with creation. This theory says that God started it all then handed it over to evolution for all the natural processes to take place. One problem with this is a scientific theory which runs contrary to the Second Law of Thermodynamics

which describes this universe as a wound-up clock which is slowly running down.

Instead, evolution has all life being built up from the simple to the complex. In an attempt to get around this, evolutionists claim that our world is not governed by the second law of thermodynamics for it receives the necessary energy from the sun to account for life. But the complexity of life calls for more than a source of energy. It also demands a purposeful direction of that energy. For example: A builder might expose bricks, sand, nails, paint, wires, wood, and other building materials to the heat and energy of the sun and to the refreshing gentle rains, but these objects would never by themselves unite and form a house!

3. **The third theory of How Life Began is Special Creation.** This theory simply affirms that God said just what He meant and meant just what He said in the first two chapters of the Bible, as He did in the remaining 1187 chapters. But the problem we humans have still comes down to faith.

In reality, no one can prove the big bang theory, evolution, or where God came from or how He created everything. This best and most logical thing to do is to look at the evidence and see where the evidence takes you. I highly recommend to everyone that you obtain the book 'Willmington's Guide to the Bible' by Dr. H.L. Willmington and read all the scientific facts concerning the three theories of origins. I think you'll be amazed at all the scientific information that points to a created order. Dr. Willmington's book will also give you answers to all the hard questions in the first eleven chapters of Genesis such as:

1. When was the Universe created?
2. How did the Universe come into being?
3. What scientific facts were put in place when God created light?
4. Did something horrible happen between verses 1 & 2 of Genesis chapter one?
5. Were the days of creation literally 24 hours long?
6. What were Adam and Eve like?
7. Where did Satan come from and how did he end up on earth?
8. What do we know about Satan?

9. Will we see Adam and Eve in Heaven?
10. How big is the universe?
11. How small is the universe?
12. What was God doing before He created?
13. Where did Cain get his wife?
14. Who were the giants on the earth in Genesis chapter 6 and where did they come from?
15. How did Noah get all those animals in the Ark?
16. How big was the Ark?
17. Is there evidence on earth of there ever being a flood that covered the entire earth?
18. How did Noah feed all those animals for an entire year?
19. Has the Ark ever been discovered?
20. Did dinosaurs and man live at the same time?

I've personally studied and preached sermons on all these topics from Dr. Willmington's work and I highly recommend his book to you. I believe you will be amazed by all that it contains to help you grow in your knowledge and understanding of God's word.

We can show you all the facts that lead to a creation account but many people on earth are just like the atheistic evolutionists who simply choose not to believe in face of the facts. Genesis stresses ten times that the entities created were to reproduce "after their own kind" while evolution says that all life came from a common ancestor. Look around you – Do people come from people – Do oak trees come from oak trees – Do squirrels reproduce squirrels or do they reproduce rabbits?

DAY ONE - CREATION OF LIGHT

> *Genesis 1:1-5 – In the beginning God created the heavens and the earth. The earth was without form, and void; and darkness was on the face of the deep And the Spirit of God was hovering over the face of the waters. Then God said, let there be light; and there was light. And God saw the light, that it was good; and God divided the light from the darkness. God called the light day, and the darkness He called night. So, the evening and the morning were the first day.*

DAY TWO - CREATION OF AIR

> *Genesis 1:6-8 – Then God said, let there be a firmament in the midst of the waters, and let it divide the waters from the waters. Thus, God made the firmament, and divided the waters which were under the firmament from the waters which were above the firmament; and it was so. And God called the firmament Heaven. So, the evening and the morning were the second day.*

This water was in two forms: regular land-based water in shallow ocean, river, and lake beds and atmospheric water in the form of invisible translucent vapor. The word firmament means air. Just as you may fill a balloon with air and try to squeeze it together you can feel the force of the air separating the sides of the balloon. So, it is with the air that separates the waters above from the waters below. God created a force to keep things from crashing together and to hold things together.

DAY THREE - CREATION OF PLANT LIFE - LIFE BEGAN ON DRY GROUND

> *Genesis 1: 9-13 – Then God said, let the waters under the heavens be gathered together into one place, and let the dry land appear; and it was so. And God called the dry land earth, and the gathering together of the waters He called seas. And God saw that it was good. Then God said, let the earth bring forth grass, the herb that yields seed, and the fruit tree that yields fruit according to its kind, who seed is in itself, on the earth; and it was so. And the earth brought forth grass, the herb that yields seed according to its kind, and the tree that yields fruit, whose seed is in itself according to its kind, and God saw that it was good. So, the evening and the morning were the third day.*

Lush green vegetation and exotic flowers now grace the newly emerged dry ground. These verses alone totally refute the harmful doctrine of theistic evolution which says life began eons ago from a glob of scum floating on some remote ocean surface. But to the contrary, the Bible tells us that life was supernaturally created on the third day of Creation and began on dry ground.

DAY FOUR - CREATION OF THE SUN, MOON, AND STARS

> *Genesis 1:14-19 – Then God said, let there be lights in the firmament of the heavens to divide the day from the night; and let them be for signs and seasons, and for days and years. And let them be for lights in the firmament of the heavens to give light on the earth; and it was so. Then God made two great lights; the greater light to rule the day, and the lesser light to rule the night. He made the stars also. God set them in the firmament of the heavens to give light on the earth and to rule over the day and over the night, and to divide the light from the darkness. And God saw that it was good. So, the evening and the morning were the fourth day.*

On the first day of creation God created physical light. He now creates special light sources. These heavenly bodies were to function in a three-fold manner.

1. <u>As signs</u> - they teach and remind us of God's creative work. Many times, God speaks to us from signs in the sky.
2. <u>As seasons</u> - they function as a calendar, dividing seasons, days, and years, enabling people to accurately plan their work.
3. <u>As lights</u> - they replace the temporary light source of the early days.

> *Psalm 8:3 – "When I consider thy heavens, the work of thy fingers, the moon and the stars, which Thou hast ordained"*

It may be asked why God created the earth on the first day, but waited until the fourth day before establishing the sun, stars, and moon? There are two possible reasons for this, one dealing with priority, the other dealing with prevention.

1. **Priority** - God created the earth first because it was the most important in His mind. It was upon earth that He planned to create man on the sixth day, made in His own image. Then, plans had

already been made, in the fullness of time, for the second person in the Trinity to come to earth and save us from our sins. Finally, it will be upon the earth, that the King of Kings shall someday touch down upon the Mount of Olives to establish His Millennial Kingdom. It will be on earth where God will eventually live with all His creation (see Revelation 21).

2. **Prevention** - Almost without exception every ancient civilization has worshiped the sun. But God wanted his people to worship the suns Creator, namely Himself. Thus, He informs us that life and light existed before the sun. *James 1:17 "Every good gift and every perfect gift is from above and comes down from the Father of lights. . ."*

DAY FIVE - CREATION OF FISH AND BIRDS

> *Genesis 1: 20-23 – Then God said, "Let the waters abound with an abundance of living creatures, and let birds fly above the earth across the face of the firmament of the heavens." So, God created great sea creatures and every living thing that moves, with which the waters abounded, according to their kind, and every winged bird according to its kind. And God saw that it was good. And God blessed them, saying, "Be fruitful and multiply, and fill the waters in the seas, and let birds multiply on the earth." So, the evening and the morning were the fifth day.*

The phrase "according to its kind" occurs ten times in this chapter, referring to vegetation and all living creatures. Creation is orderly and perpetuates itself within God's established laws.

DAY SIX - THE CREATION OF LAND CREATURES AND MAN

> *Genesis 1: 24-31 – Then God said, "Let the earth bring forth the living creature according to its kind: cattle and creeping thing and beast of the earth, each according to its kind; and it was so. And God made the beast of the earth according to its kind, cattle according to its kind, and everything that creeps on the earth according to its kind. And God saw that it was good. Then God*

said, "Let Us make man in Our image, according to Our likeness; let them have dominion over the fish of the sea, over the birds of the air, and over the cattle, over all the earth and over every creeping thing that creeps on the earth." So, God created man in His own image; in the image of God He created him; male and female He created them. Then God blessed them, and God said to them, "Be fruitful and multiply; fill the earth and subdue it; have dominion over the fish of the sea, over the birds of the air, and over every living thing that moves on the earth." And God said, "See, I have given you every herb that yields seed which is on the face of all the earth, and every tree whose fruit yields seed; to you it shall be for food. "Also, to every beast of the earth, to every bird of the air, and to everything that creeps on the earth, in which there is life, I have given every green herb for food;" and it was so. Then God saw everything that He had made and indeed it was very good. So, the evening and the morning were the sixth day.

Man, immediately becomes the highlight of this day and of the entire creation week. Note the divine account of this act. *Genesis 1:26 "And God said: Let Us make man in Our image, after Our likeness. . ."* This is the first strong evidence of the Trinity in the Old Testament. Man was made in the image of God and possessed the highest kind of life. Plant life possessed unconscious life. Animal life possessed conscious life. Man, alone, possessed self-conscious life.

DAY SEVEN - GOD RESTS

Genesis 2:1-3 – Thus the heavens and the earth, and all the host of them, were finished. And on the seventh day God ended His work which He had done, and He rested on the seventh day from all His work which He had done. Then God blessed the seventh day and sanctified it, because in it He rested from all His work which God had created and made.

This is the only place where God is described as resting. Sin would soon enter the picture and the entire Trinity would become involved in redemption.

SUMMARY OF CREATION DAYS

The Bible says that life began on dry ground (plant life being the first created thing) while evolution says that life began in some remote sea bottom. The Bible says that birds existed before insects while evolution says insects existed before birds. The Bible says that fish and birds were created at the same time while evolution says that fish evolved hundreds of millions of years before birds. The Bible says ten times that everything created was to reproduce "after its own kind" while evolution says that all life came from a common ancestor. The Bible says that Adam was made from the dust of the ground into the image of God while evolution says that Adam descended from a sub-ape creature. The Bible says that woman came from man's side while evolution says that both man and woman developed simultaneously. The Bible says that man was originally a vegetarian while evolution says that man was probably a head-hunting cannibal.

> *Hebrews 11:3 – By faith we understand that the worlds were framed by the word of God, so that the things which are seen were not made of things which are visible.*

> *John 1:1-3 – In the beginning was the Word and the Word was with God and the Word was God. The same was in the beginning with God. All things were made by Him and without Him was not anything made that was made.*

John 1:14 tells us who this word is. *"And the Word became flesh and dwelt among us and we beheld His glory – the Glory as of the only Begotten of the Father full of grace and truth."* The Bible says that Jesus is God and that He created everything there is!

> *Romans 1:18-20 – For the wrath of God is revealed from heaven against all ungodliness and unrighteousness of men, who suppress the truth in unrighteousness, because what may be*

known of God is manifest in them, for God has shown it to them. For since the creation of the world His invisible attributes are clearly seen, being understood by the things that are made, even His eternal power and Godhead, so that they are without excuse.

Hebrews 11:6 – But without faith it is impossible to please God, for he who comes to God must believe that He is, and that He is a rewarder of those who diligently seek Him.

The question comes down to "Do we believe what God said" and have we given our hearts and lives, in repentance, to the Lord Jesus Christ?

WHY DID GOD CREATE MAN IN THE FIRST PLACE?

Some have suggested that because He was lonely and needed fellowship and companionship. But God is complete within Himself. The Bible says that God is love. Jesus said, *"Greater love hath no man than this, than a man lay down his life for his friends."* Love is best expressed in giving.

1. <u>God created man because of His nature</u>. His nature is to love. He created us to love us, to have fellowship with us.

   Revelation 4:11 – Thou art worthy, O Lord, to receive glory and honor and power; for thou hast created all things, and for thy pleasure they are and were created.

2. <u>He also created us I believe to show his nature of Grace</u>. It is not unreasonable to suggest that God created Adam knowing full well he would sin (but in no way encouraging him to do so) and then, in the fullness of time, he planned to send his only Son to die in man's place and thus display his marvelous grace!

   Romans 5:20 – Moreover the law entered, that the offence might abound. But where sin abounded, grace did much more abound.

> *Ephesians 2:7 – That in the ages to come He might show the exceeding riches of his grace in his kindness toward us through Christ Jesus.*

> *Ephesians 2:8-9 – For by grace are you saved through faith; and that not of yourselves: it is the gift of God; not of works, lest any man should boast.*

3. <u>Then a third reason I believe God created us is so that we could do good on the earth and then continue to do good through all eternity</u>. An eternity that He will, in his mercy and grace, share with us.

> *Ephesians 2:10 – For we are his workmanship, created in Christ Jesus unto good works, which God has before ordained that we should walk in them.*

WHAT DOES IT MEAN THAT MAN WAS MADE IN THE IMAGE OF GOD?

We see throughout the Bible inferences of God being Three-in-One. Thus, in the image of God means, first of all, that man is three-in-one. Man is made up of a body, a soul, and a spirit.

> *1 Thessalonians 5:23 – And the very God of peace sanctify you wholly; and I pray God your whole spirit and soul and body be preserved blameless unto the coming of our Lord Jesus Christ.*

Being in the image of God points solely to the spiritual and moral nature of mankind. Like God we have a mind, we have emotion, and we have a will. We have the ability to choose. In the Garden of Eden God may have known that Adam would choose to sin, but the choice was still Adam's. Today is no different. You and I can choose to love God, to give our hearts and lives to Christ or we can choose to go our own way and not follow God. If God had made us any different than He did, then our following Him would not be because of love but rather we would be reduced to nothing more than computers or robots. God created man in such a way that we would be capable of fellowship with Him. He created us to love us and thus created us in His image.

CHAPTER 2

ARE YOU GOOD ENOUGH TO GO TO HEAVEN?

John 3:1-3 – There was a man of the Pharisees named Nicodemus, a ruler of the Jews. This man came to Jesus by night and said to Him, "Rabbi, we know that You are a teacher come from God; for no one can do these signs that You do unless God is with him. Jesus answered and said to him, "Most assuredly, I say to you, unless one is <u>born again,</u> he cannot see the kingdom of God."

There is probably no phrase in religious circles that has become more prominent than the phrase, "Born Again." There have been a lot of books written about it. Billy Graham had a best-seller, *How to Be Born Again.* Charles Colson has written about it.

In John 3:3 Jesus told Nicodemus, <u>*"Verily, verily, I say to thee, except a man be born again, he cannot see the kingdom of God."*</u> Many people confuse what Jesus is saying and believe that the phrase "being saved or being born again" belongs to a particular denomination. Many people assume if you are <u>born again</u>, you belong to this denomination or that denomination. It's not a denominational phrase, albeit some denominations don't use it. It's a Bible phrase. The very words "Born Again" came from Jesus own lips. There won't be any denominational tags such as Catholic, Episcopalian, Lutheran, Presbyterian, Assembly of God, Pentecostal, Church of Christ, Methodist, Baptist, Non-Denomination or any other in heaven. These names are just names over the door! We need to realize that everyone who goes to heaven "repents," gets "saved" and is "born again." In heaven there will only be people who

11

have been born again. If a person is not born again, they are only one heartbeat away from hell.

Jesus said, *"Except a man be <u>born again</u> - he cannot see the kingdom of God."* I don't care how formal you are, how wonderful you are, how interesting you are. If you are not "born again" you will not go to heaven. And these are not 'my words'. They're Jesus words! I don't care what denomination you are, if you are not "born again" you will not go to heaven. There is a great deal of difference between catechism and being saved. There is a great deal of difference between confessionals and being born again. The real issue is what Jesus asked Nicodemus. <u>*"Have you been born again?"*</u>

Today there are over 300 million people that live in the United States of America. Over 50 million of them claim to have been born again. That tells us something about our outreach and evangelism efforts in the United States. With 50 million Americans "born again" it is important that we seek to understand what the Bible really says about being "born again."

In John 3, a man who was a ruler came to Jesus Christ. Not only was he a ruler, he was also a wealthy, intelligent Jew who did his best to keep every law of God as recorded in the Old Testament. As far as human standards go, this man was probably one of the best men you could ever meet. But an intelligent man or a good man is not necessarily a "born again" man. There are many men who have Ph.D.'s and a lot of knowledge, but they have never been "born again." Here was a man who was a ruler, but he was not saved. He was not "born again." Not only was he a ruler, but he was equal to a pastor of a very large church. A mega-church! He was a Pharisee, was very spiritual, and did his best to be a very good man, yet Jesus looked at him and said, <u>*"Nicodemus, you've got to be born again or you will never see the Kingdom of God"*</u> let alone enter it!

What's great about knowing Christ is that when you come to know Him, he doesn't simply take the old garment of your life and put a new patch on it. Jesus said, *"you can't put a new patch on an old garment any more than you can put new wine in old wineskins."* Jesus gives you a whole new garment!

A whole new life! Being saved is not getting a new patch or turning over a new leaf! The Bible says that Jesus himself grew mentally, spiritually, physically, and emotionally. If you don't grow like that, you've never been born again because being born again means becoming a whole new person from the inside - out! It's a total Heart and Life Transformation! It's not a self-transformation but it's a God transformation. It's His Holy Spirit transforming you to become like His Son, Jesus! Used as a noun, transformation means: A radical change or alteration (a change in form, appearance, nature, and character). In math it means: A change in position or direction - and that's exactly what it is. I've been changed! I was always a creation of God but now I am a son of God. You may be either a born-again son or daughter of God. There's a song that goes: "I've been changed, I've been re-born, all my life has been re-arranged. What a difference it made when the Lord came to stay - I've been changed, oh yes I've been changed.

We grow in Christ after we've been born again but the Born-Again experience is instantaneous. When a child is born, we don't hear news that the head was born at 8:05; the right arm was born at 8:10; the left arm was born at 8:15; the legs were born at 8:30 and the feet at 8:35. When a child is born, the child is born! All the child! Some people say, "Well, I've got my mind on God," or, "I've got my body with God," or, "I've got my emotions with God," or, "I've got my finances with God." God's either got all of you or He doesn't have any of you! He's either Lord of all or He's not Lord at all!

Mankind is sinful, and we must be born again because *it is our nature to sin*. But when Christ comes into our lives, we get new bodies, new lives, and new experiences. Everything about us is new. When we're born again, everything is changed. We're different. The Bible says, "we are a new creation." "Old things are passed away."

A heard a story from another preacher who said that a senator came to his church to hear him preach but wouldn't join the church because he was afraid of being "born again." He was afraid he would change, and he liked himself just the way he was. This senator came to see the preacher one day and said "Preacher; when you preach it feels like you are preaching right at me." He said, "Preacher. . . you don't like it that I drink, do you?" The preacher said "No, Sir." "You don't like it because I have some standards other than what you have, do you?"

The preacher said, "No sir." He said "Preacher, don't you know that I'm really not a bad guy?" The preacher looked at him and said, "Senator, that's right!" "You are not a bad guy." "You are just lost and going to hell that's all." It's not that "good" people go to heaven and "bad" people go to hell. It's not that people are bad; it's just that they're lost. You do not come to Jesus as a Senator; you must come to Him as a sinner. In the alcoholics' anonymous program before healing can ever begin a person must say the words "I am an Alcoholic". And it's similar when we come to Christ. We must admit, fess up, and say the words "I am a Sinner". Get it out and let the healing begin to take place in your heart and in your life.

Someone once asked Charles Finney, "Why do you always preach on the subject, 'You must be born again'?" I love his answer. He said, "I preach on it a lot because *you MUST be born again.*" That's a good answer. Jesus said, "Nicodemus, you <u>must</u> be born again." Why must? Why can't I just be a good person? Why must I be born again? Because *Romans 3:23* says, *"All have sinned, and fall short of the glory of God." Isaiah 53:6 says, "All we like sheep have gone astray; we have turned, each one, to his own way and the Lord has laid on Him the iniquity of us all."*

> *Romans 3:10 says "As it is written: there is <u>none</u> righteous, no, not one."*

> *Isaiah 59:2 says "But your iniquities have separated you from God; your <u>sins have hidden His face from you, so that He will not hear!"</u>*

No matter how good you are you're still a sinner and before God's eyes you are not righteous! I can make a list of deadly sins, but any sin is deadly unless you are "born again." It doesn't matter how important we are or how religious we are. Some have religion, but they don't have Jesus. Religion without Jesus is still going to send you to hell. Some people say, "The devil made me do it." *The devil has never made anybody do anything they did not want to do.* The reason we have sinned in the past is because we flatly enjoyed it! People commit sins of immorality because they have pleasure and sensual fulfillment from them. In other words, they simply enjoyed it, or they never would have done it. Why does a man take that bottle? Because he enjoys it! Why does

14

a man make money through crooked business dealings? Because he enjoys it! Why will a man eat until he becomes overweight? Because he enjoys it! Why does a man look at pornography? Because he enjoys it!

The reason man enjoys sin is because he is a sinner by nature!

Once upon a time a scorpion needed to cross a pond. Wondering how he would get to the other side, he noticed a frog nearby. "Mr. Frog, will you please hop me across this pond?" The kind, gentle frog said, "Certainly, Mr. Scorpion. I will be glad to do so." So, Mr. Scorpion jumped onto Mr. Frog's back as Mr. Frog hopped from pod to pod, bringing Mr. Scorpion to the other side of the pond. But just as the frog said, "Well, Mr. Scorpion, here we are," he felt an excruciating pain in his back. Mr. Scorpion had stung him! As Mr. Frog lay dying, he looked up at Mr. Scorpion and said, "How could you do this? I brought you from one side of the pond to the other and now you sting me so that I die." Mr. Scorpion looked at Mr. Frog and said, "I can't help it. It's my nature." It's our nature to sin!

A lot of people think they are right with God because they had a great Mom and Dad. That's wonderful, but they themselves must be *"born again."* A lady said to a pastor one time, "Pastor I'm a Methodist. What do I have to do to join your church? The preacher said, "Get saved." She said, "Well, you don't believe Methodists are lost, do you?" He said, "No, I don't believe that Methodists are any more lost than any other person is lost." If you've been saved, your salvation is just as good as any person's salvation. But I want you to know that you can't just come join our church "unless you've been saved."

When someone walks the aisle to join the church I always ask them (no matter who they are) are you saved? Some people think just because they have good back grounds that everything is going to be all right; after all my grandfather was a Methodist or a Baptist preacher. My uncle was a missionary to Africa. But being "born again" means there has been a time when a person has invited Jesus into their life and committed their life to Christ.

What is the meaning of the new birth? Here are some references for the meaning of being born again.

> *1 Peter 1:22 – Since you have purified your souls in obeying the truth through the Spirit in sincere love of the brethren, love one another fervently with a pure heart.*

A Born-Again person will love & have a heart to care for others and see them get saved as well. When's the last time you talked to a stranger & your heart said. "I wonder if they're saved, born again?" - I should tell them about Jesus - I have a desire to tell them about Jesus. I have a desire to pray for them and see them get saved! If that never happens to you then maybe you need to check up on your own salvation. Perhaps you've never been born again because these things matter to born again people.

> *1 John 3:9 – Whoever has been born of God does not sin, for His seed remains in him; and he cannot sin, because he has been born of God.*

A Born-Again person will not be purposely living in sin.

> *James 1:27 says Pure and undefiled religion before God and the Father is this; to visit orphans and widows in their trouble, and to keep oneself unspotted from the world.*

A Born-Again person will be unspotted by the world. It's not that we don't have the ability to sin - it's that we no longer want to sin. We have a heart's desire to live for Jesus.

Robert Jeffers, the pastor at First Baptist Church Dallas, TX once said: "I sin all I want to - The fact is I don't want to!" When a person gives their life to Christ and is born again, they will have these characteristics. A person who has been born again is willing to obey the Word of God. He is willing for Christ to be his Master!

> *Hebrews 12:1-2 – Therefore we also, since we are surrounded by so great a cloud of witnesses, let us lay aside every weight, and the sin which so easily ensnares us, and let us run with endurance the race that is set before us. Looking unto Jesus, <u>the author and finisher</u>*

of our faith, who for the joy that was set before Him endured the cross, despising the shame, and has sat down at the right hand of the throne of God.

The reason some people have not had their faith finished or completed is because Jesus has never been the author of their lives. He has to be the author before he can be the finisher. Remember what Jesus said would happen if we have not been born again: *we will not see the kingdom of God.* You cannot go to heaven unless you have been born again! You are born again by asking Jesus to come into your life, by believing and receiving. If you ask Him to save you, He will. It's not by feeling. If you could be saved by having good feelings then Jesus wouldn't have had to die on the cross for your sins or for mine. Sin must be punished, and Jesus took our punishment upon Himself on the cross. If we don't accept His punishment for us, then we'll end up being punished for our own sins. Without Jesus we'll end up in HELL! So, are you good enough to go to HEAVEN? Not a chance! Without Jesus we are lost and doomed! But thank God there is Good News! *Romans 10:13 - For whosoever shall call upon the name of the Lord shall be saved.*

If you want to be saved, say a prayer something like this, but it must come from your heart.

"Lord Jesus, I know that I am a sinner and separated from you. I believe that you died on the cross for my sins, that you rose from the grave, and that you are alive today. Please forgive me, Lord, of my sins. I want to follow you. I want to turn from my sin and live the life you have designed for me. I turn from my sin right now and place my trust in you, and you alone, and ask for your forgiveness. Please forgive me and come into my life as my Lord, my Savior, and my Master. I promise to live for you and I commit the rest of my life to you. I receive your gift of eternal life and confess you as my Lord and my Savior. Thank you for loving me and dying for me. Thank you that you are alive today. Thank you for giving me new life. In your Holy name I pray, the name of Jesus. Amen."

After you've given your life to Christ you need to join a Bible believing church. You need to be baptized by immersion (after you've given your life to Christ). You need to start attending church on a regular basis. You need to read your Bible every day and grow closer to the Lord. You need to join a Sunday school class or a Bible study class. These things won't save you, but they will help you grow in Christ. A person who is really serious about giving their life to Christ will want to do these things. Once you've been born again by God's Spirit you have a burning desire to know more about Christ and to walk with Him as your Savior. As the old gospel song says: Do you know Him today? Please don't turn Him away! Jesus, Oh Jesus - Without Him how *LOST* I would be!

CHAPTER 3

CAN YOU KNOW FOR CERTAIN THAT YOU ARE GOING TO HEAVEN?

1 John 5:1-13 – Whoever believes that Jesus is the Christ (the Messiah) is born of God, and everyone who loves the Father also loves His Son. When we love God and keep His commandments this shows by the love we have for the children of God. This is the love of God, that we keep His commandments. God's commandments are not burdensome. Whoever is born of God overcomes the world. And this is the victory that has overcome the world – our faith. Who is he who overcomes the world? He who believes that Jesus is the Son of God! This is He who came by water and blood – Jesus Christ; not only by water, but by water and blood. It is the Spirit who bears witness, because the Spirit is truth. For there are three that bear witness in Heaven: The Father, the Word (Jesus Christ), and the Holy Spirit, and these three are one. And there are three that bear witness on earth: The Spirit, the water, and the blood; and these three agree as one. If we receive the witness of men, the witness of God is greater; for this is the witness of God which He has testified of His Son. He who believes in the Son of God has the witness in himself; he who does not believe God has called God a liar, because he has not believed the testimony that God has given of His Son. And this

> is the testimony: that <u>God has (given) us eternal life,</u>
> and this life is in His Son. <u>He who has the Son has</u>
> <u>(life); he who does not have the Son of God</u> does
> <u>not have life.</u> These things I have written to <u>you</u>
> who believe in the name of the Son of God, <u>that</u>
> <u>you may (know) that you have eternal life</u> and that you
> may continue to believe in the name of the Son of God.

O ne basic thing that every Christian ought to know beyond the shadow of any doubt is that he or she is saved and has eternal life!

WHAT DOES IT MEAN TO BE SAVED?

It means that every sin is forgiven and buried in the grave of God's forgetfulness. It means that Jesus Christ, through the Holy Spirit, has come to live in us – to give us peace with God. To be saved means the wrath of God no longer abides on us. It means that when we die or when Jesus comes again, we are going home to heaven to be with Him. We should not be saying: "I Hope I'm Saved" or "I Think I'm Saved" but <u>"Praise God, I know that I know that I am SAVED"</u>

> *John 3:36 – He who believes in the Son <u>has</u>*
> *<u>everlasting life</u>; and he who does not believe the Son*
> *shall not see life, but the wrath of God abides on him.*

I can't begin to tell you the number of people over the years who have said to me – "No one can know for sure if they are saved." I then point them to *1 John 5:13 – "These things have I written unto you who believe in the name of the Son of God that you may <u>know</u> that you have eternal life."* Of course we can know if we have eternal life! The Bible says we can know! The truth of the matter is, if you have genuine salvation, you should know it; and if it is real, thank God you can never lose it. We are not talking about denominational preference; we are talking about the eternal destiny of spirit and soul and in the end your new resurrected body that will live forever. To be a victorious Christian you need to be able to say, <u>"I know that I'm saved – "I know that I'm Heaven born, and Heaven bound."</u>

Can you be saved and have doubts about it? If it is not possible for the child of God to sometimes have doubts, then why did John write: *"These things I have written to you who believe in the name of the Son of God that you may know that you have eternal life."* Evidently there were some people who were having doubts about their salvation and he wanted to assure them. There could have been other people who thought they were saved but weren't. Doubt doesn't necessarily mean that you haven't been saved. Doubts are not good in our salvation. Arguments are not good in a marriage, but they happen. Pain is not good in our bodies, but it happens. Doubts are not good in our salvation, but they sometimes happen as well. When it comes to our salvation we need to remove those doubts. We need to have not a hope-so salvation - Not a think-so salvation - Not a maybe-so salvation - But a wonderful <u>know-so salvation</u>! Assurance of our salvation begins with the new birth.

> *1 John 5:1 – Whoever believes that Jesus is the Christ (the Messiah) is born of God, and everyone who loves the Father also loves His Son.*

Being born spiritually is much like being born physically. One thing about birth is that it makes a perfect example of salvation because all of us have experienced a physical birth and can relate to the facts of a birth.

> *John 3:1-7 – There was a man of the Pharisees named Nicodemus, a ruler of the Jews. This man came to Jesus by night and said to Him, "Rabbi, we know that You are a teacher come from God; for no one can do these miracles that You do unless God is with him." Jesus answered and said to him, "Most assuredly, I say to you, unless one is born again, he cannot see the kingdom of God." Nicodemus said to Him, "How can a man be born when he is old? Can he enter a second time into his mother's womb and be born again?"*

> *Jesus answered, "Most assuredly, I say to you, unless one is born of water and the Spirit, he cannot enter the kingdom of God. That which is born of the flesh is flesh, and that which is born of the Spirit is spirit. Do not marvel that I said to you, 'You must be born again.'"*

In this passage Jesus was talking to a religious man named Nicodemus. Nicodemus wanted to know about miracles. In essence Jesus told him that in order for him to understand miracles, he himself needed to become a miracle. He needed to be BORN AGAIN! There are some things we need to understand about the new birth in order to understand the assurance of our salvation. In a birth, a conception takes place. In verse 5, Jesus said that we must be born of Water and the Spirit in order to enter into the Kingdom of God. Water refers to the Word of God.

> *Ephesians 5:26 – "That He might sanctify and cleanse her with the washing of water by the word"*

> *1 Peter 1:23 – "Having been born again, not of corruptible seed but incorruptible, through the Word of God which lives and abides forever"*

Spirit refers to the Holy Spirit of God. When the Holy Spirit of God and the Word of God come together in the womb of faith, there is a wonderful conception that takes place. However, it will not happen without our consent. We must provide the womb of faith but even that is given to us by God so that He can save us by His GRACE. When we respond by placing our faith in Him and giving and hearts and lives over to the Lord Jesus Christ in total commitment, then we are spiritually born at that moment in time.

In a birth, a continuation is involved. In verse 6, Jesus tells us that physical life is imparted by physical life, and spiritual life is imparted by spiritual life. Parents do not manufacture babies in the true sense of the word. They pass on the life that has been given to them. Physical life is transmitted from one to the other. The term BORN AGAIN literally means BORN FROM ABOVE. Just as physical life is transmitted from one to the other, spiritual life is transmitted from one to the other. Salvation is not only getting man out of earth and into Heaven but getting God out of Heaven and into man through His Holy Spirit.

In a birth, a character is produced. In a physical birth we receive the nature of our physical parents. In a spiritual birth we receive the nature of our Father in Heaven. God transmits His character (His nature) into us! Christians are not just nice people; they are new creations.

> *2 Corinthians 5:17 – "Therefore, if anyone is in Christ, he is a new creation; old things have passed away; behold, all things have become new."*

In a birth, a completion transpires. A birth is a once-for-all experience in the physical realm and in the spiritual realm. It's important that we really understand this if we are going to have the assurance of our salvation! No one can ever be physically unborn! In like manner, no one can ever be spiritually unborn! When a physical baby is born a record is written down – A birth certificate. When a spiritual baby is born a record is written down in Heaven – in God's Book! A spiritual birth certificate! There's a song that goes like this: <u>"There's a new name written down in Heaven and it's mine oh yes it's mine and the white robbed angels sing the story – A sinner has come home"</u>

In a birth a commencement occurs. A birth is a starting place. There are no yesterdays in a birth, everything is new. There are only tomorrows! When we come to Jesus we are not yesterdays. We are all tomorrows. A physically newborn baby begins to grow. A newborn baby has all the equipment it will ever have. He or she has tiny little fingers and toes, a cute little nose and eyes, all the parts begin to grow, and the child begins to learn and grow taller and wiser. A newborn spiritual baby is no different. We have all the equipment already! We begin to grow closer to Christ in our actions, our motives, and our attitudes. We begin to be more like Christ as we begin to grow spiritually.

In a birth a certainty is expected. A birth is a definite experience. If I were to ask you this question, "Have you ever been physically born?" What would your response be? Suppose I did ask you and you were to answer me something like this: "I hope so," "I'm doing the best I can," or "I've always been born" that would be nonsensical wouldn't it.? Let's look at our spiritual birth. Now if the spiritual birth relates in kind to the physical birth and I ask you "Have you been Born Again" and you answer me "I hope so, "I'm doing the best I can," "I've always been born," do you see how nonsensical that sounds as well? Either you've been Born Again (Born Spiritually) or you haven't. It's as simple as that. The crystal-clear passage that relates to this is *Ephesians 2:8-9 "For by <u>grace</u> you have been saved <u>through faith</u>, and that <u>not of yourselves</u>; it is the gift of God, <u>not of works</u>, lest anyone should boast."*

23

This passage is so great because here the Scripture clearly tells us what saves us and what does not. What doesn't save us? Self and Works do not save us! *"Not of yourself - Not of works!"* That seems simple enough, but most people really do not understand this concept. If you asked the average person on the street the following question, "Are you going to Heaven" they would probably answer "SURE!" But then you ask them "Why?" and you may get a response something like this, "I'm doing the best I can" is the answer most often given. Think about that for a minute. I (self) am doing (works) the best I can. What does the scripture tell us does not save us? Self and Works! *"NOT OF SELF, NOT OF WORKS!"*

Many people think God is like Santa Claus. He's making a list, checking it twice, finding out who's naughty or nice. Then they think one day at the judgment we will stand before Him and He is going to weigh the good we've done against the bad and see which side the balance comes down on. Most people believe they can behave themselves into heaven. But look at the scripture again. What does it say? *"Not of yourselves"* - *"Not of works"* Ephesians 2:8-9

The devil doesn't give up easily! He will encourage you to believe something like this, "Yes, I cannot work my way into Heaven, but works will help. It is the grace of God plus what I do. I do my part and God will do His." But is that what the scripture says? If you were rowing across a stream in a rowboat using one oar (we'll call that oar *works)*, and paddled on one side of the boat only, what do you think would happen? You'd go around in circles. But what if you picked up a different oar (we'll call that oar *faith*), changed sides, and paddled only on the other side of the boat what would happen? You'd go around in circles the opposite direction. But then if you picked up both oars (*faith and works*) and paddled them together you could go straight and reach the other shore. Right? That may sound like a good illustration, but it has a fatal flaw; we're not going to heaven in a rowboat! We're going to heaven by the grace of God. It is not of self, and it is not of works! If you don't understand that then you will never have the assurance of your salvation. If any part of your salvation depends on your good works, then you will never know if you have done enough good works to get into Heaven. We need to understand this and lock it down in our head and in our heart; *it is not of self and not of works.*

If salvation is not of self and not of works, then how are we saved? Look at Ephesians 2:8 again. *"For by grace you have been saved through faith."* What saves us? Grace through Faith! What is grace? Grace is the characteristic of God's nature that makes Him love sinners such as us. God does not love us because we are valuable, we are valuable because God loves us. God's love is by His sheer grace! Grace is something we do not deserve at all. It is God's unmerited love and favor shown to sinners who deserve judgment.

GRACE - GOD'S RICHES AT CHRIST'S EXPENSE

That's Grace! When you think of God's Grace, think of Jesus dying in blood and agony upon the cross for undeserving sinners. We have nothing to commend us to God. We are sinners by birth, choice, and practice! But God loves us in spite of our sin, and that love is called GRACE! When people really understand Grace, they write songs about it like "Amazing Grace" how sweet the sound that saved a wretch like me. I once was lost but now I'm found was blind but now I see.

FAITH – FORSAKING ALL I TRUST HIM

I forsake dependence on my good intentions, my good works, my good deeds, and my own self for my salvation. I also forsake my sin! I turn my back on sin and I trust Him. I put my faith where God has put my sin – on the Lord Jesus Christ. Faith is not a mere intellectual belief; the Bible says in *James 2:19 "that the demons believe in Jesus and tremble."* It is more than belief! It is commitment! I can believe an airplane can fly, but I don't truly trust it until I get in it. I put my faith (which God gives me) in God's grace. It is not faith that saves; it is grace that saves! Faith just lays hold of that grace. Think of grace as God's hand of love reaching down from heaven, saying, "I love you, I want to save you." It's a nail-pierced hand because He has paid for our sins. Think of faith as your sin-stained hand, saying, "God, I need you. I want you." And when you put your hand of faith in God's hand of grace, that is salvation.

GRACE IS A GIFT

If you pay anything for a gift, then it ceases to be a gift. We must remember that we cannot take any praise or credit for our salvation. None whatsoever! There's not going to be any strutting peacocks in Heaven! It is all of God! It is a gift, and we cannot boast about it. When we get to heaven, God gets all the credit, all the praise and all of the glory because of His marvelous, matchless, wonderful GRACE.

Ephesians 2:9 — "Not of works less any man should boast!"

GRACE GREATER THAN OUR SIN

Marvelous grace of our loving Lord, Grace that exceeds our sin and our guilt, yonder on Calvary's mount outpoured there where the blood of the Lamb was spilt. Dark is the stain that we cannot hide, what can avail to wash it away? Look, there is flowing a crimson tide, whiter than snow you may be today. Marvelous, infinite, matchless grace, freely bestowed on all who believe! You that are longing to see His face, will you this moment His grace receive? Grace, grace, God's grace, Grace that will pardon and cleanse within! Grace, grace, God's grace Grace that is greater than all our sin!

CHAPTER 4

BIBLICAL BAPTISM

W e're going to look at something that most, if not all, of us have done. Some did it one way, some another and then still some another. Some did it as adults, some as teenagers or young people and some have even done it as babies. You may not have done it and you want to do it or you may have done it and you want to do it again. We are going to look at Biblical Baptism.

> *Matthew 28:19-20 – "Go ye therefore, and teach all nations, baptizing them in the name of the Father, and of the Son, and of the Holy Ghost: Teaching them to observe all things whatsoever I have commanded you; and, lo, I am with you always, even unto the end of the world."*

Baptism is one of the most important, meaningful, and beautiful experiences in the Christian life. When I speak of baptism I am not talking about any church tradition. I am speaking of Biblical Baptism. How was Baptism carried out in the scriptures? You might have heard someone speak of *"that Baptist doctrine of Baptism by immersion, or that Church of Christ or Assembly of God doctrine of Baptism by immersion."*

If it is a Baptist doctrine then the Baptists need to get rid of it. If it is a Church of Christ doctrine then the Church of Christ need to get rid of it. If it is an Assembly of God doctrine then the Assembly of God need to get rid of it. For that matter, if it is a Methodist doctrine the Methodist need to get rid of it, if it is Episcopalian doctrine the Episcopalians need to get rid of it, if it is a Presbyterian doctrine then the Presbyterians need to get rid of it and that goes for every other denomination as well.

What we want to look at is the doctrine of Baptism according to the Bible and not any particular denomination. If what I show you is not in the Bible, then don't believe it. If it is in the Bible, say, "That's God's Word, and that's what I'm going to stand on." We should not stand on any of our church doctrine if our church doctrine is not a Biblical doctrine.

Someone may say: "Baptism is just incidental. It really doesn't make any difference, or it's not that important any way." Baptism is not incidental; it is fundamental to our faith in Christ. Don't ever minimize what God has maximized! Think of the ministry of the Lord Jesus Christ. He had a ministry of approximately 3½ years. How did He begin His ministry? By being baptized! How did He conclude His ministry? By commanding us to be Baptized and to baptize others. It's called the Great Commission.

Jesus said: *"All authority has been given to Me . . . Go therefore and make disciples of all the nations, <u>BAPTIZING</u> them in the name of the Father and of the Son and of the Holy Spirit, teaching them to observe all things that I have commanded you." Matt. 28:18-20* Jesus commanded it! We are not to minimize what God has maximized! I'm going to show you why Baptism is such an important doctrine in the Word of God.

The Biblical Method of Baptism – Immersion
Some say, "The Bible teaches all kinds of baptism – sprinkling, immersion, pouring – but it really doesn't. In the Bible there is only one kind of baptism taught and that is total immersion.

That being said, are there times when some method other than immersion might be appropriate? The answer to that is "yes" as long as it is done with the same meaning as immersion in mind.

When a person is sick unto death and wants to be baptized it is simply not possible at times to baptize them by immersion, but you can certainly talk to them about the meaning of baptism and keep that in mind as you're sprinkling or pouring.

Let's see how Jesus was baptized. *In Mark 1:9 we read: "And it came to pass in those days, that Jesus came from Nazareth of Galilee, and was baptized by John in the Jordan."* The Jordan referred to here is the Jordan River. Jesus was not baptized near the Jordan or with the Jordan; He was baptized in the Jordan.

Mark 1:10 And straightway coming up out of the water. . . Now, if He came up out of the water, He certainly had to be down in the water. It's obvious by the written scripture that Jesus was baptized by immersion. Why did Jesus take this trip in the first place? The Bible says He came from Nazareth to where John was in Jordan. That's a distance of about 60 miles. This was not a baptism of convenience. John was not down there because of the scenery. It was not a pretty place and the water was murky at best.

Why was John down there baptizing? We don't have to guess. We know why he was there. He was there because there was much water there. *John 3:23 And John also was baptizing in Aenon near to Salim, <u>because there was much water there.</u>* If we baptize by sprinkling, we could baptize 1000 people with a jug full of water and that would certainly be convenient, but Jesus wasn't looking for convenience nor was He teaching a Baptism of convenience to His followers. The reason John was baptizing down there is simple: <u>There was much water there</u>, and it takes a lot of water to baptize by immersion.

It's not Convenient to Baptize by Immersion and it's not convenient to be Baptized by immersion

When I was a new pastor, there was a church a few miles away that got a new pastor and he spent two weeks cleaning the baptistry that was in horrible condition and had not been used in years. The church I pastored didn't have a baptistry. At another church I pastored their baptistry was a storage place. There was so much junk and filth in the baptistery that it couldn't be used without a major overhaul and over-haul it we did. After the baptistery was cleaned we baptized 18 people the first year.

I've read of missionaries who dug pits in the ground that looked like a grave, lined it with plastic, and filled it with precious water in order to baptize someone. That's really the correct depiction of Baptism. Many people over the years, and possibly even you, have been baptized in muddy creeks or rivers. You get your clothes soaking wet or you go to the expense of Baptismal robes. Women get their hair completely messed up and Pastors have to be quick change artists to Baptize someone and then get back in the pulpit to preach (sometimes wet themselves).

Why do we go to all that trouble? Why do some churches still hold to the tradition of baptism by immersion? Because of what Baptism symbolizes and the instructions given to us according to Romans 6:1-4

> *Romans 6:1-4 – What shall we say then? Shall we continue in sin that grace may abound? God forbid! Certainly not! How shall we who died to sin live any longer in it? Or do you not know that as many of us as were baptized into Christ Jesus were baptized into His death? Therefore, we were <u>buried</u> with Him through baptism unto death, that just as Christ was raised from the dead by the glory of the Father, even <u>so we also should walk in newness of life.</u>*

The idea of baptism according to verse 4 is burial and only immersion symbolizes a burial. It is a funeral of your old self, of living for yourself, of living in sin, you are being raised to newness of life in Jesus. If you get baptized before you get saved it's like having your funeral before you die!

Our old sinful lives of living for ourselves are over and done with. That life is buried in a watery grave and just as Jesus was raised to life, so we too are raised, out of the water, to walk with Jesus in newness of life. We now live for Him in total commitment from that moment forward.

While baptism doesn't save us, it certainly symbolizes the total salvation that we have received from our Lord and Savior Jesus Christ. He is now my Lord and my Savior, and I am going to totally identify with Him in His burial and resurrection! <u>Total immersion is the only baptism that identifies with Christ in that manner!</u>

Many people are looking for convenience rather than conviction and total commitment to the Lord. Remember it is not convenient to baptize by immersion and it certainly is not convenient to be baptized by immersion. It certainly wasn't convenient for Jesus to walk 60 miles to be baptized but He did it to give us an example that we are to follow.

Example of the Early Church
Baptism by immersion was originally practiced by all branches and sects of the early Christian church. Baptism by sprinkling or pouring initially

began being used as a way to baptize the sick or bedridden, but baptism by immersion was always the preferred method.

I have personally baptized by sprinkling a person who had only hours to live and could not be unhooked from his oxygen and get out of the bed. Once I baptized, by pouring, a 500-pound man because there was no way we could safely get him in and out of the water. But those are the exceptions!

Baptism by immersion was practiced by the Roman Catholic church up until the 13th century.

Tertullian, AD 200: "We are immersed."

Cyril, Bishop of Jerusalem, AD 348: "The body is dipped in water"

Vitringa: "The act of baptizing is the immersion of believers in water.

Thus, also, it was performed by Christ and his apostles."

It may surprise you to find out that many of the founders and leaders of Protestant denominations that practice sprinkling have in their writings acknowledged immersion as the original biblical method.

George Whitefield (Methodist), commenting on Romans 6:4: "It is certain that the words of our text is an allusion to the manner of baptism by immersion."

Conybeare and Howson (Episcopalians) Commenting on Romans 6:4: "This passage cannot be understood unless it is understood that the primitive baptism was by immersion."

John Calvin (Presbyterian) "The very word baptize, however, signifies to immersion, and it is certain that immersion was the practice of the ancient church."

Martin Luther (Lutheran) "I could wish that the baptized should be totally immersed according to the meaning of the word."

Baptize is an un-translated word: Did you know that the word baptize is basically an un-translated word in your Bible? It is really a Greek word, meaning "to immerse." King James of England commissioned the Biblical scholars in 1611 to translate the Scriptures into English. For the New Testament they went back to the earliest original manuscripts they could find. When they came to the word Baptize, which literally means "to immerse" it created a problem. The word was used in ordinary language and was not a religious word. A woman doing dishes would baptize her dishes, or immerse them. If two little boys were swimming, instead of saying, "I'm going to dunk you," one of them would say, "I'm going to baptize you." The word simply meant "to immerse" and was an ordinary word, not a religious word.

The word baptize has been *transliterated* – taken from one language and put into another language without change. Why didn't they translate it? The king at that time, and his church, practiced sprinkling and he was the one who gave the order to "Translate the Scriptures."

These scholars had a problem. If they took the word baptize and translated it as sprinkling they would not be true to God's Word and anybody reading it who knew the Greek language would have known what they did. If they translated it as immerse, then it would be a source of embarrassment to the king. And if you knew anything about King James, and wanted to keep you head on your shoulders, you didn't embarrass him! So, what you read in your Bible is an un-translated word. They just took the word *baptizo*, made a new English word out of it, and placed it into the English language. But the translation and definition has always been the same: "to immerse"

The Motive for Baptism: In baptism you are identified with Christ. Baptism shows that you are a new man or woman and that you have a new master. It shows that you are not ashamed of Christ. When you are baptized in front of people, you are saying, "I believe in Jesus." In the Bible the confession of faith was not walking down the church isle. The confession of faith was baptism. When one got baptized, he said, "I believe in Jesus Christ." "I identify myself with His death, burial, and resurrection." "I am not ashamed of Jesus." "I am one of His followers!"

Getting Baptized Doesn't Make You Saved; It Shows that You Are Saved. Don't ever think that baptism saves you or even helps to save you because that would be a mistake. Baptism does picture your salvation; it is a beautiful illustration of what happened when you got saved. It's like the wedding ring I wear. The ring doesn't make me married. I could be married and not wear it. Wearing it doesn't make me married and taking it off doesn't keep me from being married. The ring means I am not ashamed to call Beverly my wife. I'm not trying to fool anybody. I am a married man and I belong to my darling wife. The ring is a symbol, an emblem that I belong to her, and I'm not ashamed of it. Baptism is just your way of saying: I belong to Jesus - I have been buried with Him - His death has my name on it - I have been raised with Him - His resurrection is the resurrection life that I am living, and I belong to Him.

You Need to Get Advertised. One Sunday morning in children's church, a little boy prayed to receive Jesus into his heart. The children's pastor said, "Go tell the pastor that you've been saved, and you need to get baptized." The little boy went to the pastor, got his words mixed up, and said, "Pastor, I have been saved and I need to get advertised." I like that! That's what it is – when you get baptized, you're getting advertised. You're saying, "Hey, Look! – I belong to Jesus Christ."

A Mandate to Complete: Jesus did not request us to be baptized. He commanded us in Matthew 28:19 to be baptized.

> *Matthew 28:19 – "Go therefore and make disciples of all the nations, <u>baptizing</u> them in the name of the Father and of the Son and of the Holy Spirit. Teaching them to observe all things, whatsoever I have <u>commanded you</u>!"*

Now suppose I were to have a heart attack and fall down on the ground and try to say something. You would say, "He's dying; he's trying to say something. Listen to him. These are his last words. He must think this is important." This Great Commission was given to us right before Jesus went back to Heaven. These were His last words while He was on this earth. Jesus must have thought being baptized was IMPORTANT! It was something we needed to do after we received Him into our lives as our Savior and Lord. God has commanded us to be baptized! While baptism is not necessary to salvation, it is necessary to obedience, and obedience is necessary to joy and fruitfulness in our Christian life.

Sometimes you might wonder: Why can't I understand more of the Bible? Why don't I have more power in my life as a Christian? O God, teach me what this or that verse means. Lord, I don't understand this verse. Lord, teach me that verse.

God says: I'm not going to teach you anything. Why not, Lord? Well, I already showed you about baptism and you wouldn't get baptized, so why should I show you anything else? Why should I give you any more light when I have given you clear, plain light about this and you refuse to do it? *The Bible says in Mark 4:25: For whoever has, to him more will be given; but whoever does not have, even what he has will be taken away from him"*

The way to understand the part of the Scripture you don't understand is to obey the part you do understand. When you begin to obey the part you do understand, you'll be surprised how much more you'll begin to understand. God will give you more insight and direction as you begin to obey Him. *John 14:15 Jesus said: If you love Me, keep My commandments.* There is a Master to confess, there is a message to convey, there is a mandate to complete. God has commanded us to be baptized.

Baptism Does Not Save. Again, I want to make clear that Baptism does not save. You can be saved anytime, anyplace. If baptism is necessary to salvation, then a man in the desert can't be saved. A man in an airplane couldn't be saved. A man in a submarine surrounded by the ocean couldn't be saved because there's not enough water in the submarine to baptize him. Anytime anybody anyplace calls upon the name of Jesus in repentance and faith, they will be saved.

Bible Baptism - Baptism, as taught in the Bible, has a method, a meaning, and a motive. The method – immersion. Remember, if you change the method, you destroy the meaning. The meaning – a picture of our identification with the death, burial, and resurrection of Jesus, which is the gospel. The motive – to confess Christ, obey Him, and declare His saving gospel.

If you are saved and not yet baptized, make plans as soon as possible to present yourself for this wonderful experience. It's up to you to take the step of faith and give the Pastor your name and say – I've trusted Jesus as my Savior and Lord and I want to be Baptized by Immersion.

CHAPTER 5

THE KING ARRIVES

"Hope and Expectation"

W e begin this morning celebrating the season of ADVENT but what really is ADVENT? The word Advent literally means a coming into place, view, or being; an arrival. (The Advent of the Christ) The word Advent means the coming of Christ into the world, but in a greater sense Christ has existed before the world was ever created, He is Himself God, and all things were created by Him.

> *John 1:1-3 – In the beginning was the Word and the Word was with God and the Word was God. The same was in the beginning with God. All things were made by Him and without Him was not anything made that was made.*

> *1 John 1:1 – That which was from the beginning, which we have heard, which we have seen with our eyes, which we have looked upon, and our hands have handled, concerning the Word of life*

These verses are verbally parallel with Genesis 1:1 (*In the beginning God created the Heavens and the earth*) and speak of the beginning of creation. John in these verses establishes the preexistence of Christ in eternity past. Christ already "was" when the beginning took place. John declares that in the beginning the "Word" (*Logos*) existed. He is none other than God Himself, not only bringing the Word but incorporating it in His own Person, Life, and Being. Furthermore, this "Word" was "face to face" with God, indicating a distinction of Persons within the

Godhead as well as an equality of Persons. Finally, the "Word" is eternally God. There was never a time when the "Word" was not fully God.

> *Colossians 1:14-17 – In whom we have redemption through His blood, the forgiveness of sins. He is the image of the invisible God, the firstborn over all creation. For by Him all things were created that are in heaven and that are on earth, visible and invisible, whether thrones or dominions or principalities or powers. All things were created through Him and for Him. And He is before all things, and in Him all things consist.*

Christ's likeness or "image" to God is so genuine that it provides us with a perfect manifestation and exact representation of God. In the person of Jesus Christ incarnate, we see a revelation of the invisible God. "Firstborn" indicates that the historic Jesus was none other than the preexistent Christ, who is coeternal with the Father. The term "firstborn" is a reference to priority of position. Each person who is saved becomes a son of God by adoption; nonetheless, because of Christ deity, the Son has a priority of position over all others (who are children by adoption rather than begetting). *John 3:16 For God so loved the world that He sent His only begotten Son.* So, in a truer sense when we celebrate the arrival (advent) of Christ we must always remember that He is eternal, He has always existed, He had no beginning, He has no end, He is the Alpha and the Omega, He is Himself God.

Matthew 1:1-17 – Genealogy
The book of the genealogy means the family record of descent. Verse 18 formally introduces the birth of Jesus Christ. The words "genealogy" in verse 1 and "birth" in verse 18 translate the Greek word *genesis* which of course is the name of the first book of the Bible "Genesis." Just as the beginning of creation is recorded in the book of Genesis: *"In the beginning God created the heavens and the earth"* So the re-creation of our lives begins with Jesus Christ: *2 Corinthians 5:17 "Therefore, if anyone is in Christ, he is a new creation; old things have passed away; behold, all things have become new."*

"Jesus" is the Latin rendering of the Greek word *Iesous*, which in turn is a rendering of the Hebrew and Aramaic word *Yeshua*, meaning "Yahweh will save," or 'the salvation of the Lord." Verse 21: *"You shall call His* name JESUS for He will save His people from their sins." In the Old Testament Joshua is also translated *Iesous*. As Joshua led Israel across the Jordan and into the Promised Land, JESUS will lead His people into the Promised Land. Paradise!

The names in the genealogy are taken from 1 Chronicles 1-3. The birth of Christ is presented as the goal of Israel's sacred history, which is divided into 3 pivotal divisions. 1. From the initial promise to Abraham to the Kingdom of David. 2. From King David to the Babylonian Exile, and 3. From the Exile (the sign of Israel's sin) to the birth of JESUS (the one who is to save us from our sins)

Messianic prophecy intensified the interest in genealogy, since the promised Messiah would be:

1. **Of the seed of woman:** *Genesis 3:15 I will put enmity between you and the woman, and between your seed and **her seed**; He shall bruise your head, and you shall bruise His heel.* Eve apparently understood the prophecy but misapplied it to the birth of her first-born son, Cain. In Hebrew, Eve literally said "I have gotten a man, the Lord." Yes, the Lord would be born of a woman, but it wouldn't be Cain – it would be the Lord Jesus Christ who would come years later. **Her seed!** This is the first prophecy of a virgin birth. Women do not have seed, men do.

2. **Of the seed of Abraham:** *Genesis 22:18 In your **seed** all the nations of the earth shall be blessed, because you have obeyed My voice.* Notice that the verse does not refer to the nation of Israel. It refers to a seed, not to seeds. There would come a seed, and that seed would produce the Lord Jesus Christ, (God Himself) to save mankind from their sins and offer to them eternal life in Heaven through their salvation which comes only by the Grace of God through faith in Jesus.

3. **This seed would come through a virgin birth.** *Isaiah 7:14 Therefore the Lord Himself will give you a sign; Behold the virgin shall conceive and bear a Son and shall call His name Immanuel."* In the Old Testament, Judah's King Ahaz was shaken by the news that Syria and Israel had formed an alliance to depose him. He in turn formed an alliance with Assyria to help him in this fight. Their scheme was a

threat not just to the king personally but to the entire promise that God had given to Abraham. If the nation is destroyed then there will be no deliverer to come. But God sent Isaiah with a warning against the tactic, plus a "sign" explaining why there was no need for fear. *"The virgin will be with child and will give birth to a son and will call Him Immanuel"* The reassurance was that the kingly line would not be cut off; despite any military threat, the Messiah – Immanuel (God with us) would still come through Ahaz's lineage in the appointed way, place and time. And just as nothing could stop the arrival of the Messiah in His first advent, nothing can stop the arrival of the Christ in His second advent. We have the hope, the assurance, the expectation that Christ will soon come.

4. **This promised Messiah would be born in Bethlehem around the first century.** *(Daniel 9:25-26) Know therefore and understand, that from the going forth of the command to restore and build Jerusalem until Messiah the Prince, there shall be seven weeks and sixty-two weeks; the street shall be built again and the wall, even in troublesome times, and after the sixty-two weeks Messiah shall be cut off, but not for Himself; and the people of the prince who is to come shall destroy the city and the sanctuary. The end of it shall be with a flood, and till the end of the war desolations are determined.*

Starting with a historical decree that was then still future, the prophet Daniel established a timeline for the Messiah's presence on earth. Micah's contribution was to name Bethlehem as the place of human origin for Christ whose "goings forth are from long ago, from the days of eternity"

> Micah 5:2 – But you, Bethlehem Ephrathah, though you are little among the thousands of Judah, yet out of you shall come forth to Me the One to be Ruler in Israel, whose going forth are from old, from everlasting.

5. **The promised Messiah would be Jewish and would be a King.** In Genesis 49:10 scripture narrows the Messiah's lineage further, to the descendants of Judah: *"The scepter will not depart from Judah, nor the ruler's staff from between his feet, until He to whom it belongs shall come and the obedience of the nations shall be His."* In addition to identifying the Anointed One as a king, this verse offers

a clue about timing. The nation's genealogical records were kept in the temple, so for the Messiah's tribal affiliation to be ascertained, He would have to had been on the scene before 70 A.D., when the Romans destroyed the temple. While Matthew traces Jesus lineage through Joseph and Luke traces it through Mary both gospel writers affirm the virgin conception as fact.

To make atonement for the sin of man, Jesus had to be human. To have the authority to forgive sin and the ability to live sinlessly, He had to be God. The virgin conception is the way through which God accomplished this combination in one person, Jesus Christ.

> *Matthew 1:18-25 – "Now the birth of Jesus Christ was as follows: After His mother Mary was betrothed to Joseph, before they came together, she was found with child of the Holy Spirit."*

"Betrothed" means "engaged," but the meaning of the word in Jesus day goes beyond our own definition of "engaged." Jewish law looked upon engagement, which lasted one year in Galilee, as a formal bond that could only be dissolved by divorce thus Joseph is called Mary's husband in verse 19 though the marriage had not been consummated through sexual intimacy.

Joseph, having learned of Mary's pregnancy, was permitted to divorce her on grounds of infidelity. If she consented to this charge, she could be divorced privately in the presence of two witnesses. If she objected to the charge, she would stand before a court of three rabbis and be divorced publicly. God had to make known to Joseph what had happened to Mary so that he would be able to accept and understand.

Joseph took the news of Mary's pregnancy hard. He found her story unbelievable, but he did not want to make a spectacle of breaking off the relationship. He was leaning toward a quiet little divorce; a private transaction between himself and the synagogue leaders.

As he made his plans to do this, "an angel of the Lord appeared to him in a dream" – most likely a repeat performance by the angel Gabriel. The angel in the dream verified Mary's story; the child she carried was "of the Holy Spirit." The angel went on to reaffirm what Mary herself must have told Joseph.

1. The baby is a "Son" (Matt. 1:21).
2. His name is "JESUS" – Greek for Joshua, which means "Yahweh is salvation" – "for He will save His people from their sins" (Matt. 1:21).
3. The conception in the womb of a virgin fulfills Old Testament prophecy. *Isaiah 7:14 Therefore the Lord Himself will give you a sign; Behold, the virgin shall conceive and bear a Son, and shall call His name Immanuel.*
4. Mary's son will be "Immanuel" – no ordinary child – which is translated "God with us" (Matthew 1:23).

Joseph woke up convinced. Fear that Mary had been unfaithful vanished. He immediately changed his plans. He "took to him his wife" (Matthew 1:24). Joseph and Mary did not share physical intimacy until after the miracle child was born.

The message for us today? Joseph woke up convinced! Have we awoken to the fact of who Jesus really is? Are we convinced? Is Jesus truly your Savior and your Lord? Jesus is God! He is the Great I Am! He is the creator! He is the Savior! He is Immanuel – God with us! One day every knee will bow, and every tongue confess that Jesus Christ is Lord.

During this Christmas season and every day throughout the year let us live our lives ever mindful of who Jesus is and live our lives in hope and expectancy of His return to this earth to once again fulfill prophecy that He will be KING OF KING and LORD OF LORDS!

CHAPTER 6

A BABY IS BORN

Luke 2:1-2 — And it came to pass in those days that a decree went out from Caesar Augustus that all the world should be registered. This census first took place while Quirinius was governing Syria.

I t should be noted that this registration was for the purpose of more taxes upon the people.

A decree went out from Caesar Augustus: Caesar Augustus was the grandnephew of Julius Caesar and was adopted as his son. After the murder of Julius Caesar, young Octavius Augustus (his given name and later to become Caesar Augustus) ruled with Mark Antony and Lepidus in a triumvirate (rule by three). Then for more than forty years, from 27B.C. to 14A.D., Augustus served by himself as the first emperor of the Roman Empire. It was under his reign that the first taxation took place and during his reign that Christ was born.

From Augustus perspective, he was demonstrating his authority and power over that part of the world where he ruled. Don't you know he had a big head? He and he alone had the authority to force everyone to go to the city where their ancestors were born to register themselves for the tax. For that matter he had the authority to force the people to do whatever he pleased. And don't you know they were excited! We get to pay taxes! Not much has changed some 2,000 years later as we are still paying heavy taxes and some in the government of our land want us to continue paying even more taxes and higher taxes. However, we can learn some lessons from this story as well.

1. Never despair over what the government is doing. From God's perspective Augustus was just a pawn in God's hands to further God's agenda.

   > *Proverbs 21:1 – The king's heart is in the hand of the Lord, like the rivers of water, He turns it wherever He wishes.*

2. Augustus decree went out in God's perfect timing and according to God's perfect plan to bring His Son (Jesus) into the world.

3. Think about what is going on in our government today. Could God be preparing to bring His Son back to this earth for the second time?

Do you think the people of that day rebelled against the government and against these taxes? Of course they did! There was rebellion going on everywhere. Rebelling against a government when it is passing immoral or unethical laws is always the right thing to do and shame on us if we don't. Shame on us if we don't even take the time to go out and vote. But if we stand up to evil government and evil still persists <u>we should not fear for God is in control!</u>

Today, America is in a terrible financial situation and the economy desperately needs to be corrected. But in a nation founded on God on Godly principles we cannot, shall not, and will not fix the economy until we return to God and His principles, His statues, and His commands. You will not fix America's economy until we return to the moral and ethical foundation of this country. When things look so bleak, as they did in the days when Joseph and Mary lived, God could, and I believe is, preparing to send His Son to this earth a second time.

When it comes to America's taxes, America doesn't have an income problem, it has a spending problem. Millions and Billions of dollars are spent on waste. Remember that Rome fell because they tried to tax their way out of a moral decline.

> *Luke 2:3-6 – So, all went to be registered, everyone to his own city. Joseph also went up from Galilee, out of the city of Nazareth, into Judea, to the city of David, which is called Bethlehem, because he was of the house*

and lineage of David, to be registered with Mary, his betrothed wife, who was with child. So, it was, that while they were there, the days were completed for her to be delivered.

The government forced Joseph to make a long trip just to pay his taxes. His betrothed, Mary, who had to go with him, was going to have a baby any moment. But when they arrived in Bethlehem they couldn't even find a place to stay. When we do God's will, we are not guaranteed a comfortable life, but we are promised that everything, even our discomfort, has meaning and purpose in God's plan. God controls all history! By the decree of Augustus, Jesus was born in the very town prophesied for his birth even though his parents didn't live there.

Micah 5:2 – But you, Bethlehem Ephrathah, though you are little among the thousands of Judah, yet out of you shall come forth to Me the One to be Ruler in Israel, whose goings forth are from old, from everlasting.

Joseph and Mary were both descendants of King David. The Old Testament is filled with prophecies that the Messiah would be born in David's royal line.

Luke 2:7 – And she brought forth her first-born Son, and wrapped Him in swaddling cloths, and laid Him in a manger, because there was no room for them in the inn.

Swaddling cloths (bands of cloth) were used to keep a baby warm and to give it a sense of security. These cloths were believed to protect its internal organs. The custom of wrapping infants this way is still practiced in many Mideastern countries. The mention of the manger is the basics for the traditional belief that Jesus was born in a stable. Stables were often caves with feeding troughs (mangers) carved into the rock walls.

Despite pretty Christmas card pictures, the surroundings where Jesus was born were dark and dirty. This was not the atmosphere the Jews expected as the birthplace of the Messiah King. They thought the promised Messiah would be born in royal surroundings. We should not limit God by what we expect! God is at work in our sin-darkened and dirty world. He is at work in places where we would never even dream of setting foot on and yet people are being saved and God's Sprit is moving upon this earth even as He prepares to return.

Although our first picture of Jesus is as a baby in a manger it must not be our last. This tiny helpless baby lived an amazing life. He died for us, ascended into Heaven and will come back to this earth as King of Kings and Lord of Lords. Christ will rule the world and judge all people according to the decisions we make about Him! Make sure you don't under estimate Jesus!

> *Luke 2:8-14 – Now there were in the same country shepherds living out in the fields, keeping watch over their flock by night. And behold, an angel of the Lord stood before them, and the glory of the Lord shone around them, and they were greatly afraid. Then the angel said to them, "Do not be afraid, for behold, I bring you good tidings of great joy which will be to all people. For there is born to you this day in the city of David a Savior, who is Christ the Lord. And this will be the sign to you; You will find a Babe wrapped in swaddling cloths, lying in a manger." And Suddenly there was with the angel a multitude of the heavenly host praising God and saying: "Glory to God in the highest and on earth peace, goodwill toward men."*

From Max Lucado's book we read:

> "On the night when the Savior was born, who received an invitation to greet Him? Was it the World's Emperors? Was it the Priests or the Prophets? Was it the Theologians, the soldiers, the scholars? It was none of these. The invitation to receive the Lord Jesus was an HONOR that was reserved for the lowest of men. These Shepherds were the least educated of men. They were ranch hands who were despised by the local people. They were men whose skin glistened with sweat. These men's clothes gave off the stench of being un-kept and unwashed. They lacked the most basic of manners. Their language would be unfit for our Children's ears. They were minimum wage earners who were unlikely to

be admitted to any event of royalty or prominence. So why the shepherds? Why did God choose to announce the arrival of the long-awaited messiah to shepherds?

These Shepherds, no doubt, had names but we have no idea what their names were. Of course, there were people who knew these Shepherds and knew their names. Yet, whenever their names were mentioned in that day and whenever they are mentioned without names in our day they have graced the guest list for the most joyful moment in human history.

Shepherds were despised by the orthodox people of the day. They were unable to keep the details of the ceremonial law and they could not observe all the most meticulous hand washings and rules of the strict Pharisees. Yet it was these simple men of the field that God's message first came. Jesus first visitors were those whom religion had rejected and scorned. So why the shepherds?

Hebrew Scholar Alfred Ebershine says: "The flocks near Bethlehem were no ordinary sheep. These sheep were being raised as SACRIFICES in the TEMPLE. These were SACRIFICIAL SHEEP! They were being raised for only one purpose! They would one day be LED to the ALTAR of GOD and there they would SHED THEIR BLOOD and Give their LIVES for the SINS of God's People."

A LAMB is the most consistent picture of Christ in the Bible. When John the Baptist saw Christ coming to him he said, *"Behold the LAMB OF GOD who takes away the SIN of the world."* Who would be a more appropriate audience to share the GOOD NEWS of the BIRTH of the LAMB OF GOD than these Shepherds?"

Here the angels invited these Shepherds to meet the real "Lamb of God" who would take away the sin of the world.

> *Luke 2:15-20 — So it was, when the angels had gone away from them into Heaven, that the shepherds said to one another, "Let us now go to Bethlehem and see this thing that has come to pass, which the Lord has made known to us." And they came with haste and found Mary and Joseph, and the Babe lying in a manger. Now when they had seen Him they made widely known the saying which was told them concerning this Child. And all those who heard it marveled at those things which were told them by the shepherds. But Mary kept all these things and pondered them in her heart. Then the shepherds returned, glorifying and praising God for all the things that they had heard and seen, as it was told them.*

What a birth announcement! Usually when you hear someone has had a baby you are very excited and happy for them. Here the shepherds are terrified! Their fear is soon turned to joy as the angels announce the Messiah's birth.

First the shepherds ran to see the baby then they spread the word "Jesus is your Messiah, your Savior." I wonder, do we look forward to meeting Jesus in prayer every day? Do we look forward to reading His word on a daily basis? Have you discovered a Lord so wonderful that you can't help sharing Him with your friends and people you meet along the way? The greatest event in the history of mankind has just happened! The Messiah has been born! For ages the Jews had waited for this and when it finally occurred the announcement came to humble shepherds. The good news about Jesus is that He comes to all, including the plain and the ordinary. He comes to anyone with a heart humble enough to receive Him. Whoever you are, whatever you do, you can have Jesus in your life. Don't think you need extra-ordinary qualifications. He accepts you as you are!

Some of the Jews were waiting for a Savior to deliver them from Roman rule. Others hoped the Christ would deliver them from physical ailments but Jesus, while healing their ailments, and establishing a spiritual kingdom, came to deliver us from our sin.

His work is more far reaching than anyone can imagine. Christ paid the price for sin and opened the way to peace with God the Father. He offers us more than temporary political or physical changes. He offers us new hearts that will last for eternity.

The story of Jesus birth resounds with music that has inspired composers for 2,000 years. The angel's song is an all-time favorite. Often called the "Gloria" after its first word in the Latin translation, it is the basics of modern choral works, traditional Christmas carols, and ancient liturgical chants.

Not only during Christmas time but every day throughout the year, let's put the music of Christ in our hearts and in our minds. **Glory to God in the Highest! And on earth, Peace, Goodwill toward Men!**

CHAPTER 7

WISE MEN STILL SEEK HIM

Matthew 2:1-23 – Now when Jesus was born in Bethlehem of Judea in the days of Herod the king, behold, there came wise men from the east to Jerusalem.

These Wise Men arrived some 1 ½ to 2 years after Jesus was born.

Out of the mouth of babes: When a pastor asked the class, "Why was Jesus born in Bethlehem?", a boy raised his hand and replied, "Because his mother was there."

You do know what would have happened if it had been three wise women, instead of men, don't you? They would have asked for directions, arrived on time, helped deliver the baby, cleaned the stable, made a casserole, and brought disposable diapers as gifts.

Haggai 2:7 – And I will shake all nations, and the "Desire of all Nations" shall come; and I will fill this house with glory, saith the Lord of hosts.

Though the Christ was *"The Desire of all Nations"* his birth and young life was little observed and taken notice of. John says of Christ *"He came into the world and the world knew Him not – He came unto His own and His own received Him not"* The first who took notice of the Christ after his birth were the Shepherds (Luke 2:15ff) who saw and heard glorious things concerning Him and <u>made these things known abroad.</u> After that Simeon and Anna spoke of Him by the Holy Spirit <u>to all who would</u>

listen. You would think that with these announcements of the arrival of their Messiah the inhabitants of Jerusalem would have embraced their long-looked-for Messiah but that doesn't seem to be the case. Jesus continued for nearly 2 years at Bethlehem with no further notice of Him until the Wise Men came.

The inquiry of the Wise Men was made during the days of Herod the King. Christ was born during the closing years of his reign. The Herod family was Jewish in that they descended from the line of Esau; Jacobs's brother. They were known as Edomites. They refused to be circumcised and therefore were not considered true Jews by most of their brothers. *Genesis 36:1 Now these are the generations of Esau, who is Edom.* Edom is the name of the country lying south of Judah and the descendants of Esau populated the area. Herod the Greats grandfather was Antipas and he died in 78 BC. The Romans appointed Antipas as governor of Idumea. His father was Antipater. Julius Caesar appointed him procurator of Judea in 47 BC. He died in 43 BC. A procurator is an administrator of a province or a part of a country that is removed from the capital and major cities (an outside territory governed by ancient Rome.) Herod the Great was also known as "King of the Jews" (a title given to him by the Roman government.) He was one of Julius Caesar's triumvir's (one of 3 administrators who governed together and shared responsibilities at the same time.) Mark Antony appointed this Herod to be tetrarch of Galilee in 37 BC. Herod died on March 4 BC and was succeeded by one of his sons, Archelaus.

The better known of Herod the Greats sons were Archelaus, Herod Antipas, Herod Philip, and a second Herod Philip. Archelaus succeeded his father in ruling Judea (Matthew 2:22.) Herod Antipas ruled in Galilee when Pontius Pilate was ruling in Judea. He was known as Herod the Tetrarch (a person who ruled ¼ of an area.) Herod Philip was better known as Philip who married his brother's wife which brought the condemnation of John the Baptist which cost him his head on a silver platter. The other son named Herod Philip ruled the territory east of the Jordan River. (Now we've learned everything about Herod's family that we never wanted to know.)

We know from scripture that Jesus was born during Herod the Greats reign and that Herod died when Jesus was a young child. History records that Herod died in 4 BC. Thus, our present calendar is off in its calculation by about four to six years (this would place the birth of Christ at about 6 to 4 BC. Herod the Great was an extremely cruel man. He frequently became outraged when anyone disagreed with him. He murdered his wife and three sons who disagreed with him. In trying to murder the Christ; he murdered all the male children two years old and younger in Bethlehem. He was known as a great architect and builder. He was in the process of refurbishing the Jewish Temple that was so impressive to Jesus disciples. When they asked Jesus in Matthew 24 to look at the beautiful temple, Jesus said not one stone would be left upon another. This prophecy of Jesus actually came true in 70 AD. When Herod became sick unto death he knew that there would be no weeping at his funeral. So, in order, to make sure that everyone in Jerusalem would be mourning and crying during the time that he would die he ordered 3,000 leading citizens of Jerusalem murdered. He knew by doing this that everyone in town would be mourning and crying during the time that he would die.

THE WISE MEN
Wise Men originally were of the priestly caste among the Persians and Babylonians. These Magi from the east were experts in the study of the stars. Tradition claims there were three royal visitors who were also kings. However, there is no real historical evidence to verify this. All we are told is that wise men came from the east to Jerusalem. If they came from Babylon they could have traveled 1,000 miles to see the Christ. If they traveled from Persia they could have traveled over 1,500 miles to see the Christ. They were looking for the one Born King of the Jews. They came to Jerusalem, the royal capital of Israel seeking this new one born King of the Jews based upon their calculations of the stars. What star they saw we are not told. Why they associated this new star with the birth of a king we are not told.

Daniel and many others in the Old Testament had been exiled to Babylon (current country of Iraq), and throughout the east, and on into Persia (current country of Iran) (the story of Esther in based in Persia). They would have had contact with the people there and told of the prophecies of a coming King, a Messiah, in Israel. The star was not a natural phenomenon for it led the wise men directly to where Christ was. This was a divine manifestation by God. When they came asking this mad man, Herod the Great, where this King of the Jews would be born you can only imagine his reaction. After all, he was "King of the Jews!"

Micah 5:2 – But thou, Bethlehem Ephrathah, though thou be little among the thousands of Judah, yet out of thee shall He come forth unto Me that is to be ruler in Israel; whose goings forth have been from of old, from everlasting.

Isaiah 9:6-7 – For unto us a child is born, unto us a son is given: and the government shall be upon his shoulder; and his name shall be called Wonderful Counselor, The mighty God, The everlasting Father, The Prince of Peace. Of the increase of His government and peace there shall be no end, upon the throne of David, and upon His kingdom, to order it, and to establish it with judgment and with justice from henceforth even forever. The zeal of the LORD of hosts will perform this.

We don't really know exactly when the wise men showed up. It was some time after the birth of Christ for they were now living in a house and had moved out of the stable. I would imagine it was probably about a year and a half later. Herod feeling that if he killed all the babies born in Bethlehem two years old and younger, he would surely cover the time period and kill this rival to his throne. The Bible says of this massacre of children: *Then was fulfilled that which was spoken by Jeremiah the prophet, saying, In Ramah there was a voice heard, lamentation, and weeping, and great mourning, Rachel weeping for her children, and would not be comforted, because they are not. (Jeremiah 31:15)* Rachel was the Mother of Benjamin. She died at his birth outside the city of Bethlehem and was buried in Bethlehem.

Now the Bible says when Herod heard that this new king was born he was disturbed or your translation may say troubled. But then it says that everyone in Jerusalem was disturbed. Now why would everyone be disturbed? Isn't this what they wanted? Didn't they want the Messiah to come? Today we believe that Jesus is going to return. Does it disturb or trouble us? Most people want Jesus to return, they just don't want Him to do it today. Just think about what you lose when Jesus returns. You leave earth and go to heaven. That means that you lose your home, all the money you have saved all your life is gone, if you have family members that are not saved, you leave them behind. Everything you have ever worked for is suddenly, in the twinkling of an eye, gone and left behind. Does that disturb you?

The wise men sought Jesus by going after Him and bringing Him gifts. They brought Him gold for a King, frankincense (incense) to worship the King, and myrrh for the suffering Savior (used as a fragrance for embalming). Whatever sort of Wise Men these were before, now they began to be truly Wise Men when they began to inquire after the Christ.

The Unusual Star Appeared in the East

> *Numbers 24:17 — I shall see him but not now; I shall behold him, but not near; there shall come a Star out of Jacob, and a Scepter shall rise out of Israel. . . .*

The Wise Men perhaps heard of this star that was to come. Perhaps they had heard of stories handed down by Daniel the Prophet and many others in the Old Testament who had been exiled to Babylon and throughout the east on into Persia. They didn't follow the star as we have come to believe and sing about "We Three Kings of Orient are bearing gifts we traverse a-far — field and fountain — moor and mountain — following yonder Star." The Bible says they saw the star in the East — came to Jerusalem looking for this King and then the star appeared to them again. Exactly when the star originally appeared to them or how long they waited before leaving for Bethlehem we are not told. We do know that a camel can travel 30 to 45 miles a day (depending on the type of camel) and they possibly could have gotten there in a little over a month to a few months depending on how far they traveled per day.

How amazed they must have been that everyone in Jerusalem did not know of this event

These men were Gentiles. It is noteworthy that the Jews did not regard the Christ when He was right in their midst and yet the gentiles traveled hundreds of miles to seek Him out. The Wise Men could have reasoned "If such a Prince was born in Israel we shall hear of Him shortly in our own country and it will be time enough to pay our homage to Him." But so impatient were they to know Him that they took a long journey to enquire after Him.

NOTE: Those who truly desire to know Christ will search for Him with all their hearts regardless of the pains or perils they may encounter in seeking after Him!

The question the Wise Men asked?

"Where is He that is born King of the Jews?" Notice what they did not ask! They didn't ask if such a person had actually been born. They were sure that a King had been born! (Those who know something of Christ desire to know more of Him.) The Wise Men expected everyone to know the answer to their question. They expected everyone to be worshipping Him! So, they go door to door asking everyone, but no one seems to know what they are talking about. If someone were to ask them "What business do you have with this King of the Jews" they would have answered – "We Have Come to Worship Him" (When Christ is our KING we desire to Worship Him!) News of these Wise Men asking questions all over Jerusalem reached the ears of Herod the King and it troubled him.

> *Matthew 2:3 – "When Herod the king had heard these things, he was troubled, and all Jerusalem with him."*

Herod was troubled for he had been given the title from Rome "King of the Jews" and he would have no rival; but why was all Jerusalem troubled with him? All those except those few whose hearts were spiritually ready for the coming Messiah. Sin brings conviction and when we desire sin more than we desire God we are troubled in the presence of God. Herod calls <u>all</u> the chief priests and <u>all</u> the scribes together and inquires where the Christ is to be born. The answer they give is "In Bethlehem of Judea" to distinguish it from another Bethlehem in the land of Zebulon.

Bethlehem of Judea is also known as Bethlehem Ephrathah. There was another city known as Bethlehem in the Galilee region. Bethlehem Ephrathah is located five miles south of Jerusalem and means "House of Bread." Bethlehem was the birthplace of King David. According to Luke 2:1-7, Mary and Joseph had traveled there from Nazareth and Jesus was born in a stable after they arrived there. Bethlehem would not be important at all except for the person that would be born there.

> *Micah 5:2 – But thou, Bethlehem Ephrathah, though thou be little among the thousands of Judah, yet out of*

thee shall He come forth unto me that is to be <u>RULER</u> in Israel; whose goings forth have been from of old, from everlasting.

The ruler comes from Bethlehem, in time, but His activities have been from eternity. His goings forth were before creation. (Christ will be a Savior to those only who are willing to take Him as their RULER!)

Herod was an old man when he met the Wise Men. He had reigned in Israel for 35 years. At this time Jesus was a baby less than 2 years old. Herod would be dead many years before this child could even be a threat to him, yet he was extremely jealous. Nothing less than the blood of this infant would satisfy him, yet, *had he thought*, if this indeed was the Messiah he would be fighting a losing battle against God Himself.

In front of the Wise Men Herod covered up his sinful heart (his jealously and his hatred.) (People are often tormented with secret sins which they keep to themselves. You'll only find peace when you confess your sins to God and turn from those sins to live under God's governance; as the RULER of your life.) Herod covered his sin with the disguise of religion – *"that I may come & worship Him also"* (The greatest wickedness often conceals itself under a mask of piety.) How easily Herod could have sent spies to follow the Wise Men and have the baby killed on the spot. (When God is in control nothing can thwart His plans. You won't win when you fight against God!)

How strange that the Wise Men went alone to Worship the Christ. From Jerusalem they went to Bethlehem, resolving to seek the Christ until they had found Him. Not one person of the court, not one government official, not one religious figure, not one official from the city accompanied them on their journey to the Christ. Pure civility, that men of influence had come from another country, would have demanded that at least a city official accompany them. Perhaps people should have followed them out of pure curiosity. But nothing, they went alone! Wise Men from a far country would come to worship the Christ, the newborn King, and yet the Jews, his kinsmen, would not take one step to go to the next town to welcome Him! It might have been a discouragement to these Wise Men to find Him they sought to be so neglected at home. They might have thought or even said: "Are we come so far to honor the King of the Jews and do the Jews themselves put such a slight upon him and us?" Yet they persisted in their journey! (We must continue our devotion to Christ, though we be alone in it; whatever others do, we must serve the Lord; if they will not go to heaven with us, yet we must not go to hell with them.) The Bible records that the wise men went home a different way. It is true that they went home a different way from which they came. They took a different route. But they truly went home a different way than they came! They went home changed men; changed by the Christ whom they had given their hearts and their lives to as their Savior and their King.

After returning from Egypt, Joseph and Mary were warned in a dream not to return to Bethlehem for Herod the Greats son, Archelaus, was now reigning at the death of his father. Now Archelaus was as worse if not worse than his father. And so, they return to the land of Israel. But instead of going to Bethlehem, the land of their ancestors, they went home. They went back to Nazareth where Jesus grew up as a child and young man. They went home! Are you ready to go home, home to Jesus – renew your heart to Him – renew your love to Him – renew your life to Him? Remember Wise men (and women) still seek Him!

CHAPTER 8

JESUS REJECTED IN HIS OWN HOME TOWN

Luke 4:14 – Then Jesus returned in the power of the Spirit to Galilee and news of Him went out through all the surrounding region.

First, we see <u>the Holy Spirit descending on Jesus</u> at His baptism. <u>Then He was filled with the Spirit</u>. <u>He then was led by the Spirit</u> into the wilderness and underwent His temptation from Satan. Once He passed this test by trusting in and living by the 'Word of God', we now see that He returns to Galilee with the 'Power of the Spirit.'

Luke says that news of Him went out through all the surrounding area. What news? So far, all that Luke has recorded is that He had been baptized and tempted by Satan in the wilderness. Is this the news he was talking about? Thank you, Matthew, for filling in some of the blanks for us.

Matthew 4:23-25 – And Jesus went about all Galilee, teaching in their synagogues, preaching the gospel of the kingdom, and healing all kinds of sickness and all kinds of disease among the people. Then His fame went through out all Syria; and they brought to Him all sick people who were afflicted with various diseases and torments, and those who were demon-possessed, epileptics, and paralytics, and He healed them. Great multitudes followed Him, from Galilee, and from Decapolis, Jerusalem, Judea, and beyond the Jordan.

56

These events, scholars say, happened after Jesus temptation in the wilderness and before His return to His hometown of Nazareth.

> *Luke 4:15 – And He taught in their synagogues, being glorified by all.*

Luke summarizes all that we just read in Matthew in that one sentence: **And He taught in their synagogues, being glorified by all.**

Jesus spends one year, after the temptation in the wilderness, preaching, teaching, healing and now having a great following, He returns to His hometown of Nazareth; where He grew up.

> *Luke 4:16 – So, He came to Nazareth, where He had been brought up. And as His custom was, He went into the synagogue on the Sabbath day. . .*

Without a Jewish Temple, people began setting up synagogues as a place of worship. A synagogue was allowed to exist in any town that had at least 10 Jewish families living there. Even after the Temple was rebuilt, synagogues continued in existence. Jesus not only set an example for us to attend weekly worship services, but He also had two other customs that He observed and left for us an example to follow as well. 1) He prayed regularly and 2) He taught regularly (by His life's actions and by His words).

The Sabbath in those days was on Saturday. After the resurrection of Christ, which happened on a Sunday morning, early followers of Jesus began meeting on Sunday mornings and referred to their day of Sabbath as "The Lord's Day" which we continue to observe to this day.

> *Luke 4:16b-17a – He stood up to read and He was handed the book of the prophet Isaiah.*

It was common practice in synagogue worship, when a traveling preacher/teacher was in town and came to your service that you allowed him to read a portion of scripture. The visiting preacher would then re-join the congregation and it was up to the pastor to preach a message on what was just read. (Talk about being ready in season and out of season). Now they had scrolls in those days instead of a complete book of the Bible as we have today. The pastor could have handed Jesus any scroll from any book of the Old Testament but he (guided I believe by God's hand) handed Jesus the scroll of what we know as the book of Isaiah. The book of Isaiah was written around 700 B.C. and Jesus could have read from any of the 66 chapters in the book. But He chose a particular scripture for a particular audience and a particular point to be made. Luke tells us that Jesus stood up to read and then sat down. He goes on to say that the whole congregation was staring a hole through Him. *Their eyes were fixed on Him* is what the scripture says. It's very important that we understand what is going on here. First of all, let me ask you a question. If I stood up to read and then went and sat on any row of seats in the sanctuary, how could everyone's eyes be fixed on me? How could the people in front of me or behind me see my face, my eyes?

The people in those days did not have chairs to sit on when they came to worship. The pastor, if you will, sat on a chair, or stool, and the people sat on the floor at his feet. When the visiting preacher, Rabbi, would finish reading he would sit on the floor with the rest of the people and the pastor would sit on the stool and preach the sermon. What Jesus did was out of the ordinary. He stood up and read the scripture, then He took the seat of the pastor and began to explain what He had just read. The people were astonished, they weren't expecting this, they wondered "What in the world is He doing?" and all eyes were fixed on Him. I believe you could have heard a pin drop! He basically took over the service and began to preach a sermon after He had read from the book of Isaiah. Now we don't have the whole recorded sermon, but we do have this much: *"Today, this scripture is fulfilled in your hearing."*

Now the point is this:

1) What scripture had been fulfilled in their hearing?
2) What did Jesus read that day from the book of Isaiah?
3) What did the scripture He read mean and what did it mean to them? He read to them Isaiah 61:1-2 and is recorded in Luke 4:18-19.

> *Luke 4:18-19 – The Spirit of the Lord is upon Me, because He has anointed Me to preach the gospel to the poor. He has sent Me to heal the brokenhearted, to proclaim liberty to the captives and recovery of sight to*

the blind, to set at liberty those who are oppressed; to proclaim the acceptable year of the Lord.

Jesus applied these verses to Himself! Jewish teaching was that these verses not only had application for the "year of Jubilee" <u>when all captives would be set free and all debts and obligations would be erased</u> but they referred to the coming Messiah who would set us free from our sins and give us eternal life with Him. Jesus is telling those in His hearing, on that Saturday morning worship service, that He is the Messiah that was to come as prophesied throughout the Old Testament.

I am the Messiah — I am God in the flesh — I have come to set you free! This is what Jesus was conveying to the audience that morning. But Jesus doesn't read all of Isaiah 61:2 — He leaves out the last part of that verse which says, *"And the day of vengeance of our God."*

Jesus came the first time as our "Suffering Servant" to die for us — "A Lamb led to the Slaughter" to be punished for our sins — "To set us Free" Do you remember the old gospel hymn "HE SET ME FREE?"

Once like a bird in prison I dwelt, no freedom from my sorrow I felt. But Jesus came and listened to me and glory to God He set me free. Now I am climbing higher each day, darkness of night has drifted away. My feet are planted on higher ground and glory to God, I'm homeward bound. Goodbye to sin and things that confound. Naught of this world shall turn me around. Daily I'm working, I'm praying too and glory to God, I'm going through. He set me free, yes, He set me free and He broke the bonds of prison for me. I'm glory bound my Jesus to see for glory to God, He set me free.

Jesus will come again at the *"Day of Vengeance of our God,"* the Day of Tribulation when the Book of Revelation will be fulfilled! *Luke 4:22 So all bore witness to Him, and marveled at the gracious words which proceeded out of His mouth, and they said, "Is this not Joseph's son?"*

They marveled at His grace — His gracious words — But then they began to say among themselves (you can just imagine the whispering that was going around the room) <u>"Hey, wait a minute, who does He think He is? We know Him! This is Joseph's son!"</u> *Luke 4:23 He said to them, "You will surely say this proverb to Me, 'Physician, heal yourself! Whatever we have heard done in Capernaum, do also here in Your country."* He anticipated that they would say to Him, <u>"Physician, heal yourself."</u>

Ordinarily this would mean: 'Do for yourself what you have done for others. Cure your own condition since you claim to cure others.' But here the meaning is slightly different. It is explained in the words that follow: *"Whatever we have heard done in Capernaum, do also here in Your country."* It was a scornful challenge for Him to perform miracles in Nazareth as He had done elsewhere, and thus save Himself from ridicule.

> *Luke 4:24-27 – Then He said, "Assuredly, I say to you, no prophet is accepted in his own country. But I tell you truly, many widows were in Israel in the days of Elijah, when the heaven was shut up three years and six months, and there was a great famine throughout all the land; but to none of them was Elijah sent except to Zarephath, in the region of Sidon, to a woman who was a widow. And many lepers were in Israel in the time of Elisha the prophet, and none of them was cleansed except Naaman the Syrian."*

The Lord replied by stating a deep-rooted principle in human affairs. Great men are not appreciated in their own neighborhood. Have you ever wondered why, when churches have revivals, that they usually (not always) bring in a man that lives at least 200 miles away? Jesus then referred to two incidents in the Old Testament, 1 Kings 17:9ff and 2 Kings 5:1-14 where prophets of God were not appreciated by the people of Israel and so the prophets were sent to Gentiles! When there was a great famine in Israel, Elijah was not sent to any Jewish widows, though there were plenty of them, but he was sent to a Gentile widow in Sidon. And although many lepers were in Israel when Elisha was ministering, he was not sent to any of them. He was sent to a Gentile man named Naaman, captain of the Syrian army.

Now, imagine the impact of Jesus words on His Jewish audience. The Jewish men placed women, Gentiles, and lepers at the bottom of the social scale. But here the Lord pointedly placed all three above these unbelieving Jews! What He was saying was that Old Testament history was about to repeat itself. In spite of His miracles, He would be rejected not only by the city of Nazareth but by the nation of Israel as well. He would then turn to the Gentiles, just as Elijah and Elisha had done! And the people, that day, understood exactly what He meant! *Luke 4:28 So all those in the synagogue, when they heard these things, were filled with wrath!* They were infuriated by the mere suggestion of favor being shown to the Gentiles.

> *John 1:11-13 – He came to His own, but His own did not receive Him. But as many as received Him, to them He gave the right to become children of God, to those who believe in His name; who were born, not of blood, nor of the will of the flesh, nor of the will of man, but of God.*

> *Luke 4:29-30 – They rose up and thrust Him out of the city; and they led Him to the brow of the hill on which their city was built, that they might throw Him down over the cliff. Then passing through the midst of them, He went His way.*

Doubtless this was instigated by Satan as another attempt to destroy Jesus. But Jesus miraculously walked right through the crowd and left the city. We're reminded of Jesus later words when He said: *"No one takes my life from Me, but I lay it down of Myself. I have power to lay it down, and I have power to take it again."* You see, they got their miracle that day. His foes were powerless to stop Him from walking right through the midst of them. <u>And as far as we know, He never returned to Nazareth!</u>

There are so many lessons we can glean from this story and I hope and pray the Holy Spirit has touched your heart from the learning of God's word. But one thing we must learn today! You may only get the chance to hear and respond to the gospel one time in your life. It may be too late if you don't respond. Jesus may never walk your way again.

CHAPTER 9

HOSANNA TO THE SON OF DAVID

Luke 9:51; 19:35-36; Matthew 21:8; Luke 19:37-38; Matthew 21:9, Matthew 27:22:23 (NIV)

As the time approached for Him to be taken up to heaven, Jesus resolutely set out for Jerusalem. Then they brought the colt to Him and they threw their own clothes on the colt, and they set Jesus on him. As He went along, people spread their cloaks on the road, while others cut branches from the trees and spread them on the road. When He came near the place where the road goes down the Mount of Olives, the whole crowd of disciples began joyfully to praise God in loud voices for all the miracles they had seen. Blessed is the King who comes in the name of the Lord! The crowds that went ahead of Him and those that followed shouted: "Hosanna to the Son of David!" "Blessed is He who comes in the name of the Lord!" "Hosanna in the highest!"

One week later Pilate asked the question: "What shall I do, then, with Jesus who is called Christ?" They all answered, "Crucify Him!" "Why? What crime has He committed?" asked Pilate. But they shouted all the louder, "Crucify Him!" And so, the question begs to be asked: WHY? What crime had He committed?

Or a better question would be: What crime had I committed that Jesus would die for me? What value does He see in me that He would die in my place, for and because of my sins? *Romans 5:28 But God demonstrated His love for us in that while we were still sinners Christ died for us.*

I love the Hymn: "I Love to Tell the Story" I love to tell the story of unseen things above, Of Jesus and His glory, Of Jesus and His love. I love to tell the story because I know 'tis true. It satisfies my longings as nothing else can do. I love to tell the story! Twill be my theme in glory, to tell the old, old story of Jesus and His love.

As much as the world would try to convince us that the story of Jesus death, burial, and resurrection is not true, I'm here to tell you that it is true! The story is true down to the smallest details. And for anyone who wants to open their minds and examine the details, they will find that the Bible is true and because it is true Jesus will one day return to this earth where He will rule and reign forever. Right now, Satan, as he has been since the Garden of Eden, is sending out a great deception throughout the world. A great LIE is what the Bible calls it. There are many who deny that Jesus even died on the cross and then there are those who, while they say they believe, are apathetic about it. There are those, for example, who discount the fact that Jesus even died on the cross. They say that He escaped the cross and went on into India where he later died. But Jesus death and resurrection are not only true, they are the greatest events that have ever occurred on this earth and we should give our utmost attention to it. If not, then we do so to our own peril.

Did Jesus die on the cross?
Some say the sop that they held to his mouth was a drug that made Him pass out and then they took him down from the cross. And so, Jesus goes through a beating that would kill most men and did kill a lot of them and then he goes through the crucifixion, has spikes nailed into his hands and feet, has a sword run through his lung and heart, does not die and three days later He is in the best shape of his life. Really?

HOW DO WE KNOW THAT GOD'S WORD IS TRUE, AND THAT JESUS IS COMING AGAIN?

Daniel 9:1-19 is one of the greatest chapters in all the Bible. Daniel was reading from the book of Jeremiah and was reminded that God had determined Jerusalem must lie desolate for seventy years.

He then began an intense and prolonged prayer to God, concerning both his personal sins and those national sins of Israel which had caused the captivity in the first place. He reminds God of his covenants (the Abrahamic and the Davidic Covenants). The Davidic Covenant guaranteed Israel an everlasting king and kingdom. He contrasts the grace and goodness of God with the immorality and idolatry of Israel. He mention's Judah's kings. Two of them had been carried off into the Babylonian captivity along with the Jewish people. He fully agreed that Judah (the southern kingdom) had gotten just what she deserved, and that God meant just what he said when he warned them about disobedience and punishment. He ends his prayer by throwing both himself and his people completely upon the manifold grace of God.

> *Daniel 9:20-27 – Now while I was speaking, praying, and confessing my sin and the sin of my people Israel, and presenting my supplication before the Lord my God for the holy mountain of my God, Yes, while I was speaking in prayer, the man Gabriel, whom I had seen in the vision at the beginning, being caused to fly swiftly, reached me about the time of the evening offering. And he informed me, and talked with me, and said, O Daniel, I have now come forth to give you skill to understand. At the beginning of your supplications the command went out, and I have come to tell you, for you are greatly beloved; therefore, consider the matter, and understand the vision. Seventy weeks are determined for your people and for your holy city, to finish the transgression, to make an end of sins, to make reconciliation for iniquity, to bring in everlasting righteousness, to seal up vision and prophecy, and to anoint the Most Holy. Know therefore and understand, that <u>from the going forth of the command</u> to restore and build Jerusalem until Messiah the Prince, there shall be seven weeks and sixty-two weeks (**69 total weeks**): the street shall be built again, and the wall, even in troublesome times. And after the sixty-two weeks Messiah shall be*

> cut off, *but not for Himself*; and the people of the prince
> who is to come shall destroy the city and the sanctuary.
> The end of it shall be with a flood, and till the end of the
> war desolations are determined. Then he shall confirm
> a covenant with many *for one week* **(a total of 70**
> **weeks)**; but in the middle of the week **(3 1/2 days into**
> **the week)** he shall bring an end to sacrifice and offering.
> And on the wing of abominations shall be one who
> makes desolate, even until the consummation, which is
> determined, is poured out on the desolate.

Gabriel, an Archangel, comes to Daniel with a message from God (9:20-27). Even while Daniel was praying, God sent Gabriel the archangel to both minister to him and explain the most important, the most amazing, and the most profound single prophecy in the entire Word of God! This prophecy refers to Israel.

What is meant by the term "seventy weeks"?

The expression translated 'seventy weeks' in Hebrew is literally 'seventy sevens.' The message from God to Daniel was: *Know therefore and understand, that from the going forth of the command to restore and build Jerusalem until Messiah the Prince, there shall be seven sevens and sixty-two sevens. Then he shall confirm a covenant with many for one seven; but in the middle of the seven he shall bring an end to sacrifice and offering. And on the wing of abominations shall be one who makes desolate, even until the consummation, which is determined, is poured out on the desolate.*

Apart from the context you would not know what the 'sevens' were. You would have to inquire, 'seven' of what? This expression in Hebrew would be as ambiguous as if I were to say in English, '<u>I went to the store and bought a dozen</u>.' A dozen of what? One of the basic principles of interpretation is that you must always interpret the Bible in the light of the context, that is, in the light of the passage in which a given statement occurs. As you search the context, remembering that the vision was given in answer to Daniel's prayer, you see that Daniel had been reading in the book of Jeremiah that God would 'accomplish seventy years in the desolations of Jerusalem' (Dan. 9:2).

> *Daniel 9:2 – In the first year of his reign I, Daniel, under-*
> *stood by the books, the number of the years specified*
> *by the word of the Lord through Jeremiah the prophet,*
> *that He would accomplish seventy years in the desola-*
> *tions of Jerusalem.*

That's the clue! Daniel is told in effect, 'Yes, Jerusalem will be in captivity for seventy years; but now He is showing you that the whole history of the people of Israel will be over in a period of seventy sevens of years. In other words, if you multiply seventy times seven you get the exact number of years that God would continue to deal with Israel before bringing in everlasting righteousness. Now in case you're trying to figure that on your own, seventy times seven is 490 years.

When was the 490-year period to begin?
It was to begin with the command to rebuild Jerusalem's walls. *Know therefore and understand, that <u>from the going forth of the command to restore and build Jerusalem.</u>* The first two chapters of Nehemiah inform us that this command was issued during the twentieth year of King Artaxerxes in the month of Nisan which corresponds to our March/April. In researching historical records, the *Encyclopedia Britannica* sets this date as March 14, 445 B.C.

What are the three distinct time periods mentioned in this prophecy?
Daniel mentions 1) Seven Weeks 7x7=49 years 2) Sixty-two Weeks 62x7=434 years and One week 1x7= 7 years.

<u>First period</u>
<u>Seven weeks</u> (seven times seven is 49 years), from March 14, 445 B.C. to 396 B.C. The key events during this time were the building of the streets and walls of Jerusalem. This is recorded in Nehemiah 2-6.

<u>Second period</u>
<u>Sixty-two weeks</u> (62 x 7 = 434 years), from 396 B.C. to 32 A.D. At the end of this second time period the Messiah, Jesus Christ, was crucified! The brilliant British scholar and Bible student, Sir Robert Anderson, reduced the first two periods into their exact number of days. He did this by multiplying 483 years (49 years plus 434 years) by 360 (the days in a biblical year). The total number of days in the first 483 years is 173,880. Now this is worth looking at. If you begin counting on March 14, 445

B.C. (the day the 490 years began – the day the order was given to start rebuilding the walls of Jerusalem) and you go forward 173,880 days (483 years), you come to the date of April 6, 32 A.D. On April 6, 32 A.D. historians, of that period, tell us that was the exact day that Jesus made His triumphal entry into Jerusalem. This was Palm Sunday! Now hear what Jesus did and said as He rode into Jerusalem that day.

> *Luke 19: 41-44 – Now as He drew near, He saw the city and wept over it, saying, "If you had known, <u>even you, especially in this</u> **your day**, the things that make for your peace! But now they are hidden from your eyes. For days will come upon you when your enemies will build an embankment around you, surround you and close you in on every side, and level you, and your children within you, to the ground; and they will not leave in you one stone upon another, <u>because you did not know the time of your visitation.</u>"*

It was on this very same day that the Pharisees plotted to murder Christ, their very own Messiah. *Luke 19:47 And He was teaching daily in the temple. But the chief priests, the scribes, and the leaders of the people sought to destroy Him.* Had they known their scriptures, had they understood the book of Daniel and the prophecy given to Daniel through the angel Gabriel, they would have known that Jesus was the Christ, the Son of the living God, their Messiah.

Third period – One week (7 years)
This period is after the rapture of the church and covers the period of the 7-year Tribulation of the book of Revelation. At the beginning of this period the anti-christ will make a covenant (peace treaty) with Israel and thus begins the 7-year tribulation upon the earth. *Daniel 9:27 Then he shall confirm a covenant with many for one week.* Three and one-half years into the seven-year tribulation the Anti-Christ will break the covenant (the peace treaty) and thus begins what we know as the Great Tribulation or the last half of the seven years of tribulation that is to come to this earth.

Then he shall confirm a covenant with many <u>for one week</u>; but in the middle of the week he shall bring an end to sacrifice and offering. And on the wing of abominations shall be one who makes desolate, even

67

until the consummation, which is determined, is poured out on the desolate. At the end of the last week (and of the entire seventy-week period), the true Messiah will come and establish his perfect millennial (1,000 year) reign upon this earth.

> *Daniel 9:24 – Seventy weeks are determined for your people and for your holy city. 1. To finish the transgression. 2. To make an end of sins. 3. To make reconciliation for iniquity. 4. To bring in everlasting righteousness. 5. To seal up vision and prophecy. 6. And to anoint the Most Holy*

God stepped in and stopped the clock of prophecy at Calvary. This divine "time out" has already lasted some twenty centuries, but soon the Redeemer will blow his trumpet and the final "week" (7 years) of action will be played out upon this earth. And so, I ask you today: is the Bible true? Was it just a coincidence that Daniel, writing some five and one-half centuries before the birth of Christ, correctly predicted the very day that Christ would ride into Jerusalem and be rejected and crucified? Or will the world discover on that final day that God's Word is true?

CHAPTER 10

HOW JESUS DIED

Isaiah 53:5-7 – "He was wounded for our transgressions, he was bruised for our iniquities; the chastisement for our peace was upon him, and with his stripes we are healed. All we like sheep have gone astray; we have turned everyone to his own way, and the Lord has laid on him the iniquity of us all. He was oppressed, and he was afflicted, yet he opened not his mouth; he is brought as a lamb to the slaughter, and as a sheep before her shearers is dumb, so he opened not his mouth.

Romans 5:8 – But God demonstrated his love toward us in that, while we were yet sinners, Christ died for us.

So, it is written - So it happened!

Jesus last meal on this earth.

Matthew 26:20 – Now when the evening was come, he sat down with the twelve. And as they did eat, he said, "Verily I say unto you that one of you shall betray me." And they were exceedingly sorrowful, and began every one of them to say unto him, "Lord, is it I?" And he answered and said, "He that dips his hand with me in the dish, the same shall betray me. The Son of man goes as it is written of him; but woe unto that man by whom the Son of man is betrayed! It had been good for that man if he had not been born."

We must ask ourselves the question this morning; Lord is it I that have betrayed you?

Jesus died for us! What have we done for him? Have we surrendered our life to him? Have we invited Him into our life to be the Lord of our life; to follow His ways; His examples and to give our lives to him in total surrender. Or are we just playing the part of a Christian life. Are we make believing or are we really believing? Jesus said unto them *"One of you shall betray me."* And they were exceedingly sorrowful, and began every one of them to say unto him, "Lord is it I?"

> *Matthew 26:26-30 – And as they were eating, Jesus took bread, and blessed it, and broke it, and gave it to the disciples, and said, "Take, eat; this is my body." And he took the cup, and gave thanks, and gave it to them, saying, "Drink ye all of it; For this is my blood of the new testament, which is shed for many for the remission of sins. But I say unto you, I will not drink henceforth of this fruit of the vine, until that day when I drink it new with you in my Father's kingdom." And when they had sung a hymn, they went out into the Mount of Olives."*

As they made their way to the Mount of Olives the only light they saw would have been a fire burning somewhere or a lamp. The Mount of Olives was an olive press or orchard. It was a beautiful place with flowers all around it. It was a garden; The Garden of Gethsemane. Jesus was aware of the death that awaited him. In anguish he prays three times in the Garden to let this cup pass from me; nevertheless, not My will but yours be done. Jesus begins to sweat great drops of blood as His blood exited from the pores of His skin. Medically this is known as Hematidrosis and was first described by Aristotle 300 years before the birth of Christ. Hematidrosis is very rare. In the 20th century only 76 cases of Hematidrosis were reported. Around your sweat glands you have multiple blood vessels. Under pressure of great stress and mental contemplation the blood vessels rupture coming out as droplets of blood. The skin becomes extremely tender and fragile making Christ's pending scourging and crucifixion even more painful. Jesus death process actually starts with the shedding of his blood in Gethsemane.

Jesus is arrested and charged with blasphemy. He has nothing to drink or eat since the last supper. He is under trial all-night long. He has had no sleep. Under a mock trial he is humiliated, slapped, hit and spit upon.

The scourging begins in the morning with a flagram. A flagram is a whip with a wooden handle covered with leather to which are attached thin leather straps with little balls of lead or bone attached to the end. When the flagram is flicked with considerable strength it whips around the body and embeds in the flesh. When it is yanked out, a fine mist of blood splatters everywhere. Under scourging many people died! Jesus at this time has had extreme fluid loss from intensive sweating. He is undergoing what medical doctors call plural effusion. Across the chest area you have fluid buildup around the lungs - your blood pressure goes down while your heart rate goes up.

Jesus is raw and bleeding profusely. A circle of thorns is then put into his head. There is severe pain in the area of the thorns involving the whole head neck and shoulders. His condition becomes unbearable to his nerves! There is severe cruelty and mockery from the soldiers! A heavy rough timber is then placed on his back causing even more injury to the already ripped open skin. By this time Jesus would be going into severe shock with loss of blood, no food, and no sleep as he makes his way to Calvary.

Golgotha (Calvary) was the place where criminal's bodies were tossed without burial and where birds and rats fed on the remains. At Golgotha, for total shame and humiliation, the soldiers strip Jesus of all his clothes. They nail him to the cross with large headed nails driven through the hands and feet into the timber.

Initially the pain is in the hands and feet then goes throughout the nerves and into the whole body. During WW2 men were found in severe pain such as this and morphine would not even slow down the pain. The pain was so severe that if you even blow on the skin they would scream in pain.

Jesus is undergoing burning searing pains throughout his whole body and nerves. He is experiencing multiple suffering. His back is against the rough wood, His nerves up the arms and legs are on fire, He is cramping. He's experiencing severe joint pains and in intense thirst Jesus cries out "I Thirst". His stomach stops functioning - his heart beats faster and faster - his tongue swells against the roof of his mouth.

From noon until 3pm there is darkness over the whole land as the Father in heaven turns his back and cannot look upon the suffering and sin that Jesus is taking upon Himself. Spiritually during all this agony Jesus is taking our sins upon Himself, the sins of the world, and the Father cannot bear to look. Jesus cries out with a loud voice *"My God, My God, why have you forsaken me?"* What were these 3 hours of darkness all about? For three hours the sun is blacked out. For three hours there is complete silence. For three hours God the Father and Holy Spirit separate and leave Jesus alone on the cross. For three hours all the forces of hell that Satan has are thrown at him. Before the darkness began, the crowd yelled: *"He saved others, let Him come down from the cross and save Himself!"* It's not that He couldn't save Himself! It's that He wouldn't save Himself! If He would have saved Himself, then you and I could not be saved! We'll never know all that happened during those three hours, but we see the results in the words of Jesus after it was over. And then with one last breath he screams *"It Is Finished!"* And He dies for you and me, that we may have eternal life. He offers us eternal life in Heaven. He said, *"I go and prepare a place for you that where I am there you may also be."* But He also warned during that last week of His life on earth; if you don't receive Me and surrender your life to Me, if you hang on to your life and don't allow me to be Lord of your life, you will never see Me again. You will spend eternity in outer darkness, in the grip of Satan, in Hell itself. Jesus suffered far beyond what most of us will ever suffer. His penetrating awareness of the heinous nature of sin, its destructive and deadly effects, the sorrow and heartache that if inflicts, and the extreme measure necessary to deal with it, make the passion of Christ beyond all comprehension.

> *Revelation 3:20 — "Behold I stand at the door and knock; if anyone hears my voice and opens the door, I will come into him and sup with him and he with me."*

Do you hear Gods voice today? Have you surrendered your life to Jesus? Is Jesus truly the Lord of your life?

SONG by David Phelps: NO MORE NIGHT

The timeless theme, earth and Heaven will pass away. It's not a dream, God will make all things new that day. Gone is the curse from which I stumbled and fell. Evil is banished to eternal hell. No more night, no more pain, no more tears, never crying again, and praises to the Great I Am we will live in the light of the risen Lamb. See all around, now the nation's bow down to sing. The only sound is the praises to Christ, Our King. Slowly the names from the book are read, I know the King, so there's no need to dread. No more night, no more pain, no more tears, never crying again, and praises to the Great I Am, we will live in the light of the risen Lamb. See over there, there's a mansion, prepared just for me, where I will live with my Savior eternally. Praises to the great I AM - We're gonna live in the light of the risen Lamb.

THE ORDER OF EVENTS AT THE CRUCIFIXION

1. The arrival at Golgotha (Calvary)
2. The offer of the stupefying drink is refused
3. Jesus is crucified between two thieves
4. Jesus first words from the cross: "Father, forgive them for they know not what they do"
5. The soldiers' part His garments
6. The Jews mock Jesus
7. The thieves' rail at Him, but one repents and believes
8. Jesus second words from the cross "Today you will be with me in paradise"
9. Jesus third words from the cross "Woman, behold thy son! Behold thy mother!
10. The darkness
11. Jesus fourth words from the cross "My God, My God, why hast thou forsaken Me?
12. Jesus fifth words from the cross "I thirst"
13. Jesus sixth words from the cross "It is finished"
14. Jesus seventh words from the cross "Father, into Thy hands, I commend My spirit"
15. Our Lord dismissed His Spirit and He dies

But don't be dismayed. The following Sunday morning He arose from the grave and stayed around for another 50 days. One day soon He will return. God bless you and may you be encouraged through the reading of these messages and if you've never repented of your sin and received Christ then do so today while you still have time.

John 3:16 "For God so loved the world that He gave His only begotten Son that whosoever believes in Him should not perish but shall have everlasting life."

CHAPTER 11

HE IS RISEN! HE IS RISEN INDEED!

In reading the accounts of Matthew, Mark, Luke and John about Jesus arrest and His crucifixion we can piece together what exactly happened as each gospel writer gives us a little more information here and there. One thing seems to be missing however from each gospel writer. But then they would not have known. The missing piece is the battle that was being raged between God and Satan for the soul of men.

Going all the way back to the Garden of Eden, Satan had been trying to circumvent God's plan of redemption for mankind. The earliest account of this is found in *Genesis 3:15. And I will put enmity between you and the woman, and between your seed and her Seed; He shall bruise your head, and you shall bruise His heel.*

When the first two humans had two sons, Satan worked in the heart of the one to kill the other thinking this would circumvent God's plan. Throughout all the Old Testament we see the works of Satan as he works in the hearts and minds of men. When Jesus was on this earth He encountered Satan in the wilderness before He ever began His public ministry. Throughout His ministry He encountered numerous demons who knew well who He was as Jesus would cast them out and tell them to close their mouths.

On the cross the battle raged on! During the time that Jesus hung on the cross the sun became black as night from noon until 3pm. Father God could not look upon all the sin that Jesus was taking upon His own body and turns His back. Jesus cries out "My God My God why have you forsaken Me." Then there is a huge earthquake and rocks are split and the ground trembles.

On the cross, Satan and his demons finally believed they had won the victory. Remember, Satan doesn't know the future. In Satan, and his demons' minds, the Son of God was dead and there would be no redeemer! They had won! They had defeated God once and for all! He had captured the souls of men and women and if he had to spend eternity in hell then humans would be going with him.

But God had another plan! God would conquer sin through the death of His Son, thus defeating Satan once and for all. Unbeknownst to Satan at the time of the crucifixion Jesus would **_RISE AGAIN_** and Satan would be forever defeated!

Today, Satan has been defeated but too many people on this earth don't live as if they know this. They don't surrender their lives to Christ in order to receive victory over sin. There is a song that I love called 'It is Finished'. It is finished - the battle is over – it is finished there'll be no more war. It is finished – the end of the conflict – it is finished, and Jesus is LORD!

WHO ROLLED AWAY THE STONE?

Matthew tells us that an angel rolled away the stone. A resurrected body doesn't need a stone rolled away to get out. The stone was rolled away, so the followers of Jesus could get in. He didn't need any help getting out! He had conquered death! He was alive! He had risen just as He had told His disciples He would. Books have been written to disprove the fact that Jesus really died. They say He only swooned or went into a coma and the cool of the tomb, He was buried in, revived Him. These books say there is no resurrection. If that were true then being followers of Christ would have no meaning at all. As the apostle Paul said; *"We of all people would be the most miserable."* 1 Corinthians *15:19* - So let's examine; did Jesus really die?

> *John 19:31-34 – Now it was the day of Preparation, the next day was to be a special Sabbath. Because the Jews did not want the bodies left on the crosses during the Sabbath, they asked Pilate to have their legs broken and the bodies taken down. The soldiers therefore*

> *came and broke the legs of the first man who had been crucified with Jesus, and then those of the other. But when they came to Jesus and found that he was already dead,* they did not break his legs. Instead, one of the soldiers pierced Jesus side with a spear, bringing a sudden flow of blood and water.

These were trained executioners at Jesus death. By Roman law, if they took a prisoner down from the cross, that was not dead, then they themselves would be crucified! Do you think they made sure a person was dead before they took him down from the cross? Blood and water mixed together came out of Jesus body. Medical practitioners tell us this can only occur when the heart ruptures.

> *Matthew 27:54 – When the centurion and those with him who were guarding Jesus saw the earthquake and all that had happened, they were terrified, and exclaimed, "Surely He was the Son of God!"*

Was the Son of God, in the Greek language was past tense. They knew He was dead! There was no question in their mind! To them it was not "Jesus is the Son of God" but *"Jesus was the son of God!"* It's as if you and I would say "John Kennedy was the President of the United States" not that he is the President anymore because he is dead!

> *John 19:38-40 – And after this Joseph of Arimathea, being a disciple of Jesus, but secretly for fear of the Jews, besought Pilate that he might take away the body of Jesus; and Pilate gave him leave. He came therefore and took the body of Jesus. And there came also Nicodemus, which at the first came to Jesus by night, and brought a mixture of myrrh and aloes, <u>about a hundred-pound weight</u>. Then they took the body of Jesus, <u>and wound it in linen clothes with the spices, as the manner of the Jews is to bury.</u>*

Nicodemus brought a mixture of myrrh and aloes <u>about a hundred-pound weight</u> (about seventy-five pounds by today's standards.) Taking Jesus' body, the two of them wrapped it with spices, in strips of linen. This was in accordance with Jewish burial customs. Seventy-five pounds of myrrh and aloes were used in the embalming procedure! These myrrh and aloes were placed between the linen strips and hardened like cement! The body was rolled in strips and ended up looking like a mummy. The head was rolled last of all in separate strips. These were Jesus friends doing this! Don't you think if there was any sign of life at all that they would have stopped this procedure? Jesus was dead! He died because of my sins and yours. Yet Satan was not yet defeated. Jesus still had to conquer death not only for Himself but for us as well.

Matthew 28:1-6 – In the end of the Sabbath, as it began to dawn toward the first day of the week, came Mary Magdalene and the other Mary to see the sepulcher. And, behold, there was a great earthquake: for the angel of the Lord descended from heaven, and came and rolled back the stone from the door, and sat upon it. His countenance was like lightning, and his raiment white as snow: And for fear of him the keepers did shake and became as dead men. And the angel answered and said unto the women, do not be afraid, for I know that you seek Jesus, who was crucified. He is not here: for He is risen, as He said. Come, see the place where the Lord lay.

Mark 16:1-6 – And when the Sabbath was past, Mary Magdalene, and Mary the mother of James, and Salome, had bought sweet spices, that they might come and anoint him. And very early in the morning on the first day of the week, they came unto the sepulcher at the rising of the sun. And they said among themselves, who shall roll away the stone for us from the door of the sepulcher? And when they looked, they saw that the stone had been rolled away: for it was very large. And entering into the tomb, they saw a young man sitting on the right side, clothed in a long white garment; and they were afraid. And he said unto them, do not be afraid: you seek Jesus of Nazareth, who was crucified: He is risen; He is not here: behold the place where they laid Him.

> *Luke 24:1-6 – Now on the first day of the week, very early in the morning they, and certain other women with them, came to the tomb bringing the spices which they had prepared. But they found the stone rolled away from the tomb. Then they went in and did not find the body of the Lord Jesus. And it happened, as they were greatly perplexed about this, that behold, two men stood by them in shining garments. Then, as they were afraid and bowed their faces to the earth, they said to them, "Why do you seek the living among the dead? He is not here but is risen!*

> *John 20: 1-8 – Now on the first day of the week Mary Magdalene went to the tomb early, while it was still dark, and saw that the stone had been taken away from the tomb. Then she ran and came to Simon Peter, and to the other disciple, whom Jesus loved, and said to them, "They have taken away the Lord out of the tomb, and we do not know where they have laid Him." Peter therefore went out, and the other disciple, and were going to the tomb. So, they both ran together, and the other disciple outran Peter and came to the tomb first. And he, stooping down and looking in, saw the linen cloths lying there; yet he did not go in. Then Simon Peter came, following him, and went into the tomb; and he saw the linen cloths lying there, and the handkerchief that had been around His head, not lying with the linen cloths, but folded together in a place by itself. Then the other disciple, who came to the tomb first, went in also; and he saw and believed.*

The Christian movement could have been quickly crushed by producing the dead body of Jesus. Evidently, no one was able to produce His body. It is an undeniable fact of history that those who opposed the preaching of Christ could not disprove His resurrection. The earliest attempt to explain the empty tomb was to say the disciples had stolen the body.

> *Matthew 28:11-15 – Now while they were going, behold, some of the guard came into the city and reported to the chief priests all the things that had*

> happened. *When they had assembled with the elders and consulted together, they gave a large sum of money to the soldiers, saying, tell them, His disciples came at night and stole Him away while we slept. And if this comes to the governor's ears, we will appease him and make you secure. So, they took the money and did as they were instructed, and this saying is commonly reported among the Jews until this day."*

It is significant that even in the beginning the rulers did not deny that the tomb was empty. Paul's early testimony in 1 Corinthians 15 supports the idea of the empty tomb. The empty-tomb account is part of Mark's gospel and is very old. Many scholars believe it was written within seven years of Jesus crucifixion. The account lacked the time for legendary development. The disciples could not have preached the resurrection of Christ, in Jerusalem, had the tomb not been empty. In all the earliest attempts to spread the gospel of Christianity no one ever attempts to say that the tomb was not empty.

But an empty tomb does not necessarily mean a resurrection had happened. Perhaps grave robbers had stolen His body. *But the grave clothes were left behind!* Peter and John saw them (John 20:3-8). Grave robbers do not unwrap a body they steal from a tomb! They grab the body and run just as thieves that break into your house do not tidy up before they leave; they grab what they came for and take off with it. And remember, this body was wrapped as it were in cement. The most compelling reason the grave clothes were left behind is that the One who had been in them no longer needed them.

The events following these events over the next 40 days proved beyond any shadow of a doubt that Jesus was alive and that He had resurrected from the dead. There is an old gospel hymn that I love that goes: Do you know Him Today? Do not turn Him away! Jesus – Oh Jesus, Without Him how lost I would be

There is a very interesting fact about the grave clothes that were left behind at Jesus resurrection. The strips of cloth that covered his body were lying there as if someone had just risen right out of them. But the napkin that covered His head was folded and laid to the side. Why do you suppose that is? In the Jewish custom, as you left the dinner table, you would crumple your napkin up if you were finished eating. If you folded your napkin and laid it to the side, that meant don't touch my plate; I'm not finished eating, I'll be back. When Jesus folded the napkin that covered His head and laid it to the side; could He have been sending us a message? Could He have been saying, "I'm not finished yet, keep believing, keep being faithful, "I'll be back?"

HE IS RISEN! HE IS RISEN INDEED!

CHAPTER 12

IS FAITH REASONABLE?

Hebrews 11:6

Billy Graham steadied himself by gripping both sides of the podium. He was eighty years old, fighting Parkinson's disease, but he stared intently at the thousands of people inside the RCA Dome in Indianapolis and spoke in a steady, forceful voice. His sermon was essentially the same simple and direct message he had been preaching for fifty years. He spoke about the chaos and violence around the world. He zeroed in on the anguish, pain, and confusion in the hearts of individuals. He talked about sin, forgiveness, redemption, loneliness, despair, and depression.

All of us want to be loved he said. All of us want somebody to love us. "Well, I want to tell you that God loves you! He loves you so much that He gave us His Son do die on the cross for our sins! He loves you so much that He will come into your life and change the direction of your life and make you a new person, whoever you are."

So, he urged the people to respond to God's love. And they did! Nearly three thousand in all. Some were weeping, others stared downward in shame over their past. One woman said: "My mom died of cancer when I was young, and at the time I thought I was being punished by God. Tonight, I realized that God loves me! Tonight, a peacefulness came into my heart."

WHAT IS FAITH? IS IT REASONABLE TO HAVE FAITH?
Atheist, George H. Smith said: "Christian belief in God must be rejected by any person with even a shred of respect for reason. Reason and faith

are opposites, two mutually exclusive terms. There is no reconciliation or common ground. Faith is belief without, or in spite of, reason."

Christian educator, W. Bingham Hunter said: "Faith is a rational response to the evidence of God's self-revelation in nature, human history, the scriptures and His resurrected Son."

> *Hebrews 11:6 – Now faith is the substance of things hoped for, the evidence of things not seen, for by it the elders obtained a good report. Through faith we understand that the worlds were framed by the word of God, so that things which are seen were not made of things which do appear. By faith, Abel offered unto God a more excellent sacrifice than Cain, by which he obtained witness that he was righteous, God testifying of his gifts; and by it, he being dead, yet speaks. By faith Enoch was translated that he should not see death; and was not found, because God had translated him; for before his translation he had this testimony, that he pleased God. But without faith it is impossible to please God for <u>he that comes to God must believe that He is</u> and that He is a rewarder of them that diligently seek him.*

Can we believe, by faith, that <u>God is</u> and still be reasonable people?

> *Jeremiah 29:11-13 – For I know the thoughts that I think toward you, says the Lord, thoughts of peace, and not of evil, to give you an expected end. Then you shall call upon me, and you shall go and pray to me, and I will listen to you. <u>And you shall search for me, and find me, when you search for me with all your heart.</u>*
>
> *Job 13:3 – Surely, I would speak to the Almighty, and <u>I desire to reason with Him.</u>*
>
> *Isaiah 1:18 – <u>Come, let us reason together, says the Lord.</u> Though your sins be as scarlet, they shall be white as snow. Though they be red like crimson, they shall be as wool.*

Faith isn't always easy for people. Even for people who desperately want it. Some people hunger for faith, for spiritual certainty. But something hinders them from experiencing it. They wish they could taste the freedom of faith, but unanswered questions block their way. Their hearts want to soar to God, but their doubts won't let them. *So, God says, "Come let us reason together."*

HOW CAN JESUS BE THE ONLY WAY TO GOD?

What about other religions, aren't they just as good? Rabbi Shmuley Boteach said: "I am absolutely against any religion that says that one faith is superior to another. I don't see how that is anything different than spiritual racism. It's a way of saying that we are closer to God than you, and that's what leads to hatred."

WHY DO WE, AS CHRISTIANS, BELIEVE THAT JESUS CHRIST IS THE ONLY WAY TO GOD?

The reason we believe Jesus is the only way to God is because Jesus said so, Himself!

> *Acts 4:12 – Neither is there salvation in any other; for there is no other name under heaven given among men, whereby we must be saved.*

> *John 14:6 – "I am the way, the truth, and the life. No one comes to the Father except through me."*

AREN'T OTHER RELIGIONS JUST AS GOOD AS CHRISTIANITY?

Some people say that all religions basically say the teach the same thing, so they must all be true; if a person is really sincere in what he or she believes, he or she will get into Heaven. But the truth is that all belief systems cannot be true. They contradict each other. They do not blend together.

Buddhists deny the existence of a personal God. Hindus believe in two major gods, Vishnu and Siva, as well as in millions of lesser gods. Muslims believe in one God named Allah. Christians believe that God is a being who created humans in His own image and who loves them and wants to have a personal relationship with them.

THE SUBJECT OF SALVATION
Buddhists believe that salvation is by self-effort only. Hindus believe you achieve salvation by devotion, works, and self-control. Muslims believe that people earn their own salvation and pay for their own sins. Christians believe that Jesus Christ died for their sins. If people turn form their sins and follow Jesus, they can be forgiven and have the hope of being with Jesus in heaven.

THE PERSON OF JESUS CHRIST
Buddhists believe that Jesus Christ was a good teacher, though less important than Buddha. Hindus believe that Jesus was just one of many incarnations, or sons, of God. Yet they also assert that Christ was not the unique Son of God. He was no more divine than any other man, and he did not die for humanity's sins. Muslims believe that Jesus Christ was the greatest of the prophets below Mohammed. In addition, they do not believe that Christ died for humanity's sins. Christians believe that Jesus is God, as well as man, that He was sinless, and that He died to redeem humankind.

SO, WHO'S RIGHT?
Can we, as Christians, prove that our faith is the right faith? Absolutely! The main story of the Bible is too complex and written over too many years to be a hoax. Scientific evidence supports the Bible's accuracy. Archaeological findings have supported many of the complex historical passages found in the Bible and continue to do so on a regular basis. In addition, the Bible has greater documented accuracy than any other ancient literary work. I want to give you at least five reasons to believe and know that the Bible is the absolute Word of God.

1. The Bible is shown to be the Word of God because of its scientific accuracy.
2. The Bible is shown to be the Word of God because of its historical accuracy.
3. The Bible is shown to be the Word of God because of its wonderful unity.
4. The Bible must be the Word of God because of its fulfilled prophecy.
5. The Bible is shown to be the Word of God because of Christ resurrection.

Scientific accuracy confirms the Bible as the Word of God

It is commonly assumed that there must be scientific errors in the Bible. Before you say that, however, make sure you know two things, science and the Bible. Those who really understand science must admit that it is constantly changing. The accepted science of yesterday is not necessarily the science of today.

In 1861, the French Academy of Science wrote a pamphlet stating there were fifty-one absolute scientific facts that proved the Bible not true. Today there is not a reputable scientist on earth that believes one of those so-called absolute facts. The point is; science is always changing while God's word never changes.

The earth is suspended in Space:

All scientist today believe this to be true. But science in ancient cultures did not always believe this. The ancient Egyptians used to believe the Earth was supported by pillars. The Greeks believed the earth was carried on the back of a giant whose name was Atlas. The Hindus believed the earth was resting on the backs of giant elephants. But when you pick up the Word of God we do not find any such mythology.

> *Job 26:7 – He (God) stretches out the north over the empty space; He hangs the earth on nothing.*

Job is considered by most scholars to be the oldest piece of literature known to man. How did Job know the Earth was suspended in space? Did he orbit the earth to take a look at it? Of course not! Job could only know through divine inspiration. *2 Timothy 3:16 All Scripture is given by inspiration of God.* In other words, God who created the heavens and the earth, told Job the earth was suspended in space.

The Earth is Round, not Flat:

All scientist today believe this to be true. But scientist didn't always believe this to be true. Remember the poem we used to repeat? In 1492, Columbus sailed the ocean blue. He had three ships and left from Spain; He sailed through sunshine, wind and rain. He sailed by night; he sailed by day; He used the stars to find his way. A compass also helped him know how to find the way to go. Ninety sailors were on board; some men worked while others snored. Then the workers went to sleep; and others watched the ocean deep. Day after day they looked for land; they dreamed of trees and rocks and sand. October 12 their dream came true, you never saw a happier crew! "Indians! Indians!" Columbus cried; His heart was filled with joyful pride. But "India" the land was not; It was the Bahamas, and it was hot. The Arakawa natives were very nice; they gave the sailors food and spice. Columbus sailed on to find some gold to bring back home, as he'd been told. He made the trip again and again, trading gold to bring to Spain. The first American? No, not quite. But Columbus was brave, and he was bright.

Columbus left Spain and thought he was heading toward India! That's why he called the first people he met Indians and it just kind of stuck here in America. He was like most politicians today. He didn't know where he was going and when he got there he didn't know where he was.

In this poem; why did the men watch the ocean deep? Why were they so happy when they spotted land? These men were accomplished seamen. If they weren't afraid of the sea, then what were they afraid of? Science of that day believed the earth was flat! <u>They were terrified of falling off the earth!</u> Columbus was warned to be extremely careful on his voyage because he could sail off the edge of the earth. Imagine that; even as late as 1492 people did not know that the Earth is round.

Yet, if you look at the Word of God, in *Isaiah 40:22 It is He (God) who sits above the circle of the earth.* The word for circle in Hebrew is *chuwg,* which means 'globe or sphere.'

How did Isaiah know 750 years before Christ that the Earth is round?

> *2 Peter 1:21 – Holy men of God spoke as they were moved by the Holy Spirit.*

The Stars Cannot be Counted:
Scientist today believe this to be true. But science didn't always believe this. There was an astronomer named Hipparchus who counted the stars 150 years before Christ was born. His counted yielded 1,022 stars and that was the scientific belief for the next 250 years. That was the belief while Jesus walked this earth. Jesus must of shook his head and laughed at such a notion!

Then along came a man named Ptolemy who recounted the stars and said no, Hipparchus is wrong. There are actually 1,056 stars and that became the scientific belief for a while. Thirteen hundred years later along came a man named Galileo who invented the first telescope. When he looked beyond where the naked eye could see he exclaimed, no, there are hundreds and thousands and millions and billions and hundreds of billions of stars.

Today scientists say there are more suns like our sun in the known universe than there are grains of sand on all the seashores of the earth. But then scientist could have come to the same conclusion if they had just opened their Bible.

> *Jeremiah 33:22 – The host of heaven cannot be numbered.*

Job says the Earth is floating in space. Isaiah says it is a globe. Jeremiah says you can't count the number of the stars. Where did these men get these facts? ***All scripture is given by inspiration of God.***

Blood Circulates through the Body:
This is what scientist today believe. You and I take for granted that our blood is flowing through our body and is, what some have called, "the red river of life." Scientist didn't always believe this however. It was not until 1628 that Dr. William Harvey discovered that blood circulates throughout the body. Blood is our very life source. It carries fuel to the cells. It carries oxygen to burn that fuel, carries away waste, fights disease, and maintains a constant temperature in the body. Science used to believe when someone got sick they had '***Bad Blood.***' People thought they needed to get rid of some of that bad blood, so they would bleed these people. Can you imagine taking a person who is sick and draining their blood? <u>But that's what they did!</u>

A barber pole looks like a piece of peppermint candy but was actually meant to represent a bandage. Often, they would take sick people to a barber who would bleed them in order to make them well. Sometimes they would put leeches on them to suck the blood out of their system. As a matter of fact, Drs. were even referred to as leeches in those days.

A little-known fact is how George Washington, our first president, died. He was sick, so the physicians bled him. When he didn't get well, they bled him again. He didn't get well, so they bled him a third time. <u>They bled him to death!</u> Today they would have probably given him a blood transfusion.

But if they really wanted to know about blood all they had to do was look in the Bible. *Leviticus 17:14 For it (blood) is the life of all flesh. Its blood sustains its life.* The Bible says that blood is the life of all flesh! How did Moses know about the life-giving property of blood? Well, <u>"All Scripture is given by inspiration of God." "Holy men of God spoke as they were moved by the Holy Spirit."</u>

Rattlesnake Fat and Worm's Blood:
This is what scientist used to believe. Archeologists have uncovered an ancient Egyptian book written about 1500 years before Christ was born called the "Ebers Papyrus." This book was around during the time of Moses life on earth. The Ebers Papyrus is full of medical knowledge of the day and these were very intelligent people.

Cure for graying hair? Anoint your hair with the blood of a black cat that has been boiled in oil or with the fat of a rattlesnake. Keep your hair from falling out? Anoint your hair with six fats; those of the horse, the hippopotamus, the crocodile, the cat, the snake and the wild goat. Want to strengthen your hair? Anoint it with the tooth of a donkey crushed in honey. Want to get a splinter out of your hand? Put worm's blood and donkey dung on your hand and the splinter will come out. Other kinds of drugs they used were lizard's blood, pig's teeth, rotten meat, moisture from pig's ears, excreta from humans, animals, and even flies.

Now why would I tell you such things? The Bible says that Moses was schooled in all the wisdom of the Egyptians. Moses went to the University of Egypt and old Pharaoh paid his tuition. In Moses time he would have learned all the ways of the Egyptians and the Egyptians practiced all these cures. Aren't you glad when we open our Bible that we don't find these cures listed? Aren't you glad Moses listened to God and not the wisdom of his day?

The Answer to the Black Plaque Found in Europe.
Scientists didn't know what to do. In Europe during the fourteenth century, there was something called 'the black plaque.' One out of four people died from the black plaque. They didn't know what to do with it. They couldn't control it. Do you know what finally brought the plaque to an end? THE BIBLE! Finally, in desperation they turned to Scripture.

> *Leviticus 13:46 – All the days he has the plaque he shall be unclean. He is unclean, and he shall dwell alone; his dwelling shall be outside the camp.*

They learned to quarantine from the Word of God. I've only touched the surface of the many medical and scientific truths contained in the Bible. Aren't we glad that modern science and the Bible don't always agree? Science changes. The Bible never changes! The Bible is not primarily a science book. It is not written to tell us how the heavens go; it is written to tell us how to go to heaven. But when it speaks on science, it is always accurate! When it speaks on salvation it is always accurate!

The Bible is Shown to be the Word of God because of its Historical Accuracy

The Bible is not primarily a book of history. It is a book of His Story! The story of God! You would expect to find the history in the Bible to be accurate. As you might suspect, the Bible has been attacked on numerous fronts because of its historical inaccuracy.

In the late 1800's, Dr. S.R. Driver ridiculed the idea that Moses wrote the Pentateuch, the first five books of the Bible, because as he exclaimed "men didn't even know how to write during this period of history."

That is until the Tel el-Amarna tablets were discovered. They were written from people in Egypt to people in Palestine centuries before Moses was born. Not only did they know how to write they had a postal system to deliver the mail.

In the book of Daniel is a story about the handwriting on the wall. King Belshazzar saw the handwriting on the wall during a feast he made for a thousand of his lords and ladies. The handwriting was from God's finger and told King Belshazzar (the last king to rule Babylon) that he was weighed in the balances and found wanting. Scholars laughed and said it was a fabrication and that it never happened. Historical records from that era show that Belshazzar was not the last king of Babylon. Nabonidus was.

Is the Bible wrong? Can the Bible ever be wrong? Then one day an archeologist uncovered a cylinder, and sure enough, the name on it was Belshazzar. More records were found that show historians to be right. Nabonidus was the last king of Babylon but they were wrong when they said that Belshazzar was not the last king of Babylon. Nabonidus and Belshazzar were father and son and they had ruled together, making them both kings at the same time! Nabonidus was a big game hunter, among other things, and was often gone, leaving Belshazzar in charge.

In Daniel 5:16 king Belshazzar said to Daniel; *"If you can interpret the handwriting on the wall then you shall be clothed with purple, have a gold chain around your neck, and you shall become the **third** ruler in the kingdom."* It makes sense now that we understand there were already two kings simultaneously.

The Bible is Shown to be the Word of God because of its Wonderful Unity
The Bible is one book, Genesis through Revelation, but it is also sixty-six books; 39 in the Old Testament and 27 in the New Testament. It is a compilation of books written by at least forty different authors, and perhaps more. These people lived in a period of time that would span at least 1600 years. They lived in about thirteen different countries and on three different continents. They came from all kinds of backgrounds. They were Shepherds, Kings, Soldiers, Princes, Fishermen, Scholars, Historians, Professional men, and Common laborers.

The Bible is written in different styles and in at least three different languages. Yet when you bring all that together it makes one book that has one story beginning with Genesis and going through Revelation. The Bible has one theme, Redemption. The Bible has one Hero, the Lord Jesus, the Bible has one villain, Satan. The Bible has one purpose, the Glory of God. All its parts fit together!

Can you imagine taking forty different people over a period of 1600 years from different countries and different occupations and telling them each to write independent of one another without having read what the others had written? Put that together and see what kind of hodgepodge you would have! Yet, in the Bible, you have this wonderful unity of the Word of God! In all my years of reading and studying the Bible I find this amazing interconnectedness! God's Word, the Bible, is truly astounding!

The unity of the Bible is one of the wonderful proofs of the inspiration of God's Word – that *"All Scripture is given by inspiration of God."*

The Bible must be the Word of God because of its Fulfilled Prophecy

The Bible has predictions of things that have yet to happen but will happen. We can be sure of this because of the predictions that have come true already. It has been wisely said that you can take a child of God, put him in a dungeon with a Bible and a candle, lock him away, and he will know more about what's going on in the world than all the pundits in Washington.

We could look at all kinds of fulfilled prophecy but to make our main point let's just take a look at some of the fulfilled prophecy concerning Jesus. Scholars say that Jesus fulfilled more than 300 Old Testament prophecies. The enemies of the Bible (and of Christ) say these prophecies were rigged! They say that Christ (knowing the Old Testament) simply arranged to have these prophecies fulfilled concerning Himself.

Let's take a look of some of the prophecies that Christ arranged.

1. He arranged to be born in Bethlehem. Could you or I arrange where we were going to be born? Micah 5:2 tells the prophecy of Christ being born in Bethlehem which was fulfilled in Matthew 2: 1-5

2. Then he arranged for Isaiah to record details about His life 700 years before He was born. You can read them in Isaiah 7, Isaiah 9, and Isaiah 53. Could you or I arrange to have the history of our life written before we were born?

3. Then He arranged to be crucified by execution on a cross. If you read Psalm 22, written by David centuries before Jesus was born, you will read a description of the crucifixion of Jesus Christ that is written like a man who is standing at the foot of the cross. It tells about the piercing of His hands and feet, gambling for His garments, the very

words that Jesus would say upon the cross. *Jesus wasn't looking back and quoting David; rather David was looking forward and quoting Jesus!* It is an amazing thing that it is written as if somebody is an eyewitness to Christ's crucifixion. This one psalm contains 33 direct prophecies that were fulfilled at Calvary yet written 1,000 years before the birth of Christ. Even more interesting, when David wrote this prophecy, the form of capital punishment practiced by the Jews was stoning, not crucifixion. The Romans had not even come into power. Crucifixion was a Roman form of execution, and yet you find crucifixion described in Psalm 22 hundreds of years before the Romans ever existed.

4. Did Christ arrange to be crucified between two thieves? The Bible prophesied this is Isaiah 53:9-12 and it was fulfilled in Matthew 27.

5. In Zechariah 11:12, the Bible prophesied that Judas would betray Him for exactly 30 pieces of silver.

6. Did He arrange to rise from the dead and be seen by more than 500 witnesses? Some claim the apostles were hallucinating. 500 hallucinating at the same time? Having the same hallucination? Are people willing to die for a lie? No, absolutely not! People might live for a lie, but nobody will willingly die for a lie if they know that it is a lie. The early believers laid down their lives for the faith.

7. Most of these prophecies were not fulfilled by His friends but by His enemies, those who had the most to lose by the fulfillment of those prophecies. Fulfilled prophecy is an incredible proof of the inspiration of the Bible.

The Bible must be the word of God because of the historical facts concerning Jesus Resurrection

The following facts are all supported by scholars surrounding Jesus' death, burial, and resurrection.

1. Jesus died on a Roman cross by crucifixion.
2. Jesus was buried in a tomb not far from the crucifixion site.
3. Jesus' death threw the disciples into a state of despair and despondency, believing that their Lord was now dead.
4. Jesus' tomb was discovered to be empty shortly after His burial.

5. The disciples had real and genuine experiences that convinced them beyond a shadow of a doubt that Jesus had risen from the dead and that He was alive.
6. These experiences, with the risen Jesus, radically transformed the disciples into bold witnesses of His resurrection from the dead, a witness that led to martyrdom for most of them.
7. The message of Jesus' death, burial, resurrection was the heart of the gospel from the beginning of the church's existence.
8. This gospel was preached in Jerusalem, the very city where Jesus had been crucified and buried.
9. The good news of Christ's death and resurrection was foundational in the birth of the Christian church.
10. In celebration of the Lord's resurrection on that day, Sunday, not the Sabbath, became the day of worship for the church.
11. James, Jesus' half-brother and an unbeliever, was converted following an appearance of his resurrected brother.
12. Saul, a persecutor of Christians, was converted to Christianity following an appearance of the risen Christ.

The early disciples were willing to spend the rest of their lives proclaiming Jesus' bodily resurrection from the dead, without any payoff from a human point of view. They faced a life of hardship. The often went without food, slept exposed to the elements, were ridiculed, beaten, imprisoned and finally, most of them were executed in torturous ways. For what? For good intentions? No, because they were convinced beyond a shadow of a doubt that they had seen Jesus Christ alive from the dead! What you can't explain is how this particular group of men came up with this particular belief without having had an experience of the resurrected Christ. There's no other adequate explanation.

Jewish scholar Pinchas LaPide sees the force of this argument. Though he is not a Christian, he surprisingly believes that Jesus rose from the dead. Why? Let him speak for himself: *"The resurrection of Jesus was a real historical occurrence, and not something first and foremost taking place in the hearts and minds of the first believers. The crucifixion of Jesus by itself could not have motivated the courage of martyrdom and unquenchable hope for the cause of salvation which Jesus preached and embodied in his actions."*

JESUS CHRIST ROSE FROM THE DEAD, NOT FROM HIS SLEEP! THINK ABOUT WHAT WE ARE SAYING!

The resurrection indicates God the Father's approval of who Jesus is and what He said. And what did Jesus say?

> *John 14:6 – I am the way, the truth, and the life. <u>No one</u> comes to the Father except through Me."*

The resurrection is unlike any other miracle. Its very occurrence involves eternal life. Jesus was raised in a physical body that was transformed. Jesus is now immortal! Jesus will never die again! You can't kill Him! Nothing can harm Him! When the disciples witnessed Jesus' resurrection appearance, they were actually confronted with living, walking, talking eternal life. Jesus resurrection confirms that His existence means existence for all of His followers! The resurrection tells us that God the Father, who raised Jesus from the dead, exists! It establishes Jesus Lordship! It establishes justification for all those who repent, believe, and receive Him into their lives. The resurrection assures us victory over death!

> *John 14:2-3* (Jesus speaking) – *In My Father's house are many mansions; if that were not so I would have told you. I go to prepare a place for you, and if I go and prepare a place for you, I will come again and receive you unto Myself; that where I am, there you may be also.*

> *1 Corinthians 15:55-57 – O death, where is your sting? O grave, where is your victory? The sting of death is sin and the strength of sin is the law. But thanks be to God who gives us the victory over death through our Lord Jesus Christ.*

The resurrection is everything!

The next time you are having a bad day, Jesus was resurrected.
The next time things don't go your way, Jesus was resurrected.
The next time your health fails you, Jesus was resurrected.
The next time you are unemployed, Jesus was resurrected.
The next time you are under-employed, Jesus was resurrected.

The next time a tornado destroys your home, Jesus was resurrected.

The next time you are rushed to the emergency room, Jesus was resurrected.

The next time one of your loved ones die, Jesus was resurrected.

Romans 8:31-39 – What shall we say then to these things? If God be for us, who can be against us? He that spared not his own Son, but delivered Him up for us all, how shall He not with Him also freely give us all things. Who shall lay anything to the charge of God's elect? It is God that justifies. Who is he that condemns? It is Christ that died, yea rather, that is risen again, who is even at the right hand of God, who also makes intercession for us. Who shall separate us from the love of Christ? Shall tribulation, or distress, or persecution or famine, or nakedness, or peril of sword? As it is written, for your sake we are killed all the day long; we are accounted as sheep for the slaughter. Nay, in all these things we are more than conquerors through Him that loved us. For I am persuaded, that neither death, nor life, nor angels, nor principalities, nor powers, nor things present, nor things to come, nor height, nor depth, nor any other creature, shall be able to separate us from the love of God, which is in Christ Jesus our Lord.

SONG:

Crown Him with many crowns, the Lamb upon His throne. Hark! How the heavenly anthem drowns all music but its own. Awake, my soul, and sing of Him who died for thee, and hail Him as thy matchless King through all eternity. Crown Him the Lord of life, who triumphed o'er the grave, and rose victorious in the strife for those He came to save. His glories now we sing, who died and rose on high, who died eternal life to bring and lives that death may die.

CHAPTER 13

WHY SHOULD ANYONE BELIEVE IN THE BODILY RESURRECTION OF JESUS CHRIST?

Matthew 28:1-12 / Luke 24:1-12

Isn't this claim of resurrection unbelievable, even preposterous? Christians make a one-of-a-kind claim for an event that has never been duplicated at any time or anyplace in any part of the world by any other person other than Jesus Christ. Can we really prove beyond a reasonable doubt that the resurrection actually occurred? After all, no one actually witnessed the actual resurrection of Jesus. In fact, the Gospels never make any such claim. The belief and the proclamation of Jesus' resurrection are based on the following four facts: He died, He was buried, the tomb in which He was buried was discovered to be empty, and the disciples had experiences that convinced them that Jesus had supernaturally and bodily risen from the dead.

Mike: An Atheist
Mike is not a Christian. In fact, he considers himself an atheist or, at best, an agnostic. He is incredibly intelligent and also quite curious. That curiosity lead Mike to Criswell College in Dallas, TX to live in an evangelical community for a short period of time and write about his experience. He spent six months going to classes, attending a pastor's

conference, going on a mission trip, and observing a Southern Baptist Convention annual meeting. Afterwards he wrote his evaluation:

"After all I've studied and experienced, the bottom line issue seems to be the physical resurrection of Jesus Christ from the dead. If Jesus rose from the dead, then there is a God, and Jesus is that God. Furthermore, the Bible is true because He said it is true and believed it is true. That means heaven and hell are real, and your relationship with Jesus determines which way you go."

Mike was correct. It all rests on the physical resurrection of Christ. The apostle Paul put it this way in

> *1 Corinthians 15:14-19 – And if Christ is not risen, then our preaching is empty, and your faith is also empty. Yes, and we are found false witnesses of God because we have testified of God that He raised up Christ whom He did not raise up – if in fact the dead do not rise. For if the dead do not rise, then Christ is not risen. And if Christ is not risen, your faith is futile; you are still in your sins! Then also those who have fallen asleep in Christ have perished. If in this life only we have hope in Christ, we are of all men the most to be pitied.*

The apostle Paul was saying: If Christ did not physically, bodily, rise from the dead then none of the Bible is true. There is no God and the evolutionists are right. And we are to be most pitied for believing in fables and living our life to please a Lord who does not exist, if the resurrection is not true!

Three Basic Options
1. Jesus' resurrection is false – a great hoax. Jesus did not rise from the dead. The early disciples fabricated a lie and pulled off the greatest hoax of all time.

2. Jesus resurrection is fiction – nice mythology. The early church made Jesus into someone and something He really was not by telling stories about Him that they embellished more and more over time. Eventually, believers turned Jesus into God incarnate, who died on a cross for our sins and later rose from the dead.

3. <u>Jesus resurrection is fact – the supreme event of history</u>. Now, if we really believe this, can we give enough evidence to prove it?

We cannot prove the bodily resurrection of Jesus through a scientific formula or experiment. In fact, nothing in history can be proven this way. You can't prove that Abraham Lincoln ever existed this way. So, you must use objective evidence, historical verifiable evidence. Does the evidence persuade us that we have good reason to believe that an alleged event really happened? In a courtroom, witnesses are called, and a judgment is rendered. The question a judge or jury must answer is this: Does the evidence persuade us that we have good reason to believe that this alleged event really happened?

OBJECTIVE EVIDENCE

1. **The early disciple's faith and the radical change in their lives**. Something happened that caused Jesus' followers to believe they had genuine encounters with the risen Lord. These encounters with Jesus changed them from fearful cowards to bold witnesses of the resurrected Christ. Each disciple, with the exception of John, died as a martyr. Each disciple died alone, and yet each one died still proclaiming that Jesus had risen from the dead. Although people will die for a lie, thinking it to be the truth, they will not die for what they know to be a lie. The disciples were in a position to know without a shadow of a doubt whether or not Jesus had risen from the dead. If they weren't absolutely sure, they wouldn't have allowed themselves to be tortured to death for proclaiming that the resurrection had actually happened.

2. **The empty tomb -** The Christian movement could have been quickly crushed by producing the dead body of Jesus. Evidently, no one was able to produce this body. It is an undeniable fact of history that those who opposed the preaching of Christ could not disprove His resurrection. The earliest attempt to explain the empty tomb was to say the disciples had stolen the body (Matthew 28:11-15). It is significant that even in the beginning the rulers did not deny that the tomb was empty. Paul's early testimony in 1 Corinthians 15 supports the idea of the empty tomb. The empty-tomb account is part of Mark's gospel and is very old. Many scholars believe it was written within seven years of Jesus crucifixion. The account lacked the time for legendary development. The disciples could

not have preached the resurrection of Christ in Jerusalem had the tomb not been empty. In all the earliest attempts to spread the gospel of Christianity no one ever attempts to say that the tomb was not empty.

3. **The discarded grave clothes** - The grave clothes were left behind. Peter and John saw them (John 20:3-8). Grave robbers do not unwrap a body they steal from a tomb! They grab the body and run. The most compelling reason the grave clothes were left behind is that the One who had been in them no longer needed them.

4. **The fact that women saw the empty tomb first.** In the Jewish culture of the first century, women were not allowed to be witnesses in legal proceedings. They could not testify in a court of law. Given this fact, it is astonishing that the Bible records that women saw the risen Lord first. If the account of the empty tomb was fictional, they never would have recorded that women saw Him first. They would have made up a more convincing story than that. The only reason to record that women saw Jesus first was because women saw Jesus first.

5. **The change in the day of worship from the Sabbath (Saturday) to Sunday.** The order to worship God on Saturday was one of the 10 commandments. *Exodus 20:8-11 Remember the Sabbath day, to keep it holy. Six days you shall labor and do all your work, but the seventh day is the Sabbath of the Lord your God. In it you shall do no work; you, nor your son, nor your daughter, nor your male servant, nor your cattle, nor your stranger who is within your gates. For in six days the Lord made the heavens and the earth, the sea, and all that is in them, and rested the seventh day. Therefore, the Lord blessed the Sabbath day and hallowed it.* Now what in the world could have happened for these early disciples (who were Jewish) to abandon one of the Ten Commandments of God given by one of their most revered prophets, Moses, and begin worshipping on Sunday? The only thing of significance that happened during that period of history that involved the first day of the week (Sunday) was the empty tomb of Christ.

6. **The unexpected nature of Jesus' bodily resurrection.** The disciples did not expect Jesus to rise from the dead, though He had told

them, on several occasions, that it would happen. (Mark 8:31-33, 9:31-32, 10:32-34). When Jesus was crucified, their hopes were dashed. They *"were hoping that He was the One who was about to redeem Israel." (Luke 24:21)* They looked for and hoped for a mighty Messiah who would deliver them from Roman oppression and restore the glory of Israel, as in the days of King David. All the evidence strongly affirms that the disciples did not anticipate Jesus' resurrection. Therefore, they could not have played a role in making it appear that He had risen.

7. **The conversion of two skeptics; James, Jesus' half-brother and Saul of Tarsus.** John 7:5 *"For even His brothers did not believe in Him".* Mark 3:21 says that Jesus siblings thought that *"He was out of His mind".* The Bible is clear that James, the half-brother of Jesus, was an unbeliever in Jesus, as the Messiah, prior to His crucifixion. Yet something happened that changed James belief. He went from a skeptic to a leader in the church at Jerusalem, from one who thought his brother was "out of his mind" (Mark 3:21) to one who willingly went to his death believing that Jesus was the Messiah, the Son of the living God. James was killed in 62 A.D. for his faith in Jesus as the risen Christ. After the resurrection and ascension of Christ James became one of the pastors of the first church preaching that Jesus was the Messiah and He did rise from the dead. Saul of Tarsus violently persecuted the church (Acts 7:58; 8:1-3; 9:1-2). Acts 7:54-60; 8:1-3; and 9:1-9 describe Saul's life before he met the risen Lord on the road to Damascus. Something happened in Saul's life that changed him from a persecutor of Christ to the greatest missionary and evangelist, for Christ, that ever lived. What happened? In Paul's own words he said that he had seen the resurrected Christ. His own testimony, recorded several times in scripture, affirms that he saw the resurrected Christ (Acts 9:3-6; 22:6-10; 26:12-19; 1 Corinthians 15:8; Galatians 1:15-16)

8. **The moral character of the eyewitnesses**
    The New Testament provides the greatest teachings found in any literature on love, truth, honesty, hope, faithfulness, kindness, etc. These teachings came from the pens of men like Matthew, John, Paul, James, and Peter, all of whom claimed to be eyewitnesses of the risen Jesus. To believe in their teachings and believe they lied

about the resurrection of Jesus is nonsensical. If we accept their teachings, we must trust their testimony about Jesus.

9. **The early credal witness of 1 Corinthians 15:3-8**

The resurrection, as shown in 1 Corinthians 15:3-8, was the heart of the earliest Christian teaching. Virtually all scholars agree that Paul recorded, in these verses, a very early creed about Jesus' death and resurrection, a creed that predates Paul's letter. The usage of the terms 'delivered' and 'received' indicate the imparting of oral information. Some scholars date Paul's receiving of this creed (statement of belief) within 10 years of the crucifixion itself, or from about 30-40 A.D. Most think that Paul probably heard this testimony during his visit in Jerusalem with Peter and James, who are included in the list of resurrection eyewitnesses. (see 1 Corinthians 15:5,7 and Galatians 1:18-19). How did Bible scholars come to this conclusion? 1. All scholars agree that Paul wrote 1 Corinthians in 55-57 A.D. 2. Paul indicated in 1 Corinthians 15:3 that what he was about to write to the Corinthians was what he preached to them when he was with them on his second missionary journey (see Acts 18:1-17). The second missionary journey dates to 50-52 A.D. Note: Remember, Paul already possessed this crucifixion-resurrection information before he went to Corinth. Based on Galatians 1:13-22, Paul possessed this possibly as early as his conversion near Damascus or his visit to Jerusalem, bringing us up to 30-40 A.D. The reconstruction of the events undermines any type of mythical or fable embellishment. There was not enough time for such embellishment to occur. Eyewitnesses could provide a check and balance to any inaccuracies or exaggerated claims. Note: It is clear that from the very beginning of Christianity, Jesus' bodily resurrection was at the center of their faith.

10. **The accepted character and claims of Jesus.**

On numerous occasions Jesus spoke of His crucifixion and resurrection. He claimed he was God (see John 8:58; 10:30; 14:9), and He said He would come back from the dead (see Matthew 16:21). To claim that Jesus is a great religious figure and moral teacher while believing that His prediction of His resurrection was wrong would make Him either a liar or a lunatic. <u>The resurrection is essential to the confession that Jesus is Lord. Everything hinges on it.</u>

11. **Post resurrection appearance of Christ.** According to the Bible there were 13 distinct appearances of the resurrected Christ. We can make several important observations about these appearances. The disciples claimed that Jesus appeared at different times and to different people. Some appearances were to groups of people while others were to individuals. The differences, though complementary natures of the resurrection appearances, support their authenticity. Harmonizing the resurrection appearances is not easy. This fact provides evidence that Jesus' followers did not meet together to concoct and agree on a story. The appearances lasted for 40 days and then came to a complete and abrupt stop. Acts 1:4-11 tells us why: Jesus' ascension back to heaven occurred. No other reason for the cessation of these appearances has ever been espoused throughout history.

The Relevance of Jesus' Resurrection - The resurrection of Christ tells us that God the Father, who raised Jesus from the dead, does in fact, exist! The resurrection of Christ verifies the truths of all that Jesus said and taught! Jesus is God! The facts recorded in the gospels are true! Heaven is a real place! Hell is a real place! The resurrection of Christ tells us that God the Father approved of all that Jesus said and did! One of the things approved by God the Father were the words of Jesus in *John 14:6 – "I am the way, the truth, and the life. No one comes unto the Father except through me."*

Our spiritual bodies and souls, if we are in Christ, go immediately into the presence of God at our physical death. Our physical bodies, in Christ, will one day resurrect to new glorious physical bodies and will be forever with the Lord on the new earth. Our spiritual bodies and souls, if we are not in Christ, go immediately into hell. Our physical bodies, outside of Christ, will one day resurrect to eternal damnation in the eternal lake of fire.

The resurrection of Christ promises each of us victory over death. *John 14:1-4 Let not your heart be troubled; you believe in God, believe also in Me. In My Father's house are many mansions; if it were not so, I would have told you. I go to prepare a place for you. And if I go and prepare a place for you, I will come again and receive you to Myself, that where I am, there you may be also.*

1 Corinthians. 15:54-57 – So when this corruptible has put on incorruption, and this mortal has put on immortality, then shall be brought to pass the saying that is written: Death is swallowed up in Victory. O Death, where is your sting? O Hell, where is your victory? The sting of death is sin, and the strength of sin is the law. But thanks be to God, who gives us the victory through our Lord Jesus Christ.

The resurrection of Christ is unlike any other miracle, for its very occurrence involves eternal life. Jesus was raised in a physical body that was transformed. Jesus is now immortal; He will never die again. You can't kill Him. Nothing can ever harm Him. He will come again! When the disciples witnessed Jesus' resurrection appearance, they were actually confronted with living, walking, talking eternal life. Life that never dies! Jesus resurrection confirms that His existence means existence for all those that have been born again. All those that are His followers.

John 14:19 – "Because I live, you also will live."

I Serve a Risen Savior; He's in the World Today. I Know that He is Living, Whatever men may say. The real impact of Easter is: Has it changed my life? Has it made a difference to me? The tomb was empty! Christ arose! He's alive today! What is my response to that? Have I made a life changing commitment to Easter?

CHAPTER 14

WHY DO BAD THINGS HAPPEN TO GOOD PEOPLE?

*"I haven't prayed in over a year, every time I try to pray,
I run headfirst into the same big, black wall: 'Why God?
Why did this happen to me?"*

How many of us have ever felt this way in our lives? Have there been times in your life when bad things have happened, and you don't understand why? You were serving God the best you knew how and bad things or a very bad thing happened in your life. You know God is on His throne, but you just don't understand why? Listen to the following story.

A senior at a Christian college, I was also the supervisor for a dorm of young men. As the new school year began, we had joined together with a girls' dorm for a coed hall meeting. You need to understand that this was a fairly strict Christian college, so a coed hall meeting was an exciting event. The guys saw it as a low-key way to meet a lot of girls. Afterward, all the guys were energized, especially the freshmen. That is, all the guys except one. His name was Jim. He was in tears. I sat down next to him and asked, "What's wrong Jim?" "Nothing," he said, trying to brush back the tears. "Something's wrong," I said. "Tell me." He began to choke on tears as he answered, "I prayed tonight." I said, "Why is praying such a momentous event? This is a Christian college, and everyone prayed tonight." "Yeah," he answered. "But that's the first time I've prayed in over a year." Jim went on to tell me his story. He had grown up in a strong Christian family and had previously done well spiritually, praying daily. He had come to a Christian college because he wanted to become a pastor. Yet for the past year he had had no relationship with God. He had no faith. He had nothing inside but empty, hollow bitterness and doubt. Every time he tried to pray, one big ugly word blocked it out. *Why?* What had happened to turn him from God?

"My older sister is the best person I have ever known. She loved God, was involved in everything at church. She never did anything wrong," he explained. "A little more than a year ago, some man got a hold of her. He beat her up and viciously raped her," Jim said through clenched teeth. "She is the best person and the best Christian I know," he sobbed. The he gulped on tears and looked at me." "Why did God allow this to happen? I must admit I really did not know what to say. <u>How would you have answered his question? How would I have answered his question?</u>

What do you say in the face of such pain? Why do bad things happen to good people? It's a question we all ask. Every day in the newspaper we read the tragic tales of suffering, pain, and evil. Horribly bad things happen to very good people. Men with large families and women who are single moms lose their jobs. People get cancer and numerous other terminal diseases. Statistics indicate that around 44.6 percent of all deaths in the U.S. occur under the care of a hospice program. There are devastating floods and fires, hurricanes and tornadoes. Babies die or are born with crippling diseases. People are robbed, mugged, raped, abused, and murdered. In some parts of the world, Christians are tortured for their faith.

Why do such bad things happen to good people? It is a question that can easily bring bitterness into our lives and turn us away from God. Pain, suffering, and evil are relentless realities that will not go away until we are in heaven! Until then, what are we to do and think when bad things happen to good people? Let me begin by reminding all of us of several important truths.

1. God is under no obligation to give us an explanation for suffering.

Some say they don't want to believe in god unless they can figure him out or at least figure things out. But I have come to understand that a god that I can completely figure out is no God at all. I am so glad that the God I serve is so much bigger than I am that I cannot completely figure Him out.

Isaiah 55:8-9 – For My thoughts are not your thoughts, nor are your ways My ways, says the Lord. For as the heavens are higher than the earth, so are my ways higher than your ways, and my thoughts than your thoughts.

If I could completely figure out how God did things, exactly how he created the universe, exactly how everything is put together, exactly why everything happens the way it does then I could be God. If I could do what only God can do, then I could be God. Do you see that? What are the advantages of not being able to completely figure God out? How big is our God? Our God is bigger than we can figure out and therefore big enough to see us through our difficulties. He is a God who is beyond simple explanation. He is big enough for us to trust. Even when we don't understand, we can trust God. We don't want to hear it, but it's true. God is under no obligation to answer our questions. In this life, we may never see or fully understand why many things happen. That's what faith is about! Faith is trusting God in the *midst of*, trusting God *in spite of*, trusting God not only when we can see, but also *when we cannot see*. Peace does not mean to be in a place where there is no noise, trouble or adversity. Peace means to be in the midst of those things and still be calm in your heart. Trusting God – That's Faith.

2.   **God has given us plenty of explanation if we will only look for it and accept it.**
There are times when we get out of God's will and purpose for our lives. He warns us not to go somewhere or do some of the things we do in life. He clearly warns us many times to stay away from harmful situations and we disobey and do it anyway without any regard for obeying God's word and then we wonder why did this bad thing happen to me. And then the Bible gives us many principles and examples to point us toward reasons why bad things happen to good people. There are numerous stories of Christians who have battled severe suffering to show that God is able to produce much good from the suffering.

3. **God can do more than one good thing through the bad things that happen to us.** Have you ever had the delight of throwing a heavy rock into a still pond and seeing the many round ripples that radiate out from the center? So, it is with our episodes of suffering. They often drop like a heavy rock in a calm body of water and many good things end up coming from that heavy weight. We may not know the exact reason why bad things happen to us, but we can know that <u>good does come out of bad</u> – often times many good things come from one bad thing.

4. **God knows what it is to suffer, and He knows how to help us when we are suffering.** Sometimes we are hurting so bad that we feel all alone. Intellectually we know that God is there but emotionally we don't feel His presence, we don't sense His presence. We feel as if God has abandoned us. Realize though that this is a lie from Satan! *John 8:44 Jesus tells us that there is no truth in Satan. He is a liar and the father of lies!* God says: *I will never leave you nor forsake you. I will never abandon you!*

Two thousand years ago, God stepped out of Heaven so that He could experience our pain. He not only <u>saw our suffering</u>, but <u>He tasted it</u>, <u>He wore it</u>, <u>He lived it</u>, and <u>He died as a result of it.</u>

The ultimate and only pure picture of a bad thing happening to a good person is the cross of Jesus Christ. Jesus Christ was the only sinless person who ever lived. He was and is the Son of God and God the Son. Yet, <u>He experienced the ultimate in bad</u>. Pain, suffering, sorrow, and evil, resulting from sin, filled the cup that Jesus drank from. *The ultimate case of a bad thing happening to a truly good person was when the only truly good person was crucified for our sins.*

Are you suffering today from emotional anguish? You are not alone! Many of the people Jesus had lovingly healed and fed called for His crucifixion. His friend (Judas) betrayed Him, His best friend (Peter) denied Him 3 times, and His followers abandoned Him. He was spit upon and mocked. How do you think this made Jesus feel when His friends turned on Him? Jesus knows about emotional pain!

Are you frustrated today about an injustice that happened to you? You are not alone! Remember that the witnesses at the trial of Jesus lied about Him. The courts operated illegally to convict Him. The governor, even after plainly stating, "I find no fault with this man," condemned Him to death.

Are you in physical pain today? You are not alone! Remember that Jesus was beaten. He was whipped nearly to death with a whip designed to shred and rip the muscles, ligaments, and skin off His body. He experienced crucifixion, the most painful type of execution the Romans could imagine. Jesus died gasping for air, pulling against spikes in His wrists and feet, writhing for hours in front of a vicious crowd.

Are you in spiritual pain today? You are not alone! Remember that Jesus had the filth of our sins dumped on Him. His own Father had to turn His back on His sin-covered Son. Darkness, torment, and hell filled the cup that Jesus drank from that day. Imagine the excruciating agony of the heavenly Father, after an eternity in union with His Son, being forced to turn his back at His Son's greatest point of need. Imagine having the power to remove all the pain from His Son but knowing that to do so would leave the world cursed by sin. God knew that good was going to come out of this, so He allowed the bad!

Does God know anything about pain? You've got to be kidding. On a much higher, deeper, broader level than we can ever imagine, God experienced exactly what it is to have bad things happen to a good person! He knows what it is to suffer. He knows how to help us in our suffering.

Are you in deep anguish, battling bitterness, battling sickness, staring at a thick wall of doubts and questions, worn out by your pain? There are no easy answers and we can never make light of our pain or the pain of others. Pain is a very real thing, a very excruciating experience! You and I need God. Take your pain and turn it into prayer. Talk with God. Tell Him that you hurt. Trust Him by faith. Tell Him you need encouragement. He is there to help if we only call on Him. When we call on Him He may tell us to do something. But when we call on Him we must be willing to do what he tells us to do! Medicine is no good unless you take it.

I personally met with a man who just came from his wife's funeral two days before. He wanted me to come talk with him. His question? He said my wife was abused as a child. When we married she had a stroke at the age of 24. She lived in a crippled condition for the next 50 years before her death. He told me that she believed in Christ and according to her belief she is in heaven today. But then he said, "I am not so sure." "If there really is a loving, caring, and good God, why did all these bad things in life happen to her?"

Charles Templeton was born in 1915 and died in 2001 at the age of 86. He was a very accomplished Christian evangelist and a very good friend of Billy Graham. After the great depression there was a great spiritual vacuum in this country. From that setting came a man known as Charles Templeton. When Charles Templeton would preach evangelistic crusades, he drew crowds of 10,000, 30,000 and even 100,000. They came to hear him preach and many received Jesus Christ as their Lord and Savior. At one time he drew more crowds than Billy Graham did. Mr. Templeton began to question his faith. At one point he looked at the cover of a Time Magazine and saw a picture of a young child who died in Africa due to drought, lack of water. Mr. Templeton said, "If there is a good God then this would not have happened". He turned his back on the gospel and never preached again. He tried his best to get Billy Graham to also turn his back on God, but Billy refused and went on to lead millions of people to faith in Christ. What was the difference between the lives of Charles Templeton and Billy Graham? Was Charles Templeton, right? Is there a good God and if there is then why does He allow bad to happen?

When we ask the question "Why do Bad Things Happen to Good People" there are some assumptions behind why we even ask such a question. 1. The world is full of suffering and evil. 2. God created the world. 3. Therefore, God is the one to blame!

1. **The world is full of suffering and evil.**
   No doubt about that. Every day on the news we hear stories of pain and suffering. We know of several people in our lives that either are suffering, or they have suffered, and you may have been through a lot of suffering in your own life. Pain and suffering are truly a way of life. We really do live in a hurting world.

2. **God created the world.**
   The Bible is very clear about God being the Creator of the heavens and the earth and if we open our minds and look around us we'll

discover that everything about us screams of a created order. Evolution is no more than a religion of the atheist. And these atheists have obtained a strong foothold in the public-school systems of America and the world. Dr. Carl Baugh; scientific research director for the world's first hyperbaric biosphere and founder and director of Creation Evidence Museum in Glen Rose, Texas, wrote a book that is well worth the reading entitled "Why do Men Believe Evolution Against All Odds?

3. **Therefore, since God created the world, and bad things happen in the world, then God is the one to blame!**
Nothing could be further from the truth! People assume that if God is so good and powerful then He would prevent bad things from happening. But God doesn't stop all bad things from happening! So, we deduct that that either God is not all that good, or He is not powerful enough to stop evil from happening. But if God is good and He is powerful enough to stop bad things from happening then why doesn't He? Why do bad things happen to good people? Consider 5 Biblical truths concerning this subject.

1. **God created a good world and He created the world good.**

   Genesis 1:1 – In the beginning God created the heavens and the earth.

   Genesis 1:31a – Then God saw everything that He had made, and indeed it was very good.

God did create the world but notice the last four words from Genesis 1:31a *"it was very good."* The word "good" used here means "admirable, suitable, pleasing, fully approved." When God created the world, there were no earthquakes, hurricanes, floods, droughts, sickness, murder, suicide, or crime. The world God made was very good! It was Paradise!

2. **God created people with the ability to choose.**

   Genesis 1:27 – So God created man in his own image, in the image of God He created him; male and female He created them.

Being made in the image of God means that God created in us the ability to choose. He did this for several reasons. He created us with the ability to choose so that we would be able to love. God let us choose because He loves us and wants us to choose to love Him back. He wants us to choose to love other people. Jesus said the greatest commandment is to *"Love the Lord your God with all your heart, all your mind and all your soul and the second greatest commandment is to love your neighbor as yourself."* But if we couldn't choose then we couldn't love. If we did not have the ability to choose then we would be nothing more than robots. How would you like to be married to a chatty doll? Every morning and every night you could pull the string and get the beautiful words. "I love you." There would never be any angry words, never any conflict, never anything said or done that would make you mad or sad. But there also would never be any real love. He created us with the ability to choose because he was willing to take the risk. Evil is inherent in the risky gift of free will. God created a good world. God created people with the ability to choose.

3. People chose evil.

> *Genesis 2:16-17 – "And the Lord God commanded the man, "You are free to eat from any tree in the garden; but you must not eat from the tree of the knowledge of good and evil, for when you eat of it you will surely die."*

> *Genesis 3:6 – "When the woman saw that the fruit of the tree was good for food and pleasing to the eye, and also desirable for gaining wisdom, she took some and ate it. She also gave some to her husband, who was with her, and he ate it."*

God gave Adam and Eve a choice. What did they choose? They chose to disobey! They chose evil!

4. Their choice brought evil into the world.

> *Romans 5:12 – Therefore, just as through one man sin entered the world, and death through sin, and thus death spread to all men, because all sinned.*

"Exercise of free choice in the direction of evil is the basic reason for evil and suffering in the world." When we think of blaming God for the evil in this world, we need to stop and remember that humans introduced evil into the world. Not God.

5. Their choice has had lasting consequences.

Since the Garden of Eden, the choice of Adam and Eve has had lasting consequences. First the world is no longer good.

> *Romans 8:18 & 22 – For I consider that the sufferings of this present time are not worthy to be compared with the glory which shall be revealed in us. For we know that the whole creation groans and labors with birth pangs together until now.*

When we human beings told God to shove off, He partially honored our request. Nature began to revolt, the earth was cursed, genetic breakdown and disease began, pain and death became part of the human experience, the good creation was marred. Why are there earthquakes? The answer is that we live in a sin-cursed world. Why do you get sick? The answer is because we live in a sin-cursed world full of germs. We no longer live in Paradise. The world is now abnormal. The world is no longer good, and everything in it is flawed, from all of nature, to animals to man. People are no longer "good." *Romans 3:10 There is none righteous, no, not one.*

We ask, **"Why do bad things happen to good people?"** But if we really want to be honest, we must reword the question. Instead of asking why so many bad things happen to good people, we should be asking ourselves: **"Why do so many good things happen to bad people?"** Given the same choices that Adam and Eve had in the Garden of Eden you and I would have done the same thing. When it comes to sin, we are without excuse! So "Why does God bring so many good things into our lives when we have turned our back on Him?"

> *Isaiah 53:6 – All we like sheep have gone astray; we have turned, every one, to his own way; and the Lord has laid on Him the iniquity of us all.*

Why does God love us? Why does He continually keep drawing us to Himself? Why does He care? Why does He keep bringing us blessing after blessing? Why has He prepared a place for us in His kingdom? Why will He one day remove all pain, all suffering, all diseases, all calamities, all death? Why will He one day restore earth to the Paradise it once was? Why will He, one day, allow us to rule and reign with Him? Why does God continue to bring blessing after blessing (even among the hard times) into our lives?

"Why do so many good things happen to bad people?" One good thing that can happen in your life today. One good thing that is better than all other good things. You can receive God's free gift of salvation and eternal life today. You can receive the blessings of God by committing your entire life to Him today. As the old song goes "Count Your Blessings – Name them One by One and it will surprise you what the Lord has done"

"Why do so many good things happen to bad people?" Because amidst all your trials and tribulations God chose to love you!

> Job 1:1-3 (*Message*) – *There was a man who lived in the land of Uz, whose name was Job. Job was honest inside and out, a man of his word, who was totally devoted to God and hated evil with a passion. He had seven sons and three daughters. He was also very wealthy – seven thousand head of sheep, three thousand camels, five hundred teams of oxen, five hundred donkeys, and a huge staff of servants – the most influential man in all the East!*

In those three verses, we know several important facts about Job's life. 1. He was a good man. In fact, he was about as good a man as could be found. 2. He was a family man who enjoyed his seven sons and three daughters. Elsewhere in chapter 1, we find that he regularly prayed for his children. 3. Job had it made! One of the richest, most influential men in his part of the world, he had huge flocks and herds, and a large staff to care for them. 4. He was the envy of all! Job could truly look around and say, "Life is good! Life is very good!"

Life Turned Very, Very Bad

> *Job 1:13-19 (msg) – While Job's children were having one of their parties at the home of the oldest son, a messenger came to Job and said, "The oxen were plowing and the donkeys grazing in the field next to us when Sabeans attacked. They stole the animals and killed the field hands. I'm the only one to get out alive and tell you what happened." While he was still talking, another messenger arrived and said, "Bolts of lightning struck the sheep and the shepherds and fried them – burned them to a crisp. I'm the only one to get out alive and tell you what happened." While he was still talking, another messenger arrived and said, "Chaldeans coming from three directions raided the camels and massacred the camel drivers. I'm the only one to get out alive and tell you what happened." While he was still talking, another messenger arrived and said, "Your children were having a party at the home of the oldest brother when a tornado swept in off the desert and struck the house. It collapsed on the young people and they died. I'm the only one to get out alive and tell you what happened."*

Can you possibly imagine this happening to you? In one day, one single day, every nightmare and every unspoken fear that had ever sneaked into the corners of Job's mind exploded into reality and hit him like a train wreck. With no warning, Job's family and fortune were swept away in a landslide of loss. In one day, his job, his employees, his property, his income, his retirement, and his lifework were all totally, terrifyingly taken away. All he had worked for, all he had dreamed of, all he had owned was gone. In one day, the precious ones who proudly bore his image and carried his name, the ones he had joyfully watched take their very first steps, the ones he diligently prayed for, were cruelly killed, their promising lives prematurely snuffed out. I can't imagine losing one child, but ten! All at the same time! All gone! The agony he and his wife must have gone through. Numb? Crushed? Flattened? What words can possibly describe what they must have felt? Job's mountainous good fortune had suddenly become a gaping crater of what used to be. His very, very good life had immediately, instantaneously, turned very, very bad!

The Scene Behind the Scenes

When bad things come our way, we must always remember that God and Satan are locked in a cosmic battle for loyalty and allegiance, and often, we are the battleground. What Job was not able to see was that his sorrow was birthed out of an intriguing conversation Satan had with God.

> *Job 1:8-12 (msg) – God said to Satan, "Have you noticed my friend Job? There's no one quite like him – honest and true to his word, totally devoted to God and hating evil." Satan retorted, "So do you think Job does all that out of the sheer goodness of his heart? Why, no one ever had it so good! You pamper him like a pet, make sure nothing bad ever happens to him or his family or his possessions, bless everything he does – he can't lose! "But what do you think would happen if you reached down and took away everything that is his? He'd curse you right to your face, that's what." God replied, "We'll see. Go ahead – do what you want with all that is his. Just don't hurt him." Then Satan left the presence of God.*

As we have already seen, Satan left God and proceeded to have Job's livestock, his servants, and his children killed. Yet this situation extended far beyond Job, his animals, his employees, or his children. The question of evil and suffering on planet Earth must be understood as a spiritual battleground. There is more at stake than the comfort or heartache of a single sufferer. Massive questions hang on the response of a lone individual. Massive questions hang on our response to God when heartache comes our way. "Will a man or woman continue to loyally follow God even when they are overwhelmed by unexpected, unprovoked, inexplicable heartache, pain and evil?" "Is God worth it? "Does He merit such loyalty?"

Job's Response

So, how did Job respond when struck by a tsunami of suffering? Did Job's reaction prove Satan to be right or God to be worthy? After getting the last report that all his children had been killed in a tornado, note carefully Job's next step.

Job 1:20-22 (msg) – Job got to his feet, ripped his robe, shaved his head, then fell to the ground and worshiped: Naked I came from my mother's womb, naked I'll return to the womb of the earth. GOD gives, GOD takes. God's name be ever blessed. Not once through all this did Job sin; not once did he blame God.

Crushed, broken, aching, and numb, Job still worshipped God. Job's response to suffering proved that he believed God to be worthy of worship even when everything was taken away and life turned horribly, terribly ugly. God won! Satan lost! ROUND ONE!

Bad Turned Worse

Have you ever heard the expression "smile things could be worse, so sure enough I smiled, and things got worse?" Before Job had a chance to catch his breath or get his feet back under him, before his aching heart could begin to heal, bad turned worse – much, much worse.

The Scene Behind the Scenes

Satan does not give up easily. After Job initially responded to his loss by worshipping God anyway, Satan pulled himself off the mat to fight round two.

Job 2:3-6 (msg) Then God said to Satan, "Have you noticed my friend Job? There's no one quite like him, is there? – honest and true to his word, totally devoted to God and hating evil. He still has a firm grip on his integrity! You tried to trick me into destroying him, but it didn't work." Satan answered, "A human would do anything to save his life. But what do you think would happen if you reached down and took away his health? He'd curse you to your face, that's what." God said, "All right. Go ahead – you can do what you like with him. But mind you, don't kill him."

Satan again challenged God's integrity by attacking Job's. He said that even if Job had not given in and given up on God after losing everything, Job would certainly throw in the towel if God allowed him to attack his health.

> *Job 2:7-8 (msg) – Satan struck Job with terrible sores. Job had ulcers and scabs from head to foot. They itched and oozed so badly that he took a piece of broken pottery to scrape himself, then went and sat on a trash heap, among the ashes.*

If the inner agony of losing all your children and all your possessions weren't enough, now Job had the outer anguish of ugly, aching, pus-oozing boils over his entire body. Why would a good God possibly allow one of His most faithful servants to suffer so unjustly? What was God thinking? Why didn't He protect Job? Why did He allow this to happen?

Job's Response

> *Job 2:9-10 (msg) – His wife said, "Still holding on to your precious integrity, are you? Curse God and be done with it!" He told her, "You're talking like an empty-headed fool. We take the good days from God – why not also the bad days?" Not once through all this did Job sin. He said nothing against God.*

Anguish piled upon anguish, sorrow heaped upon sorrow, grief loaded upon grief, yet Job still worshipped God. Job's response to suffering proved that he believed God to be worthy of worship even when suffering the most intense of all emotional and physical pain.

A Reason Bad Things Happen to Good People

Let me stretch your thinking for just a few minutes. This is an amazing thought. Maybe some of our suffering has little or nothing to do with us and everything to do with God's plan to silence Satan's pride, to shut Satan's mouth. Satan wants to be worshipped like God, but he knows he is not worth it. If his followers were put to the test like Job was, they would curse him and turn on him instantly. Yet, when one of God's children, in this case Job, lost everything, he refused to turn away. God was worth it! And Satan was defeated! One little human who suffered so triumphantly had the power to shut the mouth of the prince of darkness! He did not bind the enemy with some well-worded prayer. He did not call down fire from heaven to burn up the enemy. He just remained loyal to God even though bad things were crashing in all round him. He was faithful in spite of a heart broken by grief and a body broken by

118

pain. Job did not realize it at the time, but he was winning an unseen victory. *Maybe, just maybe, we suffer some of our pain to see if we will remain loyal to God no matter what comes our way!* Maybe the entire kingdom of darkness and the entire kingdom of God are watching to see how we handle our pain. So why do bad things happen to good people? What good can come from bad?

It could be that there is an unseen victory to be won. Maybe we don't realize it now, but we may be players in an unseen battle. This scene may be played over and over throughout history.

Maybe Satan comes to God and says, "You see that woman down there; if you let her sons die in the war she will curse you to your face. And God says, "o.k. let's see." Maybe Satan comes to God and says, "You see that husband down there; if you let his wife and child die in that fire and he will curse you to your face. And God says, "o.k. let's see." Maybe Satan comes to God and says, "You see that wonderful family down there; the one that is always at church and loves you so much, the one who has those children who love their parents and love God. You let their son die in a car wreck and they'll curse you to your face." And God says, "o.k. let's see." Maybe Satan comes to God and says, "You see that woman down there, the one who goes to church all the time and claims to know you as her Savior"? You let her get cancer and she'll become so bitter that she'll turn her back on you forever! And God says, "o.k. let's see."

So, the question is, when suffering comes our way will we pass the test, as Job did, or will Satan win the victory in our lives? You see; our response to suffering may give God greater glory and get Satan to finally shut his mouth or it may just continue the battle.

> *Philippians 2:9-11 – Therefore God the Father also has highly exalted Jesus and given Him the name which is above every name, that at the name of Jesus every knee should bow, of those in heaven, and of those on the earth, and of those under the earth, and that every tongue should confess that Jesus Christ is Lord, to the glory of God the Father.*

Will we confess, no matter what comes our way, that Jesus Christ is Lord? Will we pass the test?

CHAPTER 15

LIFE CHANGING WORDS

Deuteronomy 30:19b-20a — I have set before you life and death, blessing and cursing; therefore, choose life, that both you and your descendants may live; that you may love the Lord your God, that you may obey His voice, and that you may cling to Him, for He is your life and the length of your days.

John 10:10 The thief comes to steal, kill, and destroy. <u>I am come that they might have life, and that they might have it more abundantly</u>.

Romans 10:8-11,13 (nas) — The Word is near you, in your mouth and in your heart — that is, the word of faith which we are preaching. If you confess with your mouth Jesus as Lord and believe in your heart that God raised Him from the dead, you will be saved; for with the heart a person believes, resulting in righteousness, and with the mouth he confesses, resulting in salvation. For the Scripture says, "Whoever believes in Him will not be disappointed. Whoever will call on the name of the Lord will be saved."

A little boy went out to the backyard to play with a baseball bat and a ball. He said to himself, "I am the best hitter in the whole world." Then he threw the ball up in the air and took a swing at it, but he missed. Without a moment's hesitation, he picked up the ball and tossed it in the air again, saying as he swung the bat, "I'm the best hitter in all the world." He swung and missed. Strike two. He tossed the ball up again, concentrating more intensely, even more determined, saying, "I am the best hitter in all the world!" He swung that bat with all his might. *Whiff!* Strike three. The little boy laid down his bat, smiled really big and said: "Well what do you know?" "I'm the best pitcher in all the world!"

Sometimes you simply must choose to see the bright side of situations. When things don't work out as you planned, rather than complaining, look for something good in your circumstances. Your mind is somewhat like a computer. What you program into it dictates how it will function. There's an old saying 'Garbage In – Garbage Out'

Too often we allow negative thoughts and words to have control of our minds changing us from the image we were created in. We were created in God's image. He programmed us to live life abundantly. Sometimes we go through life with a low self-esteem, with worries and fears or feelings of inadequacy and insecurity. Making matters worse, we pass on our negative attitudes to others. That's not choosing life, it's choosing death! When you recognize these things happening, you must reprogram your thoughts. You must change your thinking.

> *1 Corinthians 15:54-58a – So when this corruptible has put on incorruption, and this mortal has put on immortality, then shall be brought to pass the saying that is written: "Death is swallowed up in <u>victory</u>." O Death, where is your sting? O grave, where is your victory?" The sting of death is sin, and the strength of sin is the law. But thanks be to God, who gives us the <u>victory</u> through our Lord Jesus Christ. Therefore, my beloved brethren, be steadfast, immovable, always abounding in the work of the Lord.*

Until you get your thinking in line with the owner's manual, The Bible – God's Word, you will never operate at your full potential. Folks, you cannot go around all day long thinking about the people who have hurt you. You cannot go around all day long thinking about all the mistakes you've made and expect to live any kind of joyful, positive life. You've got to let go of the past and start dwelling on the fact that God has a great future in store for you. He has a new beginning for you. Choose to think on good things. CHOOSE LIFE.

There's a story about two brothers who were very different. One brother, no matter what bad came his way, was always positive. The other was always negative, no matter what good came his way. One Christmas his Mom and Dad decided they were going to change all that. They would get a pony for the negative son and wrap up a box of pony manure for the positive son. Christmas morning came, and the negative son went out back and saw his new pony. At first, he was so excited! But after a little bit he began to think negative thoughts. "This pony is going to make a mess in the yard and I'm going to have to clean it up. This pony is going to have to be fed and I'm the one who is going to have to feed him. This pony will need to be brushed." And all of a sudden, the negative son began to be very melancholy and depressed. When the parents went back into the house they saw the positive son opening up his box of manure and he was the most excited and positive they had ever seen him. They said, "son, why are you so excited?" "There is nothing in the box but a pile of manure." The positive son said as the dug into the pile of manure with vigor. "With all this manure there has got to be a pony in here somewhere."

When you reprogram your mental computer, your emotions will follow. Emotions are neither positive nor negative. They merely allow us to feel what we're thinking. If you go around thinking sad thoughts all the time, you're going to be sad. If you go around thinking angry thoughts, you're going to be angry. If you go around thinking joyful thoughts you are going to have joy in your life.

Choosing life is not a once-and-for-all matter. It's a choice we must make on a moment-by-moment basis. We must choose to dwell on the positive. Choose to dwell on the good. Choose to dwell on what's right, rather than on what's wrong. Choose to dwell on what you have, not on what you don't have. Dwell on the fact that God has a great plan in store for your life. When one door closes, God will always open a bigger and better door. But you must stay focused by staying in an attitude of faith. Stay filled with HOPE! <u>Faith is the substance of things hoped for.</u>

When we're always worried, upset, or depressed, all we're really doing is delaying God in bringing joy into our lives. God works where there is an attitude of faith. Jesus said, "If you believe, all things are possible." The opposite of that is also true. <u>If you don't believe, nothing is possible.</u>

If you'll do your part and keep believing, in due season, at the right time, God will bring joy into your life.

Some people take one step forward and then two steps backward. They are happy and in a good mood one day then the next day they are negative and depressed. They have a vacillating faith. They never really get to the place God wants them to be. They never experience the inner joys God has in store for them.

Jose Lima starred as a pitcher for the Houston Astros for several years in the late 1990's. He usually had a positive attitude and was very out-going. But when the Astros built Minute Maid Park, Jose was upset. The fence in left field was much closer than the fence in the Astrodome. The first time Jose Lima stepped onto the new diamond; he walked out to the pitcher's mound, noticed how close the left field fence was, and said "I'll never be able to pitch in here." The next year Jose had the worst year of his career. He plummeted from being a twenty-game winner to being a sixteen-game loser in back-to-back seasons. Never in the history of the Astros has any pitcher ever had a record like that. Why? I don't believe it was because of the fence. A lot of pitchers do well in that ball park. I believe it was because he said in his heart "I'll never be able to pitch in here."

The same thing happens to many of us every day. We get what we say. Our words become self-fulfilling prophecies. If you allow your thoughts to defeat you and then give birth to negative ideas through your words, your actions will follow. We need to be extremely careful about what we let our minds dwell on and especially careful about what words we use. Many people live discouraged lives because of their words. "Nothing good ever happens to me" - "I'll never be successful" - "I don't have what it takes" - I can't do it." - "I'll never get out of this mess." Some people even call themselves negative names. "What an idiot! You never do anything right." "You're so stupid!" "I'm just no good at anything."

Words are like seeds. By speaking them aloud, they are planted in our subconscious minds. They begin to take on a life of their own. They take root, grow, and produce. If we speak positive words our lives will move in that direction. If we speak negative words our lives will move in that direction.

James 3:4-11 – Look also at ships: although they are so large and are driven by fierce winds, they are turned by a very small rudder wherever the pilot desires. Even so the tongue is a little member and boasts great things. See how great a forest a little fire kindles! And the tongue is a fire, a world of iniquity. The tongue is so set among our members that it defiles the whole body, and sets on fire the course of nature, and it is set on fire by hell. For every kind of beast and bird, of reptile and creature of the sea, is tamed and has been tamed by mankind. But no man can tame the tongue, it is an unruly evil, full of deadly poison. With it we bless our God and Father, and with it we curse men, who have been made in the similitude of God. Out of the same mouth proceed blessing and cursing. My brethren, these things ought not to be so. <u>Does a spring send forth fresh water and bitter from the same opening?</u>

No, they don't! So why do we? I heard a story about a doctor who understood the power of words. He told his patients to say at least once every hour: "I'm getting better and better every day." The doctor's patients experienced amazing results, much better than the patients treated by many of his colleagues. When you say something often enough, with enthusiasm and passion, before long, your subconscious mind begins to act on what you are saying, doing whatever is necessary to bring those thoughts and words to pass.

If you suffer from low self-esteem you need to go overboard with faith filled positive words every day of your life. Get up each morning and look in the mirror and say: "I am valuable. I am loved. God has a great plan for my life! I'm excited about my future!" If you'll start saying those kinds of words, before long, you will rise to a new level of well-being. Life changing words are truly powerful words in your life! Have you ever started to say something and then the thought just went right out the door (so to speak)? Most of the time we say something like: "I can't remember." The next time that happens, tell yourself: "I'll remember it in a little bit." You'll be amazed at how much more you'll remember just by saying positive words instead of negative words.

> *Proverbs 18:21 – "Death and life are in the power of the tongue; and you will eat the fruit thereof."*

Guard what you say! If you're in a storm today, now more than ever you need to guard what you say and not allow any negative, destructive words to come out of your mouth. In other words, you create an environment for either good or bad with your words and you are going to have to live in the world that you've created. Instead of talking negatively or using words to describe negative situations, use your words to change the negative situation. Don't talk about the problem, talk about the solution. Jesus told us clearly to talk to our mountains!

> *Mark 11:23 – Truly I say to you, whoever says to this mountain, be taken up and cast into the sea, and does not doubt in his heart, but believes that what he says is going to happen, it will be granted him."*

Maybe your mountain is sickness; maybe it's a troubled relationship, maybe it's a floundering business. Whatever your mountain is, you must do more than think about it, more than pray about it; you must speak to your mountain. The Bible says "Let the weak say I am strong. Let the oppressed say I am free. Let the sick say I am healed. Let the poor say I am rich." Start calling yourself healed, happy, whole, and blessed. Stop talking to God about how big your mountains are and start talking to your mountains about how big God is! LIFE CHANGING WORDS!

CHAPTER 16

WHY DO I FEEL SO TIRED?

Weariness comes from bearing too heavy a burden for too long a time. If we don't have regular vacations or times of refreshment, weariness may even become fatal. Sometimes a job that seems too big can be as burdensome as a job that truly is too big. We can grow weary just thinking of an enormous job ahead. We get tired when there is too much work and the job seems too big. We get tired when we have a long sickness and grow weary of it. We get tired when we are striving too hard for something that isn't worth it. We get tired when we are depressed or discouraged.

> *Nehemiah 4:10 – Then the people of Judah began to complain that the workers were becoming tired.*
>
> *Job 7: 3 – I, too, have been assigned months of futility, long and weary nights of misery.*
>
> *2 Corinthians 11:27 – I have lived with weariness and pain and sleepless nights. Often, I have been hungry and thirsty and have gone without food. Often, I have shivered with cold, without enough clothing to keep me warm.*

We get tired when we are constantly lacking necessary resources. The apostle Paul, at this writing, was very tired. But being without these necessary resources sometimes is the mark of spiritual maturity. This marks the third time that the apostle Paul told of his trials and suffering. I believe he did so to remove the triumphalist model of gospel ministry and Christian maturity being flaunted by the false apostles not only of his day but of ours as well. True believers follow the model of the Suffering Servant Jesus for ministry and maturity. God is shown to be strong in our weaknesses and sufferings.

> *Proverbs 23:4-5 – Don't weary yourself trying to get rich. Why waste your time? For riches can disappear as though they had the wings of a bird!*

> *2 Corinthians 5:1-2 – For we know that when this earthly tent we live in is taken down – when we die and leave these bodies – we will have a home in heaven, an eternal body made for us by God himself and not by human hands. We grow weary in our present bodies, and we long for the day when we will put on our heavenly bodies like new clothing.*

As we grow older or face sickness or infirmity, we grow weary of our failing bodies and long for the new bodies we shall receive in heaven.

> *2 Corinthians 12:7-9 – I was given a thorn in my flesh, a messenger from Satan to torment me . . . Three different times I begged the Lord to take it away.*

WHAT DO I HAVE TO WATCH OUT FOR WHEN I AM TIRED?

> *Galatians 6:9 – So don't get tired of doing what is good. Don't get discouraged and give up, for we will reap a harvest of blessing at the appropriate time.*

Being tired makes us more susceptible to discouragement, temptation, and sin.

> *Proverbs 30:1-2 – I am weary, O God; I am weary and worn out, O God. I am too ignorant to be human, and I lack common sense.*

Being tired causes us to lose our perspective.

> *Job 10:1 – I am disgusted with my life. Let me complain freely . . ."*

Being tired causes us to say things we may later regret.

> *Ecclesiastes 1:8 – Everything is so weary and tiresome! No matter how much we see, we are never satisfied . . .*

Being tired can cause us to lose our vision and purpose.

HELP IS ON THE WAY! The Lord God helps us when we are weary!

> *Psalm 68:35 – God is awesome in His sanctuary. The God of Israel gives power and strength to his people. Praise be to God!*

> *Isaiah 41:10 – Don't be afraid, for I am with you. Do not be dismayed, for I am your God. I will strengthen you. I will help you. I will uphold you with my victorious right hand.*

> *Jeremiah 31:25 – For I have given rest to the weary and joy to the sorrowing.*

> *Ephesians 6:10 – Be strong with the Lord's mighty power.*

WHAT WISDOM DOES GOD GIVE US WHEN WE ARE TIRED? HOW CAN HE HELP US?

> *Matthew 11:28 – Come to me, all of you who are weary and carry heavy burdens, and I will give you rest.*

> *Psalm 127:2 – It is useless for you to work so hard from early morning until late at night . . . for God gives rest to his loved ones.*

> *Luke 10:38-42 – Now it happened as they went that He entered a certain village; and a certain woman named Martha welcomed Him into her house. And she had a sister called Mary, who also sat at Jesus feet and heard His word. But Martha was distracted with much serving, and she approached Him and said, Lord, do You not care that my sister has left me to serve alone?*

> *Therefore, tell her to help me. And Jesus answered and said to her,* <u>Martha, Martha, you are worried and troubled about many things. But one thing is needed, and Mary has chosen that good part, which will not be taken away from her.</u>

Always being tired may mean you are trying to do too much; it may be God's way of telling you to slow down and enjoy more fellowship with him. The Lord says – Whoa slow down! You're trying to do too much. There are many things to do and you can't do it all. Pick the best part and do that.

> *Isaiah 40:29-31 – He gives power to those who are tired and worn out; He offers strength to the weak. Even youths will become exhausted, and young men will give up. But those who wait on the Lord will find new strength. They will fly high on wings like eagles. They will run and not grow weary. They will walk and not faint.*

Wait on the Lord. Sit at His feet. Spend time in prayer. Spend time in God's word. Slow down and wait on the Lord. Quit doing some of the things you're doing. Don't get ahead of God. Get some rest. Don't do all the things – Do the best things.

CHAPTER 17

A DAY THAT WILL LIVE IN INFAMY

Deuteronomy 30:15-19

Turn in your Bibles to Deuteronomy 30:19. The title of today's message is "A Day That Will Live in Infamy." (Infamy: an extreme and publicly known criminal or evil act)

> *Deuteronomy 30:19 – "This day I call heaven and earth as witnesses against you that I have set before you life and death, blessings and curses. Now choose life, so that you and your children may live."*

You remember that tragic moment in American history when Pearl Harbor was bombed by the Japanese, killing thousands of our young men and women. It was December 7, 1941 and a somber President Roosevelt addressed our grief-stricken nation and said: **"This day is a day that will live in infamy."**

The same was said about September 11, 2001, when two planes took down the twin towers of the World Trade Center, another smashed into the Pentagon, and another crashed in rural Pennsylvania. America has not, and never will be the same after 9/11. We lost nearly 3,000 Americans that day, **a date that will also live in infamy.**

But did you know that almost 4,000 innocent people will be murdered in America tomorrow. It's true! In fact, we can predict these horrible deaths with chilling accuracy. One person will be murdered tomorrow every 24 seconds. When added up, that's around 1.4 million Americans a year that are murdered. Over the last 44 years over 58 million people have been murdered without mercy in the United States. These people did not have a trial. They had no legal representation. They had no opportunity to defend themselves! In fact, they didn't even commit a crime. They did nothing wrong! Yet, they have been executed in cruel, inhumane ways! Some of them have been torn from limb to limb while others have had their brains sucked from their heads as well as other cruel and inhumane treatment. Yes, that's right, this is happening every day, behind closed doors, right here in the United States of America. Do we honestly think that God is going to let that go un-punished?

What am I talking about? On January 22, 1973, the United States Supreme Court made it legal for our nation to murder nearly 60 million of its own citizens. It's called abortion. Mark down January 22, 1973 as a day that will also live on in infamy; (**an extreme and publicly known criminal or evil act.**)

But is abortion really all that wrong? Don't those who promote a woman's right to choose, have a good heart? Aren't they concerned citizens? Do they really think that what they are doing is right? The answer to those questions is yes and no. There are some who understand that it's big business and there are others who really think what they are doing is the right thing to do.

Let's examine some of their arguments and see how they hold up to scrutiny.

1. The fetus is not a baby.
2. What about rape and incest?
3. What about handicaps and birth defects?
4. What about those who cannot afford children or can't afford to raise them?
5. Doesn't a Woman have the Right to Choose what she wants to do with her body?

One – The Fetus is not a Baby

The bottom line is conclusive and biological facts show the fetus to be a living human being. A group of 60 prominent physicians, which included former presidents of the American College of Obstetrics and

Gynecology, the American Academy of Neurology, met in Cambridge Massachusetts and presented a declaration that said: "The fetus is not a sub-human species. The embryo is alive, human, and unique in the special environmental support required for that stage of human development. **The word fetus is a Latin word which translated into English is _Unborn Baby_.** The abortionists feel it is important to use the Latin word so that you and I won't know what they're talking about. It's all part of their great deception.

How far have we come in our history? The Supreme Court in 1857, in the Dred Scott case, said that a black man was not protected by the Constitution because a slave was not a person. In Nazi Germany, Hitler said that a Jew was not a person, so it was perfectly legal and moral to destroy them. Before you can get the general public to buy into your line of thinking the first thing you have to do is de-humanize the person and make people believe that what you are doing is o.k.

It's a deadly slippery slope to say that the unborn child in the womb is not human. It leads down a road where eventually all human life becomes worthless. America is heading down that slippery slope right now. Abortion is not far from rationalizing that children with defects can be put to death or that the elderly who no longer contribute to the economy should die. In Nazi Germany, Hitler not only killed millions of Jews but also children and adults, of any race, who had a physical defect

Two – What about Rape and Incest and saving the life of the Mother?
Rape, incest, and abortion, to save the life of the mother, account for less than 4 percent of all abortions yet that is where the abortionists spend 96% of their rhetoric. Sometimes an abortion may be necessary to save the life of the mother. In that instance it is certainly up to the Mom and Dad of that child to make such a decision. Yet there is a great deal of emotion attached to victims of rape and incest and rightfully so. But are we to play God in instances like these? Are you going to say that a baby conceived by rape or incest should not live? Wouldn't that be following one wrong with another wrong?

E.g. Let's say that a white man raped a 13-year-old black girl, impregnating her. Should her parents force her to abort that child? If they had, we would not have been blessed by the Gospel Singer Ethel Watters.

Three - What about Handicaps and Birth Defects?

Let's say that there's a mother who has tuberculosis, she has already given birth to four children, one died, one is blind, one is deaf, and a fourth contracted tuberculosis from the mother. She's pregnant again, should she abort? <u>Well if she had, then the world would have been robbed of the music of Ludwig von Beethoven.</u>

Are we going to be the ones to play God in such circumstances? Do we believe that defective people should be put to death? Just how defective do you have to be to be put to death? All of us are defective! All of us have sinned! *There is none righteous,* **no not one***, is what the scriptures tell us. Romans 3:10*

Where do we start when eliminating those who are defective? Where do we end? In Nazi Germany, abortion preceded the killing of the handicapped, elderly, and finally the Jews. America has started the process; where does it end?

Four – What about those who cannot afford children or afford to take care of them?

Let's say a preacher and his wife are very poor and they have 14 kids already, then she learns that another baby is on the way. Considering the burden, it would add to their family, should she abort? <u>If she had, she would have aborted John Wesley, the great 19th century evangelist and co-founder of the Methodist church.</u>

Let's say that a Mother just simply cannot afford a child. She has no way to support a child. Should she abort? <u>If she had, our adopted granddaughter would not have been born.</u>

Let's say that a teenage girl, who's very poor, discovers she's pregnant out of wedlock, and the guy she's engaged to is not the father. If he finds out, she fears he will get really upset and will call off the wedding. Should she go ahead and get an abortion? <u>If she had, she would have aborted Jesus.</u>

Five – Doesn't a Woman have the Right to Choose?

Doesn't a woman have a right to do what she chooses with her body? According to the law she doesn't! In most states, it's illegal for her to engage in prostitution. It's against the law for her to fill her body with illegal drugs. No, a woman cannot do entirely as she pleases with her body. The main argument abortionist's use is "A woman has a right to choose." **Choose what?** Choose to kill? Choose to steal? Choose to kidnap? In a civilized society a person does not have the right to do as they please. And that's especially true regarding the unborn child in the mother's womb because we're not talking about her body. Every cell in a woman's body has the same 46 chromosomes, and exactly the same genes. Every cell is identical in that way, except for the cells in her baby. The baby has a different set of chromosomes and a different set of genes. The baby has its own blood stream, maybe even a different blood type than the mother. In half the cases, the baby has a different gender. The baby is not part of the mother's body! The baby is a guest living inside the host, the mother.

Let's say a cult member comes into my home to share his propaganda with me. He is an unwanted guest from the standpoint of his religion. Do I have the right to murder an unwanted guest? It's the same faulty reasoning with abortion. If a mother delivered a baby and then decided to kill the child would that be o.k.? No, the law says that would be murder. Let me ask you. . .what's the difference? The high value God places on human life is also the justification for Capital Punishment.

> *Genesis 9:6 Whoever sheds the blood of man, by man shall his blood be shed for in the image of God has God made man.*

When you murder another person, you have committed a great evil. Why? Because God created man in His image, and the malicious attack against another human being is considered an indirect attack on God Himself. And that crime is worthy of the death penalty! Human life is precious in God's sight! We are the object of his great love! *For God so loved the world that He gave His Only Begotten Son.* Anyone who takes a life, wrongfully, is the object of God's wrath.

What does the Bible have to say about when life begins?

> *Psalm 139:13-16 – For You formed my inward parts; You covered me in my mother's womb. I will praise You, for I am fearfully and wonderfully made; marvelous are Your works, and that my soul knows very well. My frame*

was not hidden from You, when I was made in secret,
and skillfully wrought in the lowest parts of the earth.
Your eyes saw my substance, being yet unformed. And
in Your book, they all were written, the days fashioned
for me, when as yet there were none of them.

Look at the pronouns. God is not talking about an "it" here in these verses.

*"You formed **my** inward parts; you covered **me** in my*
*mother's womb. **I** will praise You. **I** am fearfully and*
*wonderfully made. **My** soul knows very well. **My** frame*
*was not hidden from You. **I** was made in secret. Your*
*eyes saw **my** substance being yet unformed. **My** days*
*are fashioned for **me.***

16. Your eyes saw my substance, <u>being yet</u>
<u>unformed</u>. And in Your book, they all were written,
the days fashioned for me, when as yet there were
none of them.

1.   After conception, a fetus seems quite formless, only a jumble of dividing cells.
2.   As time passes, specific cells with specific functions make the fetus look more like a human being with head, arms, and legs.
3.   Even though the fetus starts out looking formless, God considers the fetus a human being and values its life.
4.   While the child is still in the womb, God has a purpose for the child that extends beyond the child's birth and throughout the child's life.
5.   God treasures the life of each person. He knows what He intends the baby to become.

TRUTH: <u>God's creation of each individual, to fulfill special purposes,</u> <u>indicates the value God places on each person.</u>

1.   We too need to value each person's life.
2.   We need to work with God in protecting people at all stages of life and encourage them to fulfill their God-given purposes.
3.   We need to help pregnant mothers carry their babies to term and give their babies a chance at a full life. We need to show compassion

to the unwed mother, not condoning the sin, but caring for the mother and the child. Christians should be just as concerned before and after the pregnancy as we are during the pregnancy.

4. We need to support Pregnancy Assistance Centers who help and encourage Mother's to deliver their babies. We can go to the website www.frc.org and stay informed on the issues. (Family Research Council)

5. We need to protect children from child abuse and allow them to discover their gifts and value.

6. We need to help young people remain free of alcohol and drugs, so they can live healthy and happy lives.

7. We need to help middle-aged adults cope with the stresses of life as parents, workers, and caretakers and offer them guidance and encouragement in making decisions.

8. We need to respect our older adults, learn from them, and assist them as they lose physical strength and sometimes mental acuity.

9. We need to get involved. We need to support only political candidates that are pro-life. You can go on the website to www. ivotevalues.org to see where candidates stand on the issue of abortion. We need to be the voice for those who have no voice. We need to vote our values.

10. BE ACTIVE! *Isaiah 58:1 Shout it aloud! Don't hold back! Raise your voice like a trumpet! Declare to my people their rebellion, and to the house of Jacob their sins.*

11. BE PRAYERFUL! Above all, and more important than all the rest, we need to pray! We need to beg God to change the direction this nation is headed in. We once held to the God-given rights to life, liberty, and the pursuit of happiness in this nation, but that day has long past.

TRUTH: God has a purpose for all people at all stages of life and thus we need to value life and value all people at all stages of life.

> *Jeremiah 1:5 – Before I formed you in the womb, I knew you, before you were born I set you apart. I ordained you a prophet to the nations.*

God says that life begins at the moment of conception! ***How can a person have liberty and the pursuit of happiness if we deny them the right to have life?***

Nothing is impossible with God! This nation is not past saving! Just as slavery ended, just as the Jewish holocaust ended, the American holocaust can end.

> *2 Chronicles 7:14 — If My people who are called by My name will humble themselves, and pray and seek My face, and turn from their wicked ways, then I will hear from heaven, and will forgive their sin and heal their land.*

CHAPTER 18

WHAT IS SO ALLURING ABOUT MONEY?

Luke 12:15 – And He said to them, "Take heed and beware of covetousness, for one's life does not consist in the abundance of the things he possesses."

Luke 18:18-24 – Now a certain ruler asked Him saying, "Good Teacher, what shall I do to inherit eternal life?" So, Jesus said to him, "Why do you call Me good? No one is good but One, that is, God." "You know the commandments; Do not commit adultery, do not murder, do not steal, do not bear false witness, Honor your father and your mother." And he said, "All these things I have kept from my youth." So, when Jesus heard these things, He said to him, "You still lack one thing. Sell all that you have and distribute to the poor, and you will have treasure in heaven; and come, follow Me." But when he heard this, he became very sorrowful, for he was very rich. And when Jesus saw that he became very sorrowful, He said, "How hard it is for those who have riches to enter the kingdom of God!"

Why did the rich young ruler not accept Jesus as his personal savior? He had an interest. He heard about everlasting life. He went to Jesus. He asked Jesus the right question, "What must I do to have everlasting life." He certainly got the right answer. Jesus said, "Come Follow Me." He certainly asked the right person, Jesus who is eternal life.

He went to the right person, He asked the right question, He got the right answer, but he made the wrong decision. Why did he make the wrong decision? Jesus said "Come Follow Me" but he couldn't follow Jesus because it would cost him financially and he couldn't turn loose of his love of money. The love of money will destroy you! Maybe you think you don't have this problem with the love of money. Really? Do you give 10% of your gross income to the Lord through the local church? Do you give offerings over and above the 10%? Remember, Jesus said, where your money is there will your heart be also. If your heart is in the Lord's work, then your money will be there also. If your money is in your home, your car, your vacation resort, your boat, etc. there will your heart be also.

If you suddenly came into $25 million dollars (tax free) how would that make you feel? You'd never have to go to work, unless you wanted to. You could tell your boss what you really think of him or her (which I hope is nice). You would never have to wonder where your next meal is coming from. You would never have to stress over bills. You would never have to stress over college tuition for your children. You would never have to worry about your retirement years. You could have that vacation you always wanted but knew you could never afford. You could drive that car of your dreams. You could have that home of your dreams. There would be no limit to the amount of stress that would be forever gone if you just had that money. Yet, for all the security that money offers, it still cannot protect us from many pitfalls in life.

In Luke chapter 12 Jesus is on his way to Jerusalem to be crucified. As He travels He is teaching eternal truths; words to live by and not just to hear. He tells us to fear God. He tells us that hell is real. He tells us to know that God loves us, and we are valuable to Him. He tells us how to be sure that we have eternal life. He teaches us not to be afraid of men. He teaches us some truths about the Holy Spirit. But in the crowd is a young man who has no regard for anything that Jesus is saying. He was only concerned about his money and he wanted Jesus to settle a dispute with his brother over the money. Jesus answered the young man but then detected a problem with the man's heart: GREED

> *Luke 12: 4-15 – "And I say to you, my friends, do not be*
> *afraid of those who kill the body, and after that have*
> *no more that they can do. But I will show you whom*

you should fear: Fear Him who, after He has killed, has power to cast into hell; yes, I say to you, fear Him! Are not five sparrows sold for two copper coins? And not one of them is forgotten before God. But the very hairs of your head are all numbered. Do not fear therefore, you are of more value than many sparrows. Also, I say to you, whoever confesses Me before men, him the Son of Man also will confess before the angels of God. But he who denies Me before men will be denied before the angels of God. And anyone who speaks a word against the Son of Man, it will be forgiven him; but to him who blasphemes against the Holy Spirit, it will not be forgiven. Now when they bring you to the synagogues and magistrates and authorities, do not worry about how or what you should answer, or what you should say, for the Holy Spirit will teach you in that very hour what you ought to say." Then one from the crowd said to Him, "Teacher, tell my brother to divide the inheritance with me." But He said to him, "Man, who made Me a judge or an arbitrator over you?" And He said to them, "Take heed and beware of covetousness, for one's life does not consist in the abundance of the things he possesses."

Think about what Jesus said. <u>Your life does not consist in the abundance of the things you possess.</u> Isn't that contrary to how we live our lives? Don't we have the idea that our life does consist in the abundance of the things which we have? Don't we enjoy the golf membership that we have, that new car that we drive, that home we saved for all our life, that hunting trip we got to take, the new boat, that shopping trip, the new clothes, the new shoes and so on and so on. If we're not careful we'll come to believe that our life is all about getting and canning what we get and holding on tightly to it. The more tightly we hold on the more we begin to realize that it is squeezing the very life right out of us and we begin to wonder "Is this really what life is all about."

Luke 12:16-21 – Then He spoke a parable to them, saying: "The ground of a certain rich man yielded plentifully. And he thought within himself, saying, 'What shall I do, since I have no room to store my crops?' So, he said, 'I will do this: I will pull down my barns and build greater, and there I will store all my crops and my goods. 'And I will say to my soul, "Soul, you have many goods laid up for many years; take your ease; eat, drink, and be merry."' "But God said to him, 'Fool! This night your soul will be required of you; then who's will those things be which you have provided?' "So is he who lays up treasure for himself and is not rich toward God."

This rich man had a problem that the rest of us would die for. He had too much money. Most of us have too much month left at the end of the money. He lay awake at night worrying about what he would do with all his money. He had several choices. He could have called his family together for a service of thanksgiving to God and then donated a great deal of the money to the Lord's work. He could have used some of it to help those without work. He could have used some of it to help those who couldn't work. He could have begun to divide some of it between his heirs.

But what did he do with it? He worshipped it! He began believing that money provided protection from future problems in life. Therefore, he began to stockpile his money, so he could quit work and lead a lifestyle of luxury. Many of us think we'd like to try that out for a while but we must realize that an attitude like that is not Biblical. Why is it not Biblical?

1. **For our future, God wants us to trust Him, not our money.** King Solomon once wrote: *Two things I ask of you, O Lord; do not refuse me before I die; keep falsehood and lies far from me; give me neither poverty nor riches but give me only my daily bread. Otherwise, I may have too much and disown you and say, 'Who is the Lord?' Or I may become poor and steal, and so dishonor the name of my God. (Proverbs 30: 7-9((niv)*

   And we find that is exactly what happened to Solomon. At the end of his life he sits down to write the book of Ecclesiastes where he states that life is all in vain. Money is all in vain. Nothing matters but to love God, trust God, serve God and enjoy the work which God has given you.

2. **God never meant for us to quit working and lead lives of luxury as this rich fool desired to do.**
    Spending the last twenty or thirty years of your life with no greater purpose that self-fulfillment is a sure-fire formula for spiritual disaster. When we get to the point where our desire is to quit going to church, quit serving God, quit living for God, quit teaching others about God, and take all our wealth and live for ourselves God says, "You Fool." "This very night you are going to die and then who will own all of your wealth?" That's why God tells us to lay up for ourselves treasures in heaven where neither moth, nor rust destroys and where thieves do not break in to steal.

As powerful as money is it cannot protect you from everything. It can't protect you from the stranger who steals your husband or your wife's heart and destroys your marriage. Money can't protect you from a lawsuit that instantly wipes out your nest egg. Money can't protect you from a job loss that depletes your savings. Money can't protect you from cancer or a blood clot or Alzheimer's or any number of things that can take you to your maker. Do you see why God wants us to trust HIM and not our money? One day you are going to meet your maker. You are going to stand before Jesus, who gave His life for you, to give an account of how you lived your life.

King Solomon wrote these words in *Ecclesiastes 5:11-12 As goods increase, so do those who consume them. And what benefit are they to the owner except to feast his eyes on them? The sleep of a laborer is sweet, whether he eats little or much, but the abundance of a rich man permits him no sleep."* Having experienced great wealth, perhaps the wealthiest man that has ever lived, Solomon reminds us that money can sometimes provide more problems than solutions.

Let's review for a moment everything that money can provide: Security for the future - Fulfillment of desires – Independence. Maybe that's why Jesus pointed to money as the number one contender against God for our affections. But one day you'll stand before God to give an accounting. Perhaps you've allowed money to lure you away from God. Examine yourselves and see if you are obsessed with making money, spending money, and saving money. You may realize that your preoccupation with money has slowly strangled your love for God.

CHAPTER 19

CHRISTIAN GIVING

The parents of a young man who was killed in World War I gave their church a check for two hundred dollars as a memorial to their love one. (This is equivalent to $3,400 today). When the presentation was made, another war mother whispered to her husband, "Let's give the same for our boy." The father said, "Why, what are you talking about? Our boy didn't die in the war." The mother said, "That's just the point. Let's give because he didn't."

What is your reason for giving? Many give according to the commandment of *Malachi 3:10. Bring ye all the tithes into the storehouse, that there may be meat in My house, and try Me now in this, says the Lord of hosts, if I will not open for you the windows of heaven and pour out for you such blessing that there will not be room enough to receive it.*

We used to sing the old hymn "Trust Me, Try Me, Prove Me." I had to go back to an old Broadman Hymnal copyright 1940 to even find the song in a hymn book. It seems we don't want to sing about giving or sacrificing any more. "Bring ye all the tithes into the storehouse, all your money, talents, time and love; consecrate them all upon the altar; while your savior from above speaks sweetly, trust Me, try Me, prove Me, saith the Lord of hosts, and see if a blessing, unmeasured blessing, I will not pour out on thee."

Do we give out of God's commandment for us to give? Or do we give according to God's promise that He will give back to us more than we give to Him? Whatever the reason we give, the main reason should be because God gives.

Mark 12:41-44 – Now Jesus sat opposite the treasury and saw how the people put money into the treasury. And many who were rich put in much. Then one poor widow came and threw in two mites, which make a farthing. So, He called His disciples to Himself and said to them, Assuredly, I say to you that this poor widow has put in more than all those who have given to the treasury; for they all put in out of their abundance, but she out of her poverty put in all that she had, her whole livelihood.

In New Testament times, not only Roman but Greek, Syrian, and Egyptian coins were in common circulation. The most common coin of that day was the Roman denarius, a silver coin about 2/3 the size of the American quarter, worth about 16 cents and representing an ordinary day's wage for a laborer. The Greek equivalent to the denarius was the drachma, mentioned in Luke 15:8. The mite, the smallest coin, was worth 1/8 of our penny. It took 8 mites to make up a farthing (a penny). The widow in this story was so poor that she gave 1/4 of a penny to the church that day. And by her gift she has given us the example of true giving.

But Jesus also set the example for us as well. He gave His all! He gave sacrificially! He gave His life on the cross so that we may live! Are we following these examples of true giving? Are we giving our all?

THREE TRUTHS WE ARE GOING TO LOOK AT THIS MORNING:
1. The Lord Expects Our Gifts.
2. The Lord Exalts Our Gifts.
3. The Lord Examines Our Gifts

1. **THE LORD EXPECTS OUR GIFTS** *(Mark 12: 41)*
    Not only did Jesus teach in the temple; but He sat down and watched how the people gave into the treasury of the temple. *Now Jesus sat opposite the treasury and saw how the people put money into the treasury.*

    1. There was no rebuke in giving. Jesus watched the rich, the middle class, and the poor all put money into the treasury. The people clearly understood that God expected them to "bring ye

all the tithes into the storehouse." They were expected to give, and Jesus sat and watched them give.

2. <u>There were no reservations about their giving.</u> You would think that Jesus would have told them to stop giving into this temple. Why? *The leaders of the temple were not following God.* Jesus, time and time again, rebuked the Pharisees for their teachings. He chased the money-changers out of the temple, declaring they had made His Father's house a "den of thieves" (Mark 11:17) He knew the temple would be destroyed - he predicted it - and it was destroyed in the year A.D. 70. The leaders of this temple were the instigators and conspirators of Jesus crucifixion. Jesus, knowing all this, did not stop God's people from giving into the treasury of this temple.

3. <u>There are no reasons not to give.</u> This temple was a divine Institution and no reasons can be cited for not giving into the treasury. It is not the givers' responsibility to judge God's institutions. They and their leadership will be held accountable by God. God expects His people to give – rich and poor alike. It is expected of God's people to give through the local church.

> *Proverbs 3:9 says "We are to honor Him with our substance, with the first fruits of all our increases."*

> *1 Corinthians 16:1-2 – "Now concerning the collection for the saints, as I have given order to the churches of Galatia, even so do ye. Upon the first day of the week let every one of you lay by him in store, as God hath prospered you."*

<u>We are to give not according to how our money will be spent, but according to how God has prospered us. There are no excuses for not giving to God!</u> All throughout scripture (both Old and New Testaments) the standard for giving was and still is 10% of your income into the Lord's work through the local church plus additional offerings as the need arises.

> *2 Corinthians 9:7 – Every man according as he pur-*
> *poses in his heart, so let him give, not grudgingly,*
> *or of necessity; for God loves a cheerful giver.*

TRUTH: Jesus sat and observed the rich and the poor give into the treasury of the temple when He knew the leaders were not following God, the building was used as a den of thieves, the building would be completely destroyed, the leaders would be instrumental in His death, and yet He did not stop them from giving. Why? <u>God does not need our gifts – but we need God's blessing!</u> God's purposes will be accomplished whether you or I help or not. But God wants us to enjoy living and allows us the opportunity of blessings through giving. God's people are expected to be givers. So, the number one reason for giving is 'The Lord Expects Our Gifts.'

2. THE LORD EXALTS OUR GIFTS

> *Mark 12:43 – So He called His disciples to Him and said*
> *to them, Assuredly, I say to you that this poor widow*
> *has put in more than all those who have given to*
> *the treasury.*

<u>The Right Kind of Giving</u> – Jesus did not reject nor despise the gifts which the rich made when they cast in much. They were doing what was right. The Bible says to give according to how much God has prospered you. It is not a sin to be rich. Nowhere in Scripture is it taught that it is sinful to be rich or that in order to be spiritual, you need to be poor. Undoubtedly there were other poor givers that day, as well, which Jesus made no reference to. *It is always right to give out of simple obedience to God.*

<u>Rewarded Giving</u> – Jesus sat and watched all who gave into the treasury, but there was nothing in all the other offerings which called for the special praise Jesus bestowed upon this widow. Jesus said that her gift was of higher worth than all of the others. WHY? It was not because of the size of the gift (1/4 of a single penny). The worth of her gift was valued by the sacrifice she made in giving it. She gave all her living to the Lord. She gave herself (all of herself) to

146

the Lord that day. This was a sacrificial gift and was rewarded with a special commendation by our Lord.

Responsible Giving – The world would have you walk by sight and give responsibly. But God calls us to walk by faith and give accordingly! Jesus praised this widow for what many would condemn her for. If she had given one coin and kept the other, she would have done her duty and it would have made good sense. After all, the gift was insignificant, and the temple didn't need it as much as she did! So, she really shouldn't have given anything that day. Right? Wouldn't it have made more sense to keep it for groceries? So, her offering really was needless and irrational by the world's standards. Yet, in the eyes of Jesus, the gift was not only right, but He praised her for her sacrifice of casting in all her living! The widow did not give out of her ability but out of her poverty because she loved the Lord. It was a good thing that she didn't listen to those who might have discouraged her from giving. We rob people of God's blessings when we do not give them the opportunity to give or when we try to discourage them from giving. God exalts the gifts of His people! He can multiply our gifts by pooling our tithes and offerings with others and our gifts helps spread the gospel worldwide. This widow's gift has been used to stir the hearts of millions of Christians for the past two thousand years and has brought enumerable blessings to many.

3. **THE LORD EXAMINES OUR GIFTS**

> *Mark 12:44 – For they all put in out of their abundance,*
> *but she out of her poverty put in all that she had, her*
> *whole livelihood.*

He examines what we give. We may put into the treasury wealth, talents, prayers, time, tears, etc. None go unnoticed by our Lord. Jesus doesn't look to condemn. He looks to approve! He noticed that many who were rich cast in much and simply stated they gave out of their abundance. He also noticed that the widow gave two mites. Nothing we give goes unnoticed by our Lord!

He examines why we give. Many gave out of simple obedience and it is right to do so. But the widow gave out of her love for the Lord, giving beyond her means; giving all she had.

147

<u>3) So why do we give?</u> Many stewardship messages and testimonies challenge you to give because you cannot out give God. Jesus said *"Give, and it shall be given unto you; good measure, pressed down, and shaken together, and running over. . ." (Luke 6:38)*

God even challenges us *"Bring ye all the tithes into the storehouse, that there may be meat in my house, and prove me now herewith, saith the Lord of hosts, if I will not open the windows of heaven, and pour out a blessing for you, that there shall not be room enough to receive it" Malachi 3:10* But our real motive for giving should be as the Widow – expecting nothing, she simply gave her all because she loved the Lord.

4. **<u>DON'T EXPECT TO BE EXALTED FOR YOUR GIVING.</u>**
The Lord will not exalt you, but He will exalt your gift! True giving is expected of each and every one of God's children. It is only reasonable that we return our love for someone who gave His all for us. Jesus did not praise this widow to her face, nor in her hearing. This widow never heard Jesus say, "Well Done thou good and faithful servant." She went home that day with an inward satisfaction because she had done what was right. She had given because she loved the Lord and she had given by faith! She was unaware that the Lord was even watching that day, let alone praising her for her gift of love! This is the way we are to give – not expecting anything in return but giving as an expression of our love for the Lord and giving by faith. It truly is more blessed to give than to receive!

Biblical guidelines for giving include the following:
1. Giving abundantly *Luke 6:38*
2. Giving in obedience Matthew 23:23
3. Giving faithfully (1 Corinthians 4:1-2)
4. Giving liberally (Romans 12:8)
5. Giving freely (Matthew 10:8)
6. Giving weekly (1 Corinthians 16:1-2)
7. Giving our share (Acts 11:29 & 2 Corinthians 8:12)

I challenge all of us – Be a faithful giver!

CHAPTER 20

ROSE GARDEN CHRISTIANITY

Hebrew 2:10 – For it was fitting for Him, for whom are all things and by whom are all things, in bringing many sons to glory, to make the captain of their salvation perfect through sufferings.

Job was a righteous man. No matter how righteous Job was however – his righteousness did not exempt him from suffering. The common thought of the day was – If you were a good, ethical, moral, upright person who followed the golden rule then God would bless you. Those blessings would be visible by many good children, heath, and wealth. So, if you didn't have those things or if you had them and lost them then it must be deduced that you were a horrible sinner and a hypocrite of all the good that you had been portraying and that is exactly the way that Job's friends saw him.

Now make no mistake about it, God's word does say that He wants to bless us, and He does bless us. But his word also says that He sends the rain on the just and on the unjust.

Matthew 5:45 (CEV) – God makes the sun rise on both good and bad people. And He sends rain for the ones who do right and for the ones who do wrong.

Job once had everything. He may have been the world's richest man. His wealth did not protect him from tragedy. Disasters destroyed all of his possessions. Seven sons and three daughters also died, all on the same day and at the same time. Then his health failed. In the midst of multiple crises and affliction, Job's wife said to him, "Are you still holding on to your integrity? Why don't you just curse God and die? But Job wasn't looking for the easy way out. He said to his wife, "Shall we accept good from God, and not trouble?"

Grace is God's unmerited favor upon my life. Today there are those who preach GRACE in the same manner that Job's friends preached it. If God's favor is on your life then you will be exempt from suffering and you will receive all the good things that God has for you. The truth though is that grace will not do for you what it did not do for Job! Grace will not do for you what it did not do for CHRIST! God's favor was upon Job and yet Job suffered horribly. God's favor was upon His Son's life, but it did not exempt Jesus from suffering!

> *Hebrews 2:10 CEV – Everything belongs to God, and all things were created by his power. So, God did the right thing when he <u>made Jesus perfect by suffering</u>, as Jesus led many of God's children to be saved and to share in his glory.*

Christ was made perfect through suffering. We want to be made perfect through success. We want to have perfect health, a perfect husband, a perfect wife, a perfect job, and perfect financial resources. What's the difference? Lord, we don't want to suffer – we want your favor upon our life for our success so that we don't have to suffer. God wants our success as well. Christ was completely successful, but He suffered and died a horrible death on a cross. Was that what you call SUCCESS? Yes, for in doing so He overcame SIN and made a way into Heaven for each and everyone one of us. He paved the way for the millions who are in heaven right now and the millions who will go to heaven. That's the greatest Success in the world. There is nothing better. The Bible says, *"what does it profit a person to gain the whole world and lose their own soul?"*

But his success came through suffering! Jesus was brutally honest with people! He never left His followers in doubt as to what awaited them. He did not dazzle them with promises of riches, health, honor and power. HE DIDN'T DO THAT! He spoke to them of carrying a cross. He spoke to them of denying yourself. He spoke to them in terms of persecution and ridicule. He said to them in *John 15:18-19 "If the world hates you, you know that it hated Me before it hated you. If you were of the world, the world would love its own, yet because you are not of the world, but I chose you out of the world, therefore the world hates you."* Jesus spoke in terms of losing in order to find. He spoke of dying in order to live. In other words, Jesus said – "I beg your pardon – I never promised you a ROSE GARDEN. Along with the sunshine there's going to be a little RAIN sometimes."

JESUS ON THE SEASHORE

John 21 records for us the story of Jesus, after His resurrection, meeting His disciples on the seashore. They were all out in their boat. They had fished all night and had caught nothing. Jesus cooks up some fish for them on the seashore. He looks out to sea and calls out: "Hey boys - Have you caught anything?" At this point they do not realize that it is Jesus calling out to them. They reply: "No. Try another fishing hole. We've fished here all night and have caught nothing." Jesus calls out to them – "Cast your net on the other side of the boat and you'll catch plenty of fish." They cast the net and immediately it is full of 153 very large fish. They are amazed at the catch! They are amazed that their net did not break! Then one of them squints and looks at the shoreline. He says: "It's the Lord!" "It's the Lord!" Peter throws his clothes back on and swims to shore while the rest catch up to him dragging the net of huge fish behind them.

After breakfast Jesus says to Peter: **Let's take a walk.** As they walk Jesus asks Peter: *"Peter, do you love me more than these?"* The question begs to be asked: More than these what? More than the other disciples love me? More than the fish you just caught? You see, Peter was a commercial fisherman. It's how he made his living and he had just made a huge catch that would be worth an enormous amount of money to him. He had enough to pay his bills, to share, and probably put a substantial amount of money into his savings account. So, Jesus asks: *"Peter do you love me more than these"*, more than your livelihood? "Do you love me more than anything else in this world?" He asks Peter this question 3 times.

Peter replies that he does. Then Jesus says to him – then this is what I want you to do. I want you to spend the rest of your life fishing for men. I want you to give up your fishing business and spend every day of your life telling others about my great love for them. I want you to care for them, to love them, to bring them to SALVATION.

BUT LISTEN TO WHAT HE TELLS HIM NEXT

Now Peter, if you will do this, this is what I will do for you. I will make you famous. You will have all the money you ever want. You will live a healthy life until you are an old man. You will preach the most famous sermon ever to be preached on the earth, the Pentecostal sermon. Thousands will come to Christ when you preach this message. You will write part of the Bible that will have your name on it. Millions and millions of people will call you the first Pope. Your name will become a household name for thousands of years to come. You will be known as the gatekeeper of heaven.

And Peter would say yes Lord, I will do it! That's the kind of sales pitch you hear in a lot of churches today. People want to be successful. They want to be happy. They want to have lots of money. They want to be healthy. They want to WIN at life. And there's nothing wrong with wanting these things. In fact, there's everything right in wanting these things. We should have a positive realistic view of life.

The most popular churches today are power-based churches. Everything is interpreted in terms of POWER. Power Religion, The Hour of Power, Power Languages, Power Images. We talk about Power, Might, Success, WINNING! And we want to have a WINNING church. But remember these words this morning. GRACE WILL NEVER DO FOR YOU WHAT IT DID NOT DO FOR CHRIST. Christ was successful through suffering! What makes us think life will be any different for us?

LISTEN TO WHAT JESUS REALLY TOLD PETER

"When you were younger you dressed yourself and went where you wanted; but when you are old you will stretch out your hands, and someone else will dress you and lead you to where you do not want to go." He said this, John tells us, <u>"to indicate the kind of death by which Peter would die."</u>

WHAT HAPPENED TO JESUS?

He stretched out his hands and others led Him where He did not want to go. Jesus says to Peter: <u>Follow me and you'll be crucified too!</u> That's all I'm promising you Peter. The world will hate you, they will mistreat you, they will kill many of your followers, and eventually the world will crucify you. NOW DO YOU LOVE ME? – THEN FOLLOW ME!

THAT'S NOT THE WAY WE WANT TO WIN! THAT'S NOT THE KIND OF SUCCESS WE WANT IN LIFE! IF JESUS HAD SAID THAT TO US WOULD WE BE WILLING TO FOLLOW HIM?

What's the difference? We love <u>Him</u> for wearing the thorns on <u>His</u> brow. But me? Wear the thorns on my brow? **No way!**

I want SUCCESS, but I don't want to go through suffering to get it. I want all the good things of life and none of the bad. But the Bible says – "The rain falls on the just and on the un-just!"

<u>When the rain falls – will you still love Jesus?</u>

CHAPTER 21

ARE YOU SUFFERING?

When hardships come we seem to want to escape, to run from it all. No one really wants to go through hardships. You can't turn Christianity into a religion of escape. As important as positive thinking is, you can't just think positive and expect to be exempt from all the difficulties of life. If you think Christianity is going to exempt you from the hardships of life, then you really don't understand Christianity at all.

Last week I preached a message entitled 'Rose Garden Christianity.' Jesus would say this to us: "I beg your pardon, I never promised you a Rose Garden." Grace will never do for you what it did not do for Christ; that is exempt us from hardships and suffering.

When Jesus was praying is the garden, before His crucifixion, He could have escaped the hardship. The Bible says, "He could have called 10,000 angels." There is a song that goes like this: They bound the hands of Jesus in the garden where He prayed. They led Him through the streets in shame. They spat upon the Savior so pure and free from sin. They said, "Crucify Him; He's to blame." Upon His precious head they placed a crown of thorns. They laughed and said, "Behold, the King." They struck Him, and they cursed Him and mocked His Holy Name. All alone He suffered everything. He could have called ten thousand angels to destroy the world and set Him free. He could have called ten thousand angels, but He died alone for you and me.

Jesus _could have_ escaped hardship, but He chose instead to endure. We _can't escape_ hardship, but we die trying. And the more we try to escape the hardships of life, the less strength we have to endure the hardships.

> *Hebrews 11:6 – Without Faith it is impossible to please God.*

Faith however is not necessarily the power to make things the way we want them to be; it is the courage, many times, to face things the way they are and to endure to the end knowing that no matter what happens to us that God is with us and if God is with us then that is all we need!

Faith surrenders everything to God! At times, Faith seems crazy. We can't do this, just look at the finances – look at the situation! Faith obeys God no matter what the circumstances may be! Faith has a motto: THE LORD WILL PROVIDE! Faith will always be tested. God will determine your heart. Will you be faithful?

Perseverance has been well defined as "courage stretched out." Although God sometimes delivers his people from difficult or painful circumstances, He more often calls us to a courageous and enduring faithfulness in the midst of our trials. Perseverance, according to the Bible, is not only enduring situations of suffering and hardships but over-coming them with obedience, faithfulness, hope, and joy. Perseverance sometimes means obeying God even when God's way doesn't seem to make sense. We don't want to obey, we want to escape! We want to get away from this disease – we want to get away from this trouble – we want to get away from this situation – we want to get away from this circumstance! And we don't understand why God has not taken it away. Remove it God; I DON'T WANT IT!

But God seems to be silent! God says endure it. God says to persevere through it. God says it is for a reason that you have it. God says, *"Trust me in this situation." 2 Peter 1:5-8 – says that patient endurance leads to Godliness.*

> *Romans 5:3-5a – And, not only that, but we also glory in tribulations, knowing that tribulation produces perseverance; and perseverance produces character and character produces hope and hope does not disappoint us.*

155

Romans 5:5b – The love of God has been poured out in our hearts by the Holy Spirit whom God gave to us.

SERENITY PRAYER (Un-troubled, calm, peaceful heart)
God grant me the serenity (calm assurance) to accept the things I cannot change, the courage to change the things I can, and the WISDOM to know the difference.

Philippians 4:4-7 – Rejoice in the Lord always, Again I say Rejoice! Let your gentleness be known to all men, the Lord is at hand. Be anxious for nothing. In everything by prayer and supplication, with Thanksgiving, let your request be made known to God and the peace of God, which passes all understanding, will guard your hearts and minds through Christ Jesus our Lord.

<u>Why is it that many times we don't experience this peace in our hearts?</u>
Rejoice in the Lord sometimes? Let your gentleness be known to some men? Be anxious for everything? Ask God for what you want then complain and not understand when you don't get it?

Mark 4:35-41 CEV – That evening Jesus said to His disciples, let's cross over to the east side of the lake. So, they left the crowd and His disciples started rowing across the lake with Him onboard. Some other smaller boats followed along. Suddenly a great windstorm struck the lake. Waves started splashing into the boat, and it was about to sink! Jesus was in the back of the boat with His head on a pillow, and He was asleep! His disciples woke Him and said, Teacher, don't you care that we're about to drown? Jesus got up and ordered the wind and the waves to be quiet. The wind stopped, and everything was calm. Jesus asked his disciples, why were you afraid? Don't you have any faith? Now they were more afraid than ever and said to each other, Who is this? Even the wind and the waves obey Him!

Now notice what Jesus didn't do! He didn't rebuke them for not having enough faith to calm the storm. He knew that He was the only one who could do that! He rebuked them for not having enough faith to stay calm in the storm; especially with Jesus onboard.

Remember the Serenity Prayer? God grant me the serenity to accept the things I cannot change. God grant me the courage to change the things I can. God grant me the WISDOM to know the difference.

I'm not talking about passive resignation when I say that Jesus rebuked them for not having enough faith to stay calm in the storm. It takes a lot of courage; it takes a lot of faith to stay calm when there's a storm going on in your life.

God grant me the courage to change the things I can
1. If I can change things for the better then I should change things for the better.
2. If you need a better job, then pray for the one you've got or go look for another one.
3. If you have a headache, take an aspirin or a Tylenol.
4. If you are really sick, first pray in faith, and then go to the doctor.

Resignation means that you give up. . .You enclose yourself in a shell of self-pity. You're unable and unwilling to see any purpose for your condition. You are powerless to see any good in it.

> *1 Thessalonians 5:18 – In everything give thanks for this is the will of God in Christ Jesus concerning you.*

As far as finding meaning in suffering and hardship, it only has meaning if it is unavoidable. If it is avoidable, the meaningful thing to do is to remove the cause of the suffering. If on the other hand, you cannot change a situation that causes suffering, you can choose your attitude about the suffering. You can choose to have the faith to endure the hardship especially when Jesus is in your boat.

> *Hebrews 11:1 – Faith is the substance of things hoped for, the evidence of things not seen.*

Faith is the wisdom to see Treasure in Trash. Faith is the courage to face things as they are. Faith is the boldness to get out of our self-pity and go through the storm, knowing that with God on my side I can't lose even if I die. The Apostle Paul said: *to live is Christ, to die is Gain!*

> *Proverbs 3:5-6 – Trust in the Lord with all you heart and lean not on your own understanding; in all your ways acknowledge Him, and He will direct your paths.*

ONE DAY AT A TIME

I'm only human – I'm just a man (woman). Help me believe in what I can be and all that I am. Show me the stairway I have to climb. Lord, for my sake, teach me to take one day at a time. Do you remember when you walked among men? Well, Jesus, You know if You're looking below it's worse now than then. Pushing and shoving – crowding my mind - So for my sake Lord teach me to take one day at a time. One day at a time sweet Jesus; that's all I'm asking from You. Just give me the strength to do every day what I have to do. Yesterday's gone sweet Jesus and tomorrow may never be mine. Lord, help me today – show me the way - One day at a time.

Live one day at a Time. Enjoy one moment at a time. Accept hardships as the pathway to peace. Take, as Christ did, this sinful world as it is, not as I would have it. Trust that He will make all things right, if I surrender to His will, that I may be reasonably happy in this life, and Supremely happy with Him forever in the next!

CHAPTER 22

HOW'S YOUR LOVE LIFE?

I ntroduction: God has truly been good to us! He has given us more than we ever deserved. Think of it! He has provided a means of salvation that will save even the vilest sinner. He has given us so many wonderful promises.

> *Hebrews 13:5 – Let your conversation be without covetousness; and be content with such things as you have; for God has said, "I will never leave you, nor forsake you."*

> *Philippians 4:19 – But my God shall supply all your need according to His riches in glory by Christ Jesus.*

> *John 10:28 – And I give unto them eternal life; and they shall never perish, neither shall any man pluck them out of my hand.*

When a person is saved, they are given spiritual gifts so that God can use them in His kingdom work. Yet, the greatest gift the LORD has ever given us is HIS LOVE! The love of God for His people is everlasting.

> *Jeremiah 31:3 – The Lord has appeared of old unto me, saying, Yes, I have loved you with an everlasting love.*

His love is what motivated Him to send Jesus to die on the cross. John 3:16 – For God so love the world. . .

The greatest evidence of the love of God is the death of Christ on the cross. *Romans 5:8 – But God demonstrated His love for us in that while we were yet sinners, Christ died for us.*

Yet, God did not stop by just giving HIS LOVE to us, He has also placed HIS love within us. That is why Jesus said in John 13:35 that the world would know we are Christians by our love.

The first characteristic mentioned in Galatians 5:22-23, concerning the Fruit of the Spirit is LOVE. - *Now the fruit of the spirit is LOVE, joy, peace, longsuffering, gentleness, goodness, faith, meekness, and self-control*

Here was one of the primary problems with the church in Corinth when this letter was written. They were manifesting every other spiritual gift, but they were not manifesting love to each other. Paul wrote this letter to remind us that of all the great spiritual things we can do, the greatest spiritual exercise is to LOVE in the right way.

LOVE IS PRIMARY

1 Corinthians 13:1-3 – Though I speak with the tongues of men and of angels, but have not love, I have become sounding brass or a clanging cymbal. And though I have the gift of prophecy, and understand all mysteries and all knowledge, and though I have all faith, so that I could remove mountains, but have not love, I am nothing. And though I bestow all my goods to feed the poor, and though I give my body to be burned, but have not love, it profits me nothing.

You may be a great speaker but without love you are simply a clanging cymbal. Can you imagine the only musical instrument of accompaniment is a clanging cymbal? Even if we knew all about prophecy, understood everything, had so much faith that we could literally make a mountain physically move, we would still be worth nothing at all without love. Even if we make the greatest sacrifice to feed the poor and sacrifice our own lives we would still be worth nothing at all, in God's eyes, without love.

THE PORTRAIT OF LOVE

1 Corinthians 13:4-6 – Love suffers long and is kind; love does not envy; love does not parade itself, is not puffed up; does not behave rudely, does not seek its own, is not provoked, thinks no evil; does not rejoice in iniquity, but rejoices in the truth;

Long Suffering:
This word means "patient endurance under provocation." Love does not retaliate! This kind of love endures all attacks. Stephen was a great example of this kind of love. While he was being stoned to death for his faith in Christ, he looked up to heaven and said "Lord, do not charge them with this sin." The Lord Jesus gives us the greatest example of this kind of love when He was under trial.

Kind:
This word refers to active goodness that goes forth in behalf of others. Genuine love is never hateful or mean, but it respects others and reaches out to them.

Does not Envy:
True love is not jealous over the abilities or possessions of another. Instead of being jealous when others prosper or excel, love is pleased when they do well.

Love does not parade itself:
Love does not brag! It does not draw attention to itself or to what it is doing. People who parade themselves are hurt when they are not the center of attention.

Is not puffed up:
Love is not arrogant or proud. A person realizes that all they have and all they are; are gifts from God. No matter how great our talents or how spectacular our gifts, everything we are and everything we have is the result of God's grace.

Does not behave rudely:
Love always treats others with compassion, consideration and respect!
Love controls the emotions. It is not friendly one day and rude the next.
Genuine love always makes Jesus look good.

Love does not seek its own:
True love is never selfish and self-centered, but it is actively interested
in what will profit others. It never looks at itself first, but it always considers another ahead of itself.

Love is not easily provoked:
True love keeps no record of evils done to it. This kind of love does not
demand its own rights! True love only responds in anger to that which
angers God! All other things are handled through forgiveness.

Love thinks no evil:
This phrase literally means "takes no worthless inventory." True love
does not attribute evil motives to people. That is, every action is not
seen in its most negative light. It thinks the best of others. True love does
not keep a record of evils done. In other words, you do not dwell on the
evils that others have done to you. Real love does not: 1. Remember
injury 2. Believe all it hears about another 3. Look for faults in others

Love does not rejoice in iniquity:
Love does not rejoice in sin, whether its own sins, or the sin of others.
Love hates sin! Love does not rejoice with another falls into sin. Believe
it or not, there is a part of us that is glad when another believer falls
because we think it makes us look better. (E.g.: That is why we go and
gossip and tell someone else about it. "Did you hear what happened
to so and so? Did you hear what so and so did?) True love does not
gossip or rejoice when another believer falls but it hurts with the
injured member!

Love rejoices in the Truth:
While love hates all forms of evil, it loves the truth! Love is glad for the
truth, even when the truth hurts.

How's your love life this morning? Do these attributes characterize
your life?

LOVE'S PERSISTENCE

1 Corinthians 13:7-12 – Love bears all things, believes all things, hopes all things, endures all things. Love never fails. But whether there are prophecies, they will fail; whether there are tongues, they will cease; whether there is knowledge, it will vanish away. For we know in part and we prophesy in part but when that which is perfect has come, then that which is in part will be done away. When I was a child, I spoke as a child, I understood as a child, I thought as a child; but when I became a man, I put away childish things. For now, we see in a mirror, dimly, but then face to face. Now I know in part, but then I shall know just as I also am known.

Bears all things:
Love patiently endures and overlooks the faults in others. The word literally means "to cover." Instead of parading the faults and failures of others before the world, love covers them and continues to love despite those things.

Love believes all things:
Love always places the best possible interpretation on everything that happens. Love believes that good will triumph in any situation. Basically, love trusts, love believes, and love has confidence in the one being loved. The Living Bible puts it this way: *If you love someone you will be loyal to them no matter what the cost. You will always believe in them, always expect the best of them, and always stand your ground in defending them.*

Love hopes all things:
Love always expects the best possible outcome. Love refuses to accept failure. Love does not give up but holds out hope that things will work out right in the end.

Love endures all things:
This is a military term and means that loves does not give up the fort! It stands its ground and continues despite everything that can be thrown against it. It continues in spite of persecution and ill treatment.

Love bears the unbearable, believes the impossible, holds on to the incredible and never gives up. The word STOP does not exist in the vocabulary of love!

Love never fails:
Love may lose a battle here and there but has already won the war. The idea here is on endurance. When everything else in this world has passed away, love will still exist. Love does not give in, Love does not give up, Love does not give out - Love that is real is love that lasts!

THE PREEMINENCE OF LOVE

1 Cor. 13:13 – And now abide faith, hope, love, these three; but the greatest of these is love.

The Bible says that three things abide: **Faith, Hope, and Love**. Yet faith and hope are encompassed inside of love. Therefore, the greatest of all things a believer can possess is love! If our love is right, then faith is no problem! If our love is right, then our hope is in the right place. When our love is right, then we are right! What makes love so great? Well, love is the defining characteristic of Who God Is. When the Bible wanted to describe God in one sentence, it said, **God is Love**.

God does not have faith! After all, who would God place His faith in? God does not have hope! What could God who already controls everything possibly hope for? Yet, GOD IS LOVE! Therefore, we are never more God-like than when we learn to love like God.

HOW'S YOUR LOVE LIFE THIS MORNING?

CHAPTER 23

RUN YOUR RACE, TO WIN!

1 Corinthians 9:24-27 — But I discipline my body and bring it into subjection, lest, when I have preached to others, I myself should become disqualified.

Ayoung mother once approached Confederate General Robert E. Lee with her baby, wanting the famed general to bless her son. General Lee took the infant in his arms and then, looking at the mother, said, "Teach him he must deny himself." What a strange thing to say to a young mother and her child! But General Lee understood what the masses fail to comprehend: Discipline is the key to success in every area of life including our relationships with God.

Unfortunately, the prodigal son never learned that "he must deny himself." (Luke 15:11-32) The promise of pleasure in that distant land caused him to pack his bags and leave his father. How can you keep yourself from becoming addicted to pleasure? The apostle Paul understood the importance of refusing to allow pleasure to rule his life. He realized that the inability to control both his natural and sinful desires could have disastrous consequences in his relationship with God. In fact, Paul had an overwhelming concern that a lapse in self-control could one day ruin his life and ministry, and more importantly, damage the reputation of Jesus Christ. Thus, Paul continually battled with discipline and self-control in his life.

What does Paul mean by "I discipline (buffet) my body?" To fully appreciate his imagery, you need to read the entire paragraph.

1 Corinthians 9:24-27 – Do you not know that those who run in a race all run, but one receives the prize? Run in such a way that you may obtain it. And everyone who competes for the prize is temperate in all things. Now they do it to obtain a perishable crown, but we for an imperishable crown. Therefore, I run thus: not with uncertainty. Thus, I fight: not as one who beats the air. But I <u>*discipline my body and bring it into subjection,*</u> <u>*lest, when I have preached to others, I myself*</u> <u>*should become disqualified.*</u>

If you read between the lines of Paul's writings, you'll conclude that he was a sports enthusiast. He uses many metaphors from the athletic realm to describe the Christian life. For example, he describes the Christian life as a wrestling match in Ephesians 6:12 and as a boxing tournament in 1 Corinthians 9:26. But his favorite metaphor for the Christian life is a footrace. Paul says that a competitor in a footrace has one goal in mind: to win! It isn't enough just to be in the competition; a runner must have an insatiable desire to win. And that strong desire to win translates into some specific steps of action.

Let's consider Paul's command to "run in such a way as to win." Paul says that if we desire to win in the Christian life and receive rewards at the Judgment Seat of Christ, we must commit ourselves to the same discipline a runner commits himself to in order to win a race. How do we cultivate that kind of discipline? By adopting four actions, all of which involve breaking our addiction to pleasure, I believe we can cultivate that kind of discipline in our lives. 1. Remove any excess weight. 2. Say no to a specific pleasure every day. 3. Allocate your energy wisely. 4. Keep your eye on the finish line.

1. Remove any excess "weight"
A Runner doesn't carry any excess pounds if he or she is intent on winning the race. When is the last time you saw an obese person crossing the finish line? Can you ever recall seeing a relay runner dressed in a wool suit or overcoat? Of course not! Runners know that to win they must travel as lightly as possible.

The writer of Hebrews (who also must have been a sports enthusiast) wrote:

> *Hebrews 12:1 — Therefore, since we have so great a cloud of witnesses surrounding us, let us also lay aside every encumbrance, and the sin which so easily entangles us, and <u>let us run with endurance the race that is set before us.</u>*

<u>The author of Hebrews identifies the excess weight we need to shed:</u> <u>SIN.</u> Wrong attitudes, actions, or thoughts will weigh you down in your Christian life and cause you to lose both the race and ultimately your reward. To win in the Christian life, you must decisively deal with sin now. Ask yourself the following questions. Am I entangled in relationships that I know displease the Lord? Do I have any secret habits that are constantly dragging me down in my spiritual life? Do I hold any wrong attitudes, such as bitterness or a critical spirit that is poisoning me?

Those who are addicted to pleasure find it easy to rationalize detrimental relationships, habits, and attitudes. Eliminating them involves too much pain, and the pleasure addict finds it difficult to willingly endure discomfort. But if you want to regain control over your spiritual life, you have to lay aside those wrong relationships, actions, habits, and attitudes. But some people may say; "I'm not strong enough to lay aside the wrong relationships, the wrong actions, the wrong habits, the wrong attitudes." I just simply pray and ask God to remove any wrong doing from my life. But if you adopt this kind of attitude you will fail miserably in trying to overcome the sins which so easily beset us.

WHY?

1. <u>We are responsible for laying aside our own sin!</u> It's not God's responsibility; it's ours!

    > *Hebrews 12:1 Therefore we also, since we are surrounded by so great a cloud of witnesses, let <u>US</u> lay aside every weight, and the sin which so easily ensnares us, and let us run with endurance the race that is set before us.*

    Does that say to let God lay aside every weight and sin which so easily ensnares us, or does it say let <u>US</u> lay aside every weight and sin which so easily ensnares us? God says that it's your responsibility, not His, to remove sin from your life. We cannot delegate to God something that does not belong to Him. God isn't responsible for removing sin from my life. I AM!

2. <u>We are capable of removing sin from our lives.</u> God never asks us to do something that He hasn't empowered us to do.

    Romans 6:4-6 reminds us that God has already given us the power to remove sin from our lives.

    > *Therefore, we have been buried with Him through baptism into death, in order that as Christ was raised from the dead through the glory of the Father, so we too might walk in newness of life. For if we have become united with Him in the likeness of His death, certainly we shall be also in the likeness of His resurrection, knowing this, that our old self was crucified with Him, that our body of sin might be done away with, that we should no longer be slaves to sin.*

    When you become a Christian, the same power that raised Jesus Christ from the grave operates in your life to give you power over sin. Sin has no more power over your life than you choose to allow it to have.

3. <u>Not only do we have to remove any excess weight, but we have to say NO to a specific pleasure every day if we are going to run the Christian life to win the race.</u>

    > *1 Corinthians 9:27 – Paul says that he would constantly "buffet his body" – literally, he beat it black and blue – to make his body his slave.*

An athlete determined to win the race must discipline himself or herself. The athlete must make a slave of desire instead of remaining a slave to desire.

John MacArthur Jr. provides us with some great insight into Paul's statement: Most people, including many Christians, are instead slaves to their bodies. Their bodies tell their minds what to do. Their bodies decide when to eat, what to eat, how much to eat, when to sleep and when to get up, and so on. An athlete cannot allow that. He follows the training rules, not his body. He runs when he would rather be resting, he eats a balanced meal when he would rather have a chocolate sundae; he goes to bed when he would rather stay up, and he gets up early to train when he would rather stay in bed. An athlete leads his body; he does not follow it. It is his slave, not the other way around.

All of us tend to allow pleasure to dominate our lives. That's why we must regularly practice self-discipline. In order to take control of our bodies a good idea would be to say - "NO" - to at least one thing in your life every day, just to remind your body who is in charge. Make it a daily practice to refuse something from which you derive pleasure – a piece of pie, an extra hour of sleep, a television program – not because there's anything sinful about the pleasure, but because you need to practice maintaining control over your desires. St. Francis used to refer to the human body as "Brother Donkey" because we are to ride the donkey instead of allowing the donkey to ride us. By saying no to something pleasurable every day, we can remain in control!

4. <u>We must allocate our energy wisely.</u> In Paul's day, an athlete didn't have the luxury of excelling in only one sport; instead, he had to train for several events. The most popular Greek contest was the pentathlon which involved a footrace, the discus throw, wrestling, the javelin throw, and the long jump.

Paul mentions two sports, running and boxing, in 1 Corinthians 9:24-27. He says: *"Everyone who competes in the games exercises self-control in all things."* If an athlete hoped to win the victor's crown at the end of the competition, he had to exhibit proficiency in many areas, not just one. Thus, the athlete had to wisely allocate his training time to cover all areas in which he would compete. This same truth applies to the Christian life. To avoid allowing pleasure to take first place in our lives (the love of pleasure), we must learn to wisely allocate our time and energy among the various responsibilities God has given us. What are those responsibilities? 1. Fulfill the Great Commission. This is our greatest responsibility but not our only responsibility. 2. Be responsible for our families.

3. Be responsible for our jobs. 4. Be responsible for our financial affairs. 5. Be responsible for our health. 6. Be responsible for our friendships and a number of other areas.

If we want to win both in this life and at the Judgment Seat of Christ, we must give attention to all these areas. What happens when a person devotes too much time to their work, neglecting their families? We say such people are unbalanced. But what happens when a person devotes all his time to reading the Bible and spiritual matters and neglects making a living for his family. This person too is unbalanced. What happens when a person goes to work and makes a living for their family, witnesses for Christ and reads his Bible and then lets his health go to pieces through lack of discipline and lack of exercise? This person too is unbalanced.

God expects us to be well allocated in all areas of our lives. If we want to run to win, we must give appropriate attention to all the life-areas over which God holds us accountable.

5. Keep your eye on the finish line.
A runner who allows the weather, spectators in the stands, or other runners to distract him or her will eventually stumble. If a runner really wants to win, he must keep his thoughts on making it across the finish line. A winner runs the race with the end in mind. In the same way, we must live our lives with the end clearly in focus. And the end is not graduation, marriage, the presidency of our company, or retirement. Our finish line is the Judgment Seat of Christ. Paul describes it this way.

> *2 Corinthians 5:10 – For we must all appear before the Judgment Seat of Christ, that each one may be recompensed for his deeds in the body according to what he has done, whether good or bad.*

To keep the Judgment Seat of Christ in mind means we constantly evaluate every word, thought, action, and attitude based on how Jesus Christ will one day judge it.

The strongest motivation for breaking our natural addiction to pleasure is realizing that one day the trumpet will sound, and our Holy God will summon us to give an account for the ways we have spent our days; for the ways we have spent our lives.

Remember as we go through this life to evaluate: 1. Every word we say 2. Every thought we think 3. Every action we take 4. Every attitude we have - For one day we will give account as we stand before our Lord and Savior Jesus Christ

CHAPTER 24

ARE OUR GOALS OUR GOD?

Goals, Desire, Determination, Persistence – Keep on Keeping On – Put one foot in front of the other – Go for the Gusto - We've all been taught this ever since we were little kids. Is there anything wrong with goal setting, the desire to accomplish something great and the determination to keep going on in spite of all the opposition? Many great people in this world were determined and accomplished great things through their dogged determination and their positive thinking.

I read a story of a young boy who the doctors said would never walk again. They said his legs must be amputated due to an explosive fire. But the boy and his parents refused to amputate his legs. When the legs finally healed his left leg was two and one-half inches shorter than the right and his right foot was missing most of its toes. The boy was told he would never walk again without crutches. But the boy did walk; then he began to jog and against all odds Glen Cunningham became an Olympic gold medalist and won the title "the world's fastest human being." Glen Cunningham lived on this earth from 1909 – 1988. He had a positive attitude as well as a strong faith. His favorite Bible verse was *Isaiah 40:31 "But those who wait on the Lord shall renew their strength; they shall mount up with wings like eagles, they shall run and not be weary, they shall walk and not faint."*

Thomas Edison made 1,800 attempts to invent the electric light bulb before he succeeded. Babe Ruth struck out 1,330 times and George Bernard Shaw received rejection notices for his first five novels. Most of us have heard of Ludwig Van Beethoven but many of us have never heard of the great handicap he had to overcome. In his 20's he began to lose his hearing and by the time he was 50 he was tone deaf.

We admire people who know what they want in life and will do whatever it takes to achieve their goals. <u>But there's also a dark side to ambition.</u> <u>Sometimes our thirst for success can actually lead us away from God.</u>

<u>WHEN IS AMBITION WRONG IN OUR LIVES</u>

1. **When it becomes the Predominant desire of our Lives**
   God labels as idols anything that commands our complete attention and devotion. And He *hates* idols.

   > *Exodus 20: 3, 5 – You shall have no other gods before Me. . .for I, the Lord your God, am a jealous God.*

   > *Deuteronomy 6:5 – And you shall love the Lord your God with all your heart and with all your soul and with all your might.*

   God considers an idol anything or person we love more than Him. And if we are not careful; ambition, goals, desires can certainly take first place in our lives and choke out our love for God.

2. **When it comes at the expense of others**
   Jesus said that if we really want to become great in this world then we must learn to be a servant. A servant serves – he does not dominate! He does not climb the ladder at the expense of someone else. He does not push others down or demean others to make himself look good.

   When Jesus was having his last supper with his disciples he took a towel and wrapped it around his waist and began to wash the disciple's feet. He demonstrated for us what a real servant looks like.

3. **When it disallows God's will for our Lives**
   While the Bible never belittles planning, goal setting, or ambition, it does remind us that sometimes God has a different plan for our lives than we do.

   > *James 4:13-16 – Come now, you who say, today or tomorrow, we shall go to such and such a city, and spend a year there and engage in business and make*

a profit. Yet you do not know what your life will be like tomorrow. You are just a vapor that appears for a little while and then vanishes away. Instead, you ought to say, "If the Lord wills, we shall live and also do this or that." But as it is, you boast in your arrogance; all such boasting is evil.

James doesn't condemn planning. Nothing is wrong with making plans in our lives. But James says we shouldn't formulate our plans without any regard for God's plans for our lives. How would you complete this sentence? "My greatest desire in life is to _____."

Your answer might involve a job, a degree, or a certain lifestyle you'd like to have, or it might be a dream you have for your kids or grandkids. Does your greatest desire lead you to God or away from God?

1. Do I spend most of my free time thinking about this desire?
2. Have I mistreated or neglected others (such as family members) in pursuit of this goal?
3. How would I feel toward God if He said no to my desire?

Your honest answers to these questions might reveal that you have allowed your greatest desire to become your god. We've already looked at two desires that can lead us away from God; the love of money and the love of pleasure and now we look at a third: The Love of Ambition.

Nothing is inherently wrong with wanting to achieve something significant in life. Ambition in and of itself is not necessarily sinful any more than money or pleasure are inherently sinful. However, Satan can take our natural desire to achieve and use it to gradually lure us away from God. It was Satan's own ambition that drove him out of heaven. Satan had a strong desire to reach the top of his profession, regardless of the cost, and that resulted in his downfall.

Ezekiel 28: 11-17 – Moreover the word of the Lord came to me, saying, "Son of man, take up a lamentation for the king of Tyre, and say him, 'Thus says the Lord God; You were the seal of perfection, Full of wisdom and perfect in beauty, you were in Eden, the garden of God; every precious stone was your covering; the sardius, topaz, and diamond, beryl, onyx, and jasper, sapphire, turquoise, and emerald with gold. The workmanship of your timbrels and pipes was prepared for you on the day you were created. You were the anointed cherub who covers; I established you; you were on the holy mountain of God; you walked back and forth in the midst of fiery stones, you were perfect in your ways from the day you were created, till iniquity was found in you. By the abundance of your trading you became filled with violence within, and you sinned; therefore, I cast you as a profane thing out of the mountain of God; and I destroyed you, O covering cherub, from the midst of the fiery stones. Your heart was lifted up because of your beauty; you corrupted your wisdom for the sake of your splendor; I cast you to the ground, I laid you before kings, that they might gaze at you."

Although Ezekiel delivered this message to the King of Tyre, a king in ancient times, He intended the message for Satan. The King of Tyre did not possess "the seal of perfection" nor was he "full of wisdom and perfect in beauty." He was definitely not in the "Garden of Eden" when God created all things.

Why would Ezekiel refer to him as "the anointed cherub" who was "blameless in all your ways from the day you were created?" The passage obviously explains how Lucifer, God's chief angel, fell from heaven. God told Lucifer that everything was going great until iniquity was found in you. Lucifer became known to us as Satan! What was Satan's sin?

Isaiah 14:12-17 – How you are fallen from heaven, O Lucifer, son of the morning! How you are cut down to the ground, you who weakened the nations! For you have said in your heart: "I will ascend into heaven, I will exalt my throne above the stars of God; I will also sit on the mount of the congregation on the farthest sides of the north; I will ascend above the heights of the clouds, I will be like the Most High." Yet you shall be brought down to Sheol, to the lowest depths of the pit. Those who see you will gaze at you, and consider you, saying: is

> *this the man who made the earth tremble, who shook kingdoms, who made the world as a wilderness and destroyed its cities, who did not open the house of his prisoners?*

It was Satan's own ambition; his desire to succeed; his desire to make a name for himself; his determined desire to reach his goals that was his downfall.

1. *"I will ascend into Heaven"*
   Lucifer had access to Heaven. He was the "anointed cherub." He was the head angel over all the other angels. He was the most beautiful creation that God had ever made. But Satan wanted more than access to heaven, he wanted to rule heaven.

2. *"I will exalt my throne above the stars of God."*
   The term stars here refers to angels. Although God gave Lucifer responsibility over the other angels, he wanted absolute authority over the angels.

3. *"I will also sit on the mount of the congregation on the farthest sides of the north."*
   Satan not only wanted to rule the angels but to rule the entire universe from Heaven.

4. *"I will ascend above the heights of the clouds."*
   In the Old Testament clouds often represented God's glory. In this statement, Lucifer wanted to have a glory that surpassed God's glory.

5. *"I will be like the Most High."*
   Just in case anyone missed Satan's point, his goal in life, he spells it out clearly here. Although he was a created being who owed his very existence to God, he wanted to supplant God and reign as absolute monarch over the universe.

And What About Us?
Would we ever do such a thing as Satan did? Would we ever dare to be our own god; our own Lord; Lord over our own life? Would we ever dare to think that we can rule our own personal universe? Our own

lives? What was wrong with Satan's desire? There was nothing sinful about Lucifer wanting to excel in the role God had created for him, just as there is nothing wrong with our desire to succeed. But Satan made two mistakes. 1. He wanted absolute control over his own life, 2. He wanted freedom from God's authority. In the story of the rich man in the New Testament the man said: 1. "I have many goods" 2. "I will store my goods" 3. "I will take my ease" 4. "I will eat, drink, and be merry" 5. "I will be in control of my own destiny." Jesus said of this man; "You fool" – tomorrow your soul will be required of you and then what will you do? Just as Satan has his five "I WILLS" even so man has his five 'I WILLS!"

CHAPTER 25

OVERCOMING DEPRESSION

What is depression?

We all go through ups and downs in our mood. Sadness is a normal reaction to life's struggles, setbacks, and disappointments. We may feel "down in the dumps" for a short period of time, but if these feelings of sadness don't go away or if they are so intense that they interfere with our ability to work, study, eat, sleep, and enjoy life, we may be suffering from depression.

What are the signs and symptoms of depression?
Some people describe depression as "living in a black hole" or having a feeling of impending doom. They can't escape their unhappiness and despair. Some people feel lifeless and empty. They are unable to experience pleasure. They feel as if they are just "going through the motions." People suffering from depression often show distorted thinking. Everything looks bleak to them, and they hold extremely negative views about themselves, their situation, and the future. Trapped in their pessimism, they obsess over their problems and blow them out of proportion. Feeling hopeless and helpless, they may even start to see suicide as their only way out.

Thoughts of Death or Suicide
Suicidal thoughts are a symptom of severe depression and must always be taken seriously. If you or someone you know is threatening suicide or talking of wanting to hurt themselves, seek professional help right away.

What are the causes of depression?

There is no single cause of depression. Early life experience, genetic predisposition, lifestyle factors, and certain personality traits all play a part in causing depression. Feeling connected to people in our daily lives makes an enormous difference in our ability to surmount stress that might trigger depression. Individuals who feel unknown or unseen, or who avoid the support and comfort of others, are at risk for depression and depressive disorders.

Chronic Depression

A sermon is not a sufficient platform to deal with a subject as complex as CHRONIC depression – which is caused by a biochemical imbalance and can be treated very effectively with medication these days. Drug treatment may cause unwanted side effects, so educating yourself about your medication and its risks is important.

Talk Therapy

In psychotherapy for depression, you are taught the facts about your depressive disorder and how to manage it. Working with a mental health professional, you will learn how to cope with negative feelings, identify and change distorted thinking patterns, improve your relationships with others, and deal with problems constructively.

Defeating Depression from a Biblical Viewpoint

Depression is not a new thing. It has been around for thousands of years. As far back as the 4th century B.C. Hippocrates, the father of modern medicine, was familiar with depression and referred to it as "melancholia." Today we call it "the blues" or "a slump" or "feeling gloomy." But whatever designation you give it, depression is the most widespread form of emotional illness. It has been called, "the common cold of emotional disorders." Statistics say that each of us has one in ten chances of becoming severely depressed and all of us have our regular skirmishes with its milder form. We should also understand that depression is not always easy to cope with. You can't just ignore it! It hurts too much to ignore! In fact, recent studies of more than 11,000 individuals found depression to be more physically and socially disabling than arthritis, diabetes, lung disease, chronic back problems, hypertension, and gastrointestinal illnesses. The only medical problem that is more disabling is advanced coronary heart disease. So, battling depression is not an easy thing.

A stigma attached to depression

Some depression is the result of a person's willful disobedience of God. However, as Christians it is important for us to realize that this is not always the case. There seems to be a stigma attached to depression. Many people think that if a person is walking in close relationship with God and making progress as a Christian, they will never suffer the blues. But the truth is if you are normal and love God deeply, there are still going to be days, sometimes weeks, and maybe even seasons when you wrestle with depression. That doesn't mean you are a bad person or an ungodly person. It just means you are a real person.

Many great Christian servants, whose walk with God is not in doubt, have suffered from depression. The Bible records the fact that Moses and Jeremiah went through times of deep despair. Job did as well – often to the point of his being suicidal. Listen to Job's anxiety-filled words, *"I cannot eat for sighing; my groans pour out like water. . .my life flies by. . .day after hopeless day. . .I hate my life. . .my heart is broken, depression haunts my days, my weary nights are filled with pain. . .I cry to you, O God, but You do not answer me."* But notice that even with his constant, deep, agonizing depression, Job 1:22 says *"In all this Job did not sin."* So, the Bible teaches that depression is not always related to sinful actions. Many faithful servants of Christ also struggled with depression. For example, the great reformer, Martin Luther, fought with depression on and off through his entire life. In 1527 Luther wrote, "For more than a week I was close to the gates of death and hell. I trembled in all my members. Christ was wholly lost. . .the content of the depressions was always the same, the loss of faith that God is good and that He is good to me." The famous preacher Charles Hadden Spurgeon, whom God used to light the "fires" of the 19th century revival movement, struggled so severely with depression that he was forced to be absent from his pulpit for two to three months a year. In 1866 he told his congregation of his struggle saying: "I am the subject of depressions of spirit so fearful that I hope none of you ever get to such extremes of wretchedness as I go through." He explained that during these depressions, "Every mental and spiritual labor. . .had to be carried on under protest of spirit." There are numerous other examples that I could use such as John Bunyan, J.B. Phillips, Rick Warren and even myself. So, despair is not always linked to sin. Mature Christians can suffer from depression.

<u>Christianity does not always equal happiness</u>. Now, Christians are urged to rejoice – and they should – at all times. But the truth is, Christian joy can sometimes be mixed with cheerless despondency. The Apostle Peter spoke of this in *1 Peter 1:6* when he wrote, *"In this you greatly rejoice, even though now for a little while, if necessary, you have been distressed by various trials."*

Basic tools for dealing with the more common form of Depression
Elijah, the man of God, was God's prophet during a time in the life of the nation of Israel when its rulers were leading the people to worship the false gods known as Baal and Asherah. Well, to shock them into turning from this sin God withheld any dew or rain from the land for three years and a severe famine resulted. At the height of this drought, Elijah challenged Ahab and his false prophets to a public contest on the top of Mt. Carmel to demonstrate both the POWER of God and the weakness of Baal and Asherah. You may remember that two bulls were chosen. Elijah sacrificed one to God and the false prophets sacrificed theirs to Baal and Asherah. The contest was to see whose god was capable of sending fire to consume the sacrificed bull. Well, the 850 false prophets went first. You may remember they tried from early morning until late in the afternoon in vain to get their "god" to respond. They ranted and raved and cut themselves to get his attention – all to no avail. Then Elijah's turn came, and he had barely ended his petition when God answered by sending fire to consume not only the bull which Elijah had drenched with water, but the stone altar as well. The Israelites who witnessed this demonstration of God's unlimited power responded in true belief and worship. They fell on the ground and confessed that truly Yahweh alone was God.

Then Elijah commanded that those 850 prophets of Baal & Asherah be seized and executed according to the law of God written in Deuteronomy 7. And when that was done, Elijah prayed that God would end the drought. You may remember that Elijah sent his assistant to watch for approaching clouds while he prayed seven times and finally a small cloud the size of a man's fist could be seen on the distant horizon. Then Elijah advised Ahab to head for Jezreel and avoid the approaching downpour – and as the rain fell, Elijah tucked his robe into his belt, so he wouldn't trip over it, and ran ahead of the royal chariot the entire 17 miles back to the city gates. Can you imagine running that far in leather sandals? Now, you may wonder, why would Elijah associate with Ahab – why he would accompany this wicked king to Jezreel? I don't know for sure but perhaps he was hoping that the Lord would enable him to put the final nail in Baal's coffin with the elimination of the evil queen Jezebel and that Ahab would repent of his sin and lead the entire nation to return to worshiping God and God alone. Elijah may even have had dreams of being placed in King Ahab's palace as the "prophet in residence."

The scene in our text opens as Ahab arrives home at his summer palace in Jezreel with Elijah running ahead of him. I imagine that this weak-kneed king was still excited about the events of the day – the amazing presence of Jehovah on Mt. Carmel and the joy of the rain falling on his kingdom once again. As he enters the palace he calls for Queen Jezebel to share the adventures he had experienced with Elijah. But the story about the power of the living God, the fire from heaven, and the thunder and rain that came after Elijah prayed – well, all this was drowned out when the king got around to mentioning the elimination of all 850 of Jezebel's prophets as per Elijah's order. And, at that point all the wrath of hell poured out of the mouth of this demonic woman and she expressed her desire to end the life of one more prophet. Then King Ahab's excitement faded as he stood by passively and let his queen take matters into her own hands as she proceeded to put a contract out on the life of Elijah. So, there's no doubt who wore the "pants" in that family! Take your Bibles and follow along as I read, and you'll see what I mean. All this is recorded in *1 Kings 19:1-4.*

> *Now Ahab told Jezebel everything Elijah had done and how he had killed all the prophets with the sword. So, Jezebel sent a messenger to Elijah to say, 'May the gods deal with me, be it ever so severely, if by this time tomorrow I do not make your life like that of one of them.' Elijah was afraid and ran for his life. When he came to Beersheba in Judah, he left his servant there, while he himself went a day's journey into the desert. He came to a broom tree, sat down under it and prayed that he might die. "I have had enough Lord," he said, "Take my life; I am no better than my ancestors."*

Now, I want you to notice that Jezebel was not only vicious but clever. She could have ordered Elijah killed immediately, then again, without her own prophets to protect her, she might have lost her life at the hands of the people who had just recommitted themselves to following God and not Baal. But if she threatened to kill Elijah within twenty-four hours, he might slip into a posture of self-defense and flee. And if he did this, the people might be spiritually demoralized without their prophet leading them and Jehovah might be discredited – and her plan basically worked. Elijah did flee. The Bible records that he ran 115 more miles all the way to Beersheba, where he left his servant. Then he continued another day's journey into the Negev (South) where he pulled up under a Juniper tree and succumbed to deep depression saying, *"I have had enough Lord, take my life."*

Application: What can we learn from Elijah's experience that will help us in our own battles with depression?

1. **What goes UP must come DOWN.**
   You see, the truth is life is full of ups and downs. You can count on it. After every down there is an up and after every UP there is a DOWN. Life is not just one long joy ride that gets better and better. No, there are mountains and valleys. And Elijah had just climbed an 'Everest" of accomplishment! Remember? He had prayed, and God had instantly answered in the presence of thousands of people – proving once and for all that Jehovah was the one true God. And because of this, Elijah had just seen the people turn from idol worship to the one true God and obey his command to kill 850 false prophets of Baal and Asherah. He had prayed again, and a 3-year drought had ended. So, talk about a high! I don't think it gets much better than that!

   And when we have great times of accomplishment and joy in life we should learn to anticipate the inevitable lows like the one that hit Elijah. You see, our lives cannot stay at a constant emotional high. There are downs after ups. That's the way common depression is – it is part of the natural cycle of ups and downs in life. After ups come downs! So, when we are in a "down" we should remember that an "up" will come. When we are depressed, we tend to picture ourselves in a "bottomless pit." Someone once said that if you want to imagine what depression feels like, just imagine that you have red eye jet lag, combined with an overwhelming grief. (I know! In 1970, after an escape mission from Vietnam, and no sleep for over 4 days, I flew home, non-stop, (8.600 hundred miles) to attend my father's suicide death. My mother had died of cancer 6 years earlier. My body was in total shock and believe me when I say I went into a deep, deep depression.)

Instead of picturing depression as a "pit" we should think of it as a "tunnel." You see depression is not something to climb out of as much as it is something to "go through." **Like a tunnel as soon as we enter depression we are already on the way out.** One of my favorite Christian comedians is Mark Lowery and I remember hearing Mark say that his favorite verse of scripture is "It came to pass." They remind Mark, and us, that when problems come they also go. They "come to pass." As the Psalmist says, "weeping may remain for a night. . .but JOY comes in the morning." Depression does not last forever. It will come to pass. You will get through it. And Elijah did get through this time of depression in his life.

2.   **We make ourselves especially susceptible to depression when we take our eyes off God. Or perhaps our eyes have never been on God.** Remember, when Elijah heard of Jezebel's threat he responded with fear. Verse 3 says, *"Elijah was afraid."* He took his eyes off God and looked at Jezebel and when he did he became afraid and slipped into the pits of despair. So, when depression approaches, keep your eyes on God. Dwell on God's greatness and power. Remember all the ways He has been faithful to you. In short, KEEP THE SON IN YOUR EYES!

> *Romans 8:28 says: And <u>we know</u> that all things work together for good to those who love God, to those who are the called according to His purpose.*

The Bible never claims that all things are good but that all things (good and bad) work together for good. Salt is made of two poisons, sodium and chloride. If you eat either one by itself, it could kill you but mix them together and you have something good. This is something the Bible says we <u>can know</u>. But this promise is only for those who love God, to those who are saved (called according to His purpose).

If you are not saved, then today can be your day of salvation. You need to understand that you, just like the rest of us, have sinned and your sins have separated you from God. The only way to get right with God and have peace with Him is to confess your sins to Him. Name them one by one. Then be willing to repent (turn from your sins, turn from living for yourself only) and ask Christ, beg Him if you will, to come into your life and save you.

Believe that He died for and with your sins upon Himself and ask Him for forgiveness. Know that He rose from the dead and you will face Him one day! Promise to give Him your life and live for Him the rest of your life and really mean it. If you'll do that, He'll give you peace of mind a new lease on life like you have never imagined. The Bible says you will be "born again."

He may lift your depression from right off your shoulders immediately if you'll just love Him and give your life to Him. He loves you so much that He was willing, and did, die a horrible death with your sins all upon Him. He voluntarily was punished for all our sins and you may have lived a life acting like you could care less.

When you face Him one day, and you will face Him, you can either face His wrath or His mercy. It all depends on whether you are willing to accept His love and His gift of salvation.

> *Ephesians 2:8-9 – For by grace are you saved through faith and that not of yourselves, it is the gift of God, not of works lest anyone should boast.*

3. **Physical stress can cause emotional stress.**
   Remember that just prior to the onset of Elijah's depression he had put his body through incredible stress. He had run over 100 miles without stopping. He was physically exhausted. And might I add in tremendously great shape. Prior to his 100-mile sprint Elijah had put in a full day of exhausting ministry on the top of Mt. Carmel. So, I think depression was inevitable, because physical stress negatively affects our emotional health.

The Bible says that the first thing God did to help Elijah's depression was to minister to his physical fatigue. God fed him fresh baked bread and cool water and then told him to sleep. Then He fed him again. And you know, that is the most practical thing some of us can do when we deal with depression. We need to stop running ourselves into the ground and take care of this physical body that God has given us. We need to quit abusing it and learn to eat right and sleep right. There's an old Greek saying that goes like this: "You will break the bow if you keep it always bent." In other words, if you're living under constant, relentless physical stress, you will eventually break under the pressure. You have to give yourself some time for rest and refreshment. Just remember when your body becomes weak and ill so does your spirit. Physical stress can cause emotional stress.

4. **We are more susceptible to depression when we are alone**
   Remember, Elijah went off by himself and sat under that Juniper tree wanting to die. When we get depressed and discouraged, the first thing we tend to do is get alone and that is usually the WORST thing we can do. You see, loneliness is one of the greatest contributors to depression. When we draw into a shell and cut ourselves off from others we naturally begin to feast on self-pity. This is one reason we should go to church. Hebrews 10:25 tells us not to forsake the assembling of ourselves together. You see, God didn't design us to live like hermits in a cave. No - He built us such that life works best for us when we live in friendship and fellowship and community with others. That's why the church, the body of Christ, is so very important, because that is where we are drawn together in love and mutual encouragement. We are meant to be a part of one another's lives. When we gather in a Sunday School or Bible study class of caring people - when we come into a church service in the house of God with Christian friends we draw strength for life's battles.

5. **Elijah's experience also shows that when it comes to depression, doing affects feeling.**
   In other words, idleness breeds despair. Sitting alone with nothing to do but focus on his own problems magnified Elijah's despair. So, God put him to work! In verses 15-17 God told Elijah that he had a job to do. Two kings needed crowning. He also had his prophetic successor, Elisha, to appoint. And from this chapter in Elijah's life, we can learn that when depression attacks we should not go somewhere and simply dwell on it. No, instead we should get our bodies moving because physical activity can be

like an emotional medicine. You see our emotions are rebellious at times. They won't take orders! They easily ignore commands such as "Stop being angry" or "Don't feel sad" or "Be happy." It is difficult if not impossible to control our emotions. But we can control our bodies. And FORCING our bodies to do something that needs doing can have the effect of MAKING us feel better. One thing we can do to help ourselves out of depression is to DO non-depressive things – even if we don't feel like doing them. Martin Luther once said: "A good way to exorcize the Devil is to harness the horses and spread manure on the fields." In other words, get to work! Do something productive and you will feel productive because doing affects feeling.

6. **Focusing on other people's worries helps us forget our own**
   God reminded Elijah that there was an entire nation that needed his ministry. And this tells us that one way to deal with depression is to help others - to focus on meeting their needs. This is what Philippians 2:4 encourages us to do, *"look not only to our own interest, (needs) but also to the interest of others."*

Dr. Carl Menninger once "gave a lecture on mental health and was answering questions from the audience. Someone said, "Dr. Menninger, what would you advise a person to do if that person felt a nervous breakdown coming on?" Most people thought he would say, "Go see a psychiatrist immediately," but he didn't. To their astonishment, Dr. Menninger replied, "Lock up your house, go across the railroad tracks, find somebody in need, and help that person." To overcome discouragement, "Don't focus on yourself, get involved in the lives of other people." You see, when we focus on the needs of others our own needs fade into the background. So sometimes the best thing you can do when you are in the midst of deep despair is go and help someone else.

We've listed six lessons we can learn from Elijah's experience with depression but the greatest lesson we can learn is to follow God's example in relating to people who battle with depression. Remember? God was compassionate in His treatment of Elijah. Far from criticizing him, our Lord allowed him to rest and twice sent an angel to feed him. And we must be just as compassionate in our dealing with people who are suffering from depression or emotional problems. If we really want to help them, we must be their angel. I guess you could say that there are two types of people in the world. . .people who are drowning in despair without hope and others who have called out to God and experienced His rescue.

CHAPTER 26

TO LIVE WELL IS TO GRIEVE WELL

And now let us talk about grief in depression. Grief can and does bring on depression. Grief is a wound of the spirit, a spiritual wound that hurts clear to the bone. Death takes away those you love, and you are helpless to do anything to stop it. The death of a loved one is something you cannot fully prepare for ahead of time. Coming to grips with its reality, intellectually and emotionally, is something that happens only by experiencing such a loss. It is as if a part of you has been taken away. There is no hurt like death brings. No friend or loved one can fully identify with your personal loss. There comes with the death of a love one: numbness – shock – disbelief – yearning – protest – anger – loneliness – restlessness – an aching void – tears (sometimes many tears).

Many times, there is guilt when a loved one dies. There are two types of guilt: Real Guilt and False Guilt. Real guilt happens when we knowingly choose to disobey God or do something we know is wrong. False guilt is feeling guilty about something over which you have no control. Sometimes there are feelings of guilt when one feels relief over a loved one dying who has endured prolonged suffering. If we are to overcome our false guilt; if we are going to live again and enjoy life to its fullest extent again then we must learn how to move well through our grief.

First, recognize that grief is a necessary and important part of our lives. We need the freedom to grieve. It is an important part of closure because it allows us to honestly express the way we feel. And while we may ask the question: "Why God", the important question – the one that gets us moving again and living again is "What now God?" Second, we need to participate in the process of grief. Take time to personally mourn, but also become involved in the necessary steps to bring closure to your loss. We grieve because what we lost was important to us. How do we get through it? How do we go on? How do we live again?

Ecclesiastes 3:4 – There is a time to cry and a time to laugh -A time to grieve and a time to dance

When we grieve well we will dance again, we will live again, we will laugh again, we will have joy again. Grief has its season, but then it is time to move on to another season, it is time to dance again. God wants to wipe our tears but then He wants us to move on and be a help to other people who are grieving. Remember above all else that God loves you!

Romans 5:8 God demonstrated His love to us in that while we were yet sinners Christ died for us. In John 15:3 Jesus said, "Greater love hath no man than this that a man lay down his life for his friends." And then he proved His love for us when He laid down His life for us, for the forgiveness of our sins.

God knows we grieve. He understands our sorrow and He comforts us. He does not promise to keep us from grief but to help us through it. Grief can and does bring on depression. When you are in physical pain you need to seek help. When you are in spiritual pain you need to seek help as well. There are many places where you can go for help. Go to God, to your family, to your church (go to the place where you get spiritual help). If your grief is severe you may need to go to a professional counselor. But the bottom line is GO!

Grief is an emotional response to a loss. The greater the loss the more emotional the response. A sudden loss produces even a greater emotional response. The Bible says: *"In this world we will have sorrow and tribulation."* When was the first time you remember experiencing grief in your life? When did grief actually begin in your life? It began the moment you were born. You were born into grief. For 9 months you were secure in your environment then suddenly everything you knew was gone and you find yourself in a new and scary environment.

Throughout our lives we are constantly saying goodbye. We experience grief in a thousand different ways. Loss is a universal experience for all of us. Many times, when we are grieving God seems so far away and we don't know how to connect to Him. What we need to do is to hold a hand that is holding the hand of God. When you help someone through the process of grief you can be that hand!

THE COMMON CAUSES OF GRIEF

1. Death – The number one cause of grief

2. Divorce – The death of a relationship; a death that never stops dying especially when children are involved.

3. Mobility – When we move we lose a lot. We lose friends, doctors, churches, work, school, etc. You need closure when you move. In order for you to move on to new adventures in your life you need to say so long, goodbye to friends and your surroundings. God will help you when you reach out and say, "What now God.?"

4. Retirement – The death of what has given your life meaning and purpose

SIX OBSERVABLE STEPS TO GRIEF REACTIONS

1. Shock and Denial – Shock is a natural anesthesia.
    In order to help someone, you don't do what Job's friends did. (book of Job) You remain quiet, but your presence is needed. It's called the "Ministry of Presence." Be there to listen to the grieving person – they'll be able to work through it if they are allowed to talk. Repeat words of reassurance to them without giving suggestions. Don't use religious clichés (E.g.: "It was God's will"). God can speak through your presence more than your words. People will talk themselves back into orientation.

2. Disorganization and Disorientation – Am I losing my mind?
    You are not losing your mind. This is a natural response to grief. A good book to read is called "Good Grief"

3. Unleashing of volatile emotions – throwing things – screaming at God

   Don't suggest to a person that they shouldn't scream at God. They are not really turning their backs on God, they are venting their hurt, their grief. Let them do so. God says in Isaiah 1:18 "Come let us reason together saith the Lord." Say: "Hurts like heck doesn't it?" They will get over their volatile emotions. Allow them to get through it. Allow them to vent.

4. Guilt – If only I'd done this or that differently

   If only I'd called the doctor sooner. If only I'd been by my loved one's side when death occurred. If only I'd spent more time with my loved one. If only I had told my loved one how much I loved him/her. We must learn to ask the right questions. What good do all the what if questions accomplish? What if questions just keep us emotionally upset to where it is extremely hard for us to move forward and deal with the death. Death still would have come. The Bible tells us "It is appointed unto men once to die."

5. Depression – Many times extreme depression

   Depression is normal but it's something we need to go through, not stay in. Psalm 23 tells us *"Yea though I walk **through** the valley of the Shadow of Death"* You must put one foot in front of the other and make yourself do what needs to be done and depression may start to gradually go away.

6. Relief and Re-establishment

   Get involved in Sunday school, Bible study, life groups, Church worship, neighborhood events, get involved with friends, do volunteer work, etc. As Ecclesiastes tells us *"Learn to Dance Again"* In John 10:10 Jesus tells us: *"I came that you might have life and that you might have it more abundantly."*

THINGS NOT TO DO WHEN YOU ARE TRYING TO HELP SOMEONE THROUGH GRIEF

Don't ask, "Is there anything I can do for you?"
Don't say, "If I can ever do anything for you please let me know."
Don't say, "I know how you feel."
Don't say, "Time heals all things."

You don't say these things because: 1. People won't call you. 2. They won't ask for help. 3. Even though you might have been through a similar experience, every experience is different, in many ways, and we can't possibly understand how that person really feels in their personal situation. Time does not heal all things! Time just passes, that's all it does! It puts distance between you and the hurt but it's what you do with the time that's important. What you do with the time is what begins to heal you.

THINGS TO DO WHEN TRYING TO HELP SOMEONE THROUGH GRIEF

Do say something like this: "I'm going to the store and I'm coming by to pick you up." It's not an option! Don't give them a choice. In their state of mind, they cannot make a choice. You've got to get them moving. You've got to be there to help them get moving.

But don't do it too soon. Give people time to grieve. Spend time with them without saying a word. There is always hope if we tap into the help that is available. And always remember that a hug, during time of grief, is better than all the theology in the world. To live well is to grieve well.

We know from experience that the Lord will hear the cries of all people and according to *Psalm 40:2 ". . .I will lift them out of the pits of despair. . .out of the mud and mire and set their feet on the rock. . .I will establish their steps and put a new song in their heart"*

> *Psalm 42:5 says, "Why are you downcast, O my soul?*
> *Why so disturbed within me? Put your hope in God."*

If you are not a Christian, then why not put your faith in Christ? Claim Him as your Savior and Lord. Give your life totally to Him and He will give you a new life, a new hope, a new job, a new purpose and a complete fulfillment in your life.

CHAPTER 27

SWALLOWED BY A WHALE – REALLY?

I decided to include this sermon because, of all the miracles in the Bible, none is better known or more disbelieved than this one. The question is often asked as to whether a whale could actually swallow a man and if he could, could the man live inside the whale. Well, let's take a look.

There are three basic interpretations of the book of Jonah. There is the **mythological view** (e.g. Robinson Crusoe, Gulliver's Travels). There is the **allegorical or parable view** (for example: Jonah is actually Israel, the sea is actually the gentile nations, the fish is actually Babylonian captivity, the regurgitation is the return to Israel during Ezra's time). And then there is the **literal view**.

The literal view, the historical view, I believe is the correct view. The account presents itself as actual. The Jews and early Christians believed it to be literal. 2 Kings 14:25 refers to Jonah as an historical person *("He restored the coast of Israel from the entering of Hamath unto the sea of the plain, according to the word of the Lord God of Israel, which he spoke by the hand of his servant, Jonah, the son of Amittai, the prophet, who was of Gath Hepher."). Jesus testified to the literal account of Jonah in Matthew 12:38-41 and Luke 11:29-32.*

> *Matthew 12: 38-41 – Then some of the scribes and Pharisees answered, saying "Teacher, we want to see a sign from You." But He answered and said to them, "An evil and adulterous generation seeks after a sign, and*

no sign will be given to it except the sign of the prophet Jonah. For as Jonah was three days and three nights in the belly of the great fish, so will the Son of Man be three days and three nights in the heart of the earth. The men of Nineveh will rise up in the judgment with this generation and condemn it, because they repented at the preaching of Jonah; and indeed, a greater than Jonah is here."

Luke 11:29-32 – And while the crowds were thickly gathered together, He began to say, "This is an evil generation. It seeks a sign, and no sign will be given to it except the sign of Jonah the prophet. For as Jonah became a sign to the Ninevites, so also the Son of Man will be to this generation. The queen of the South will rise up in the judgment with the men of this generation and condemn them, for she came from the ends of the earth to hear the wisdom of Solomon, and indeed a greater than Solomon is here. The men of Nineveh will rise up in the judgment with this generation and condemn it, for they repented at the preaching of Jonah, and indeed a greater than Jonah is here."

Jonah was from Gath Hepher of Zebulun north of Nazareth in Galilee. He was the first foreign missionary. Thus, the Pharisees were in error concerning their statement in John 7:52: They answered, and said unto him, *"Art thou also of Galilee? Search, and look, for out of Galilee ariseth no prophet."*

1. Jonah Protesting

The command of God was to go! (Jonah 1:1-2). God orders Jonah, his prophet, to go to Nineveh and preach out against the city's exceeding wickedness. Jonah says NO! (Jonah 1:3). Jonah foolishly attempts to hide from God and run away from the presence of God. (Psalm 139:7-12). He purchases a ticket to Tarshish (ancient name for Spain) from the port of Joppa. Eight centuries later Peter received a similar command to share the gospel with Gentiles while he was staying in a tanners house whose name was Simon in the port city of Joppa. He obeyed God.

2. **Why did Jonah refuse to obey God?**
    Because he was a coward? NO! (See Jonah 1:12). Because he hated the Ninevites? YES! Nineveh was the capital of Assyria. The Assyrian army was on the move and many felt it would only be a matter of time before the army came marching into Israel.

    Consider the following testimonies from various authors:
    Some of the victims were held down while one of the band of torturers inserts his hand into the victim's mouth, grips his tongue, and wrenches it out by the roots. In another spot, pegs are driven into the ground. To these, another victim's wrists are fixed with cords. His ankles are similarly made fast and the man is stretched out, unable to move a muscle. The executioner then applies himself to his task and beginning at the accustomed spot, the sharp knife makes its incision. The skin is raised inch by inch till the man is flayed alive. These skins are then stretched out upon the city walls to terrify the people and leave behind long-enduring impressions of Assyrian vengeance. For others, long sharp poles are prepared. The sufferer, taken like all the rest from the leading men of the city, is laid down; the sharpened end of the pole is driven in through the lower part of the chest; the pole is then raised, bearing the writhing victim aloft. It is then planted in the hole dug for it and the man is left to die. Pyramids of human heads marked the path of the conqueror. Boys and girls were burnt alive or reserved for a worse fate. Men were impaled, flayed alive, blinded, or deprived of their hands and feet, or their ears and noses, while the women and children were carried into slavery. The captured city, plundered, reduced to ashes, and the trees in its neighborhood cut down.

    Some of Jonah's friends and family probably died like this. Is it any wonder that Jonah did not want God to grant repentance and forgiveness to these people? Jonah wanted them punished, not forgiven! He hated these people and he was not about to obey God and go preach repentance and forgiveness to them!

3. **The Command of God – Blow! (Jonah 1:4-12)**
    Jonah boards a ship to get as far away from Nineveh and as far away from God as he can. Out at sea, God sends a terrible storm and the ship is about to go under. The frightened sailors pray to their pagan gods and frantically throw the cargo overboard to lighten the ship.

Jonah is asleep at the bottom of the ship. The captain wakes him up and orders him to pray. They cast lots to determine who had angered his god and brought the storm upon them. The lot falls on Jonah. Jonah admits what he has done and advises them to throw him overboard.

4. **The action of the mariners – Throw! (Jonah 1:13-17)**
    The mariners struggle to bring the ship to land but without success. They ask for forgiveness in what they are going to have to do and they throw Jonah overboard. As Jonah hits the water, the waters become calm and the storm ceases. The amazed sailors give thanks to Jehovah God. As Jonah is sinking into the waters and about to die, suddenly, he is swallowed by a huge fish. A fish which God had previously arranged for.

As stated above, of all the miracles in the Bible, none is better known or more disbelieved than this one. The question is often asked as to whether a whale could actually swallow a man. And if he could, could the man live inside the whale. It needs to be pointed out that nowhere in the original Old Testament or New Testament language does the Bible say a whale swallowed Jonah. The Hebrew word for fish is *dag* and refers to a great sea monster. In Matthew 12:40, the words translated whale by the KJV is the Greek word, *Ketos*, which again refers to a sea monster. In the second place, God could have used a whale had He chosen to.

Numerous cases have been reported in more recent times of men who have survived the ordeal of being swallowed by a whale. The Princeton Theological Review (October 1927) tells of two incidents, one in 1758 and the other in 1771, in which a man was swallowed by a whale and vomited up shortly thereafter with only minor injuries. One of the most striking instances comes from Francis Fox, *Sixty-Three Years of Engineering* (P. 298-300), who reports that this incident was carefully investigated by two scientists (one of whom was M. DeParville, the scientific editor of the *Journal Des Debats* in Paris). In February 1891, the whaling ship, Star of the East, was in the vicinity of the Falkland Islands, and the lookout sighted a large sperm whale three miles away. Two boats were lowered and in a short time, one of the harpooners was enabled to spear the creature. The second boat also attacked the whale but was then upset by a lash of its tail, so that its crew fell into the sea. One of them was drowned, but the other, James Bartley, simply disappeared without a trace. After the whale was killed, the crew set to work with axes and spades removing the blubber. They worked all day and part of the night. The next day they attached some tackle to the stomach, which was hoisted on deck. The sailors were startled by something in it which gave spasmodic signs of life, and inside was found the missing sailor, doubled up and unconscious. He was laid on the deck and treated to a bath of sea water which soon revived him. At the end of the third week, he had entirely recovered from the shock and resumed his duties. His face, neck, and hand were bleached to a deadly whiteness and took on the appearance of parchment. Bartley affirms that he would probably have lived inside his house of flesh until he starved, for he lost his senses through fright and not through lack of air. (*A Survey of Old Testament Introduction*), p. 302

Whether these stories are true or not they are certainly intriguing. Remember, from the original language of the Bible, never does the Bible say that Jonah was swallowed by a whale, but rather by a great sea creature. This possibly could have been a sea creature especially created by God for this very purpose. In any event, according to Jesus own words, the story in the Bible does appear to be true.

5. **Jonah praying while being in the belly of this sea creature – Jonah chapter 2**
Jonah begins an earnest and all out one-man prayer meeting. From Jonah's words we assume he is at the point of death. Perhaps he is repeating the 23rd Psalm (Yea, thou I walk through the valley of the shadow of death). Can you imagine calling out to God from inside a fish's belly with seaweeds wrapped around your head? Jonah mentions a scientific fact totally unknown by humans of his day when he speaks of the mountains rising from the ocean floor. Just one more proof that the Bible is the very word of God. Jonah renounces his sin and re-consecrates his life to God (vs. 8-9). He ends his prayer with a five-word summary of the entire Bible and, indeed, the very plan and purpose of God. **"Salvation is of the Lord"** (vs. 9). He is vomited up on dry land by the fish who gives his life to God. <u>(a huge creature like this who beaches itself would not be able to get back into the sea and so it dies obeying God)</u>

6. Jonah's mission field (Jonah chapter 3)

Nineveh, the capital of Assyria, lay on the eastern side of the Tigris River and was one of the greatest cities in ancient times. So large was its metropolitan area that it would take three days to go around it. It had 1,200 towers, each 200 feet high, and its wall was 100 feet high. Three chariots could drive abreast on top of the wall. It was 60 miles in circumference, and could, within its walls, grow corn enough for its population of 600,000. The basement of its wall was of polished stone, and its width 50 feet. In the city was a magnificent palace, with courts and walls covering more than 100 acres. The roofs were supported by beams of cedar, resting on columns of cypress, inlaid and strengthened by bans of sculptured silver and iron. Its gates were guarded by huge lions and bulls sculptured in stone. Its doors were of ebony and cypress encrusted with iron, silver, and ivory, and paneling the rooms were sculptured slabs of alabaster, and cylinders and bricks with cuneiform inscriptions. In their temples, palaces, libraries and arsenals were beautiful, rich, hanging gardens and rare animals, all to enrich and adorn the city and were all built by the labor of foreign slaves.

7. Jonah's Message

Jonah 3:4 – And Jonah began to enter into the city a day's journey, and he cried, and said, *"Yet forty days, and Nineveh shall be overthrown."*

8. The Result of the Message
The greatest revival in the world breaks out!

Jonah 3:10 – And God saw their works, that they turned from their evil way; and God repented of the evil that He had said that He would do unto them, and He did it not.

9. The lesson that Jonah learned – Jonah chapter 4

But it displeased Jonah exceedingly and he became angry. So, he prayed to the Lord, and said, "Ah, Lord, was not this what I said when I was still in my country? Therefore, I fled previously to Tarshish; for I know that You are a gracious and merciful God, slow to anger and abundant in loving-kindness, one who relents from doing harm. Therefore now, O Lord, please take my life from me, for it is better for me to die than to live!" Then the Lord said, "Is it right for you to be angry?" So, Jonah went out of the city and sat on the east side of the city. There he made himself a shelter and sat under it in the shade, till he might see what would become of the city.

And the Lord God prepared a plant and made it come up over Jonah, that it might be shade for his head to deliver him from his misery. So, Jonah was very grateful for the plant. But as morning dawned the next day God prepared a worm, and it so damaged the plant that it withered. And it happened, when the sun arose, that God prepared a vehement east wind; and the sun beat on Jonah's head, so that he grew faint. Then he wished death for himself, and said, "It is better for me to die that to live."

Then God said to Jonah, "Is it right for you to be angry about the plant?" And he said, "It is right for me to be angry, even to death!" But the Lord said, "You have had pity on the plant for which you had not labored, nor made it grow, which came up in a night and perished in a night." (in other words: "You feel sorry for yourself because you've lost your discomfort of the shade) And should I not pity Nineveh, that great city, in which are more than one hundred and twenty thousand persons who cannot discern between their right hand and their left – and much livestock?"

10. What can we learn from this story?

Would you feel the same way that Jonah felt? Remember what the people of Nineveh had done to others, how they had tortured and killed! But also remember that we all have sinned and no matter how small or great the sin, it will still, without repentance, send us to HELL! Do we think we are so self-righteous that we should escape the punishment for our sin? Remember the thief on the cross with Jesus who simply, in his heart, asked for forgiveness and Jesus said, *"Today you will be with me in Paradise."* We don't know what the thief did but apparently it was worthy of the death penalty.

The Bible says in *Romans 3:23 "For all have sinned and fall short of the glory of God."* And in *Romans 6:23 "For the wages of sin is death, but the gift of God is eternal life in Christ Jesus our Lord."*

Would we, like Jonah, wish for the total destruction of the Ninevites or would we wish for their repentance and change of heart? What happens to us, on the inside, when we hold on to hate and a lack of forgiveness? Aren't we damaged, and don't we retain our anger and our hurt to our own detriment?

What would happen in this world today if everyone in the world would turn to Christ in repentance and a change of heart? Well, I'll tell you what would happen! All wars would immediately cease, and everyone would start living by doing unto others what they would have them do unto them. Can you even imagine a world where there is no crime or hatred?

And isn't this what God desired for the people of Nineveh? Not an easy escape for the consequences of their sin but for repentance and forgiveness so as they never do it again. And wasn't God thinking about all the people in the future that would be tortured and killed by the Ninevites if they did not change?

So, God had the goodness and welfare of all people on His mind when His desire was for repentance and forgiveness of the people of Nineveh. And what did Jonah have on his mind? The comfort and welfare of Jonah.

And what about you? What about me? Is our heart right with God? Are we concerned about whether others go to Heaven or Hell or are we just concerned about ourselves?

Another thing we can learn from this story is to act on what you hear God say and not run from it! Hearing is not doing! Only doing is doing!

James 1:22 – "But be ye doers of the word and not hearers only, deceiving your own selves."

Renew your commitment to obey God for the sake of others. Even if others have hurt you, even if you don't understand, even if things don't seem fair to you, OBEY GOD!

CHAPTER 28

WHAT HAPPENS WHEN A CHRISTIAN SINS?

Psalm 51:1-2 – Have mercy upon me, O God, according to Your loving kindness; according to the multitude of Your tender mercies, blot out my transgressions. Wash me thoroughly from my iniquity and cleanse me from my sin.

There was a Scottish tradesman, a painter called Jack, who was very interested in making a dollar where he could. So, he often would thin down his paint to make it go a wee bit further. As it happened, he got away with this for some time. Eventually the Presbyterian Church decided to do a big restoration job on one of their biggest churches. Jack put in a painting bid and because his price was so competitive, he got the job. And so, he set to, with a right good will, erecting the trestles and putting up the planks, and buying the paint and yes, I am sorry to say, thinning it down with the turpentine. Well, Jack was up on the scaffolding, painting away, the job nearly done, when suddenly there was a horrendous clap of thunder. The sky opened, and the rain poured down washing the thin paint from all over the church and knocking Jack fair off the scaffold to land on the lawn. Now, Jack was no fool. He knew this was a judgment from the Almighty, so he fell on his knees and cried, "Oh God! Forgive me! What should I do?" And from the thunder, a mighty voice spoke, "Repaint! Repaint! And thin no more!"

What Happens When a Christian Sins?

> *If we can't lose our salvation, does that mean we*
> *have nothing to lose when we sin?*

I heard a story about a former prizefighter. He had been converted, and he thought God had called him to preach. The only problem was, while he thought he had the gift of preaching, nobody else had the gift of listening, so he couldn't get a church to preach in. He got a little pulpit, found a street corner, and preached to those who passed by his corner. He had 2 or 3 friends that liked him and came to hear him preach but that's about the entire crowd he ever had. One day an atheist heard him preach and shouted out "I don't believe any of the Bible." As time went by the atheist continued to come and the two of them would get into arguments over the Bible. One day the former prizefighter was ready for him. He said to the atheist, "Listen, if I can prove to you just one verse in the Bible is true, will you apologize to me?" And the atheist said, "Yes, indeed I would." With that the former prizefighter reached out and took this man by the nose and twisted it so severely that the blood ran down both nostrils; and then with a smile on his face, he opened his Bible and read *Proverbs 30:33 "The churning of milk produces butter, and wringing the nose produces blood."* Then he said, "I want you to apologize to me because I proved to you at least one verse in the Bible is true."

There is another truth in the Bible that I want us to see this morning, *"If you are bound to sin, you are bound to suffer – whether you are saved or not."* Suffering follows sin just as sure as night follows day

CONSEQUENCES OF SIN IN THE LIFE OF A CHRISTIAN

SIN DIRTIES THE SOUL.
In Psalm 51 King David is praying, *"O God, wash me; O God, cleanse me."* If you are a child of God and you sin, spiritually you are going to feel dirty. If you don't feel dirty when you sin, you need to ask yourself if you've ever been saved. No pig has ever said, "Woe is me, I'm dirty." A pig has no concept of being dirty because that is his element. A child of God realizes that he is dirty when he sins. A true child of God, when he (or she) sins, feels unclean. If you are a child of God and you've sinned, you've felt that!

SIN DOMINATES THE MIND.

In Psalm 51:3, David says, *"For I acknowledge my transgressions, and my sin is always before me."* Think about that: **"My sin is <u>always</u> before me."** Day and night, night and day, what David had done had so etched itself upon his consciousness, so reverberated through his spirit, that he was conscious of it all the time. A test as to whether you're saved is not if you can sin but if you can sin and just ignore it. If you are a child of God, the Holy Spirit will not let you ignore it. He will not let you forget it! The Holy Spirit will put His finger on the sore spot and push! David said, *"My sin is always before me!"* It dominated his mind! Now that doesn't mean that he was necessarily consciously thinking about it all day long. But that doesn't mean that your sin is not always there. It is there either in your conscious mind or, perhaps worse, in your subconscious mind. It will show up in your subconscious as an irritable temper, the inability to concentrate, sleepless nights, and lack of joy. Your sin is there night and day. There are two kinds of wounds that can come to the human soul. One is guilt and the other is sorrow. Sorrow is a clean wound. Give it time and it will heal. But guilt is a dirty wound. It just festers and festers and festers and never stops until it is cleansed. So here David is saying to God, *"O God, my soul feels dirty; my mind is dominated by this thing that I have done."*

SIN DISGRACES THE LORD

In Psalm 51:4 David is speaking to God: *"Against You, You only, have I sinned, and done this evil in Your sight, that You may be found just when You speak, and blameless when You judge."*

Think about the first part of that verse. He says, *"Against You, <u>You only</u>, have I sinned."* Now against whom did David sin? When you think about it, you might say, well, he committed adultery, so he sinned against his own body. He certainly committed sin against his wife when he committed adultery. He also sinned against his children and his family. He sinned against the woman he committed adultery with. He certainly sinned against the woman's husband, who he committed adultery with, as he had him put to death. And because he was the King, he sinned against his nation. David mentioned none of these offences. He saw his sin for what it actually was: AN AFFRONT TO ALMIGHTY GOD

David loved God. That's the reason his heart was broken. He said, *"O God, against You, <u>You only</u>, have I sinned and done this evil in Your* *sight.*" When people want to commit adultery, sometimes they go off to some secret rendezvous, some secret liaison, some hidden place. But it dawned on David, <u>"My God, You were watching me. Your eyes saw what I did. O God, my God, God, the God that I love, Lord, I have sinned against You. Not only have I broken Your law, but I have broken Your heart."</u> An unsaved man sometimes feels bad about what his sin does to him. A saved man feels bad about what his sin does to God. When a slave disobeys, what's he afraid of? The whip! But a son, when he disobeys, is hurt because of his father's displeasure. When you love the Lord God, you can know that you're saved when it's not the punishment, but the sin, that stings your conscience.

SIN DEPRESSES THE HEART

In Psalm 51:8 David is talking about the consequences of sin. He says: *"Make me hear joy and gladness, that the bones You have broken may rejoice"* He's depressed; there's no joy, no gladness. Oh, it seemed thrilling while he was doing it, while he was committing the sin. The Bible says, *"sin is pleasurable for a season"* Proverbs 20:17 *"Bread gained by deceit is sweet to a man, but afterward his mouth will be filled with gravel"* David had lost his joy. Look at verse 12 which says, *"Restore to me the joy of Your salvation."* He's not saying *"Lord, restore my salvation"* He had his salvation, but he had lost the joy of his salvation. Only one thing can take joy from your heart – not two, three or four – only one and that one thing is sin. And only one kind of sin can destroy your joy – YOUR SIN! When someone sins against you, that is their SIN.

Your reaction to what they do to you can take away your HAPPINESS, but it can't take away your JOY unless you allow it to. If you want to see what a person is, don't watch their actions, watch their reactions because their reactions are what they really are. If you want to see what a person is full of, just see what spills out when they are jostled; when things don't go their way. If you jostle somebody and anger spills out, then that's what they are full of – ANGER. If you jostle somebody and JESUS spills out, then that's what they are full of – JESUS. If you want to know what a person is full of, just watch what happens when somebody steals their parking spot. Watch what happens when someone cuts them off on the freeway and see how they react – then you'll know the real person. What I'm saying is that JOY can be constant no matter what anybody else does to you. There's a difference between HAPPINESS and JOY. HAPPINESS depends on what HAPPENS – that's why it's called HAPPI-NESS.

You wouldn't want to be HAPPY all the time! You'd get sick and tired of being HAPPY all the time. Jesus was a man of sorrows; Jesus wept. He was not HAPPY all the time – but He was full of JOY. When He was facing the CROSS, He spoke to His disciples and said: *John 15:11 "These things I have spoken to you, that MY JOY may remain in you and that your joy may be full."* When Jesus was facing the cross, He was speaking of JOY! When the apostle Paul was in a dismal prison He wrote to us as recorded in *Philippians 4:4 "Rejoice in the Lord ALWAYS"* The JOY of the Lord can be a constant in your life and the JOY of the Lord is your STRENGTH! Happiness is like a thermometer; it registers conditions. Joy is like a thermostat; it controls conditions. Something wonderful really happens when you get Happiness and Joy at the same time. Those are great times! Maybe you're having a wonderful Holiday season, all your family is there, all your family members are dedicated Christians, and everyone is having a great time together in the Lord. Maybe you're with other Christians who love the Lord, you're praying for one another, having a fellowship meal afterwards, everyone is happy and enjoying one another's company. Happiness and Joy have come together and it's a great day. There are days though when HAPPINESS is gone and during those times JOY becomes all the more important. Sometimes God gives you JOY, not to take away the pain but to help you bear it! In the midst of excruciating pain, you can have supernatural JOY. *PAIN IS INEVITABLE, BUT MISERY IS OPTIONAL!!*

SIN DISEASES THE BODY

Sin in your life, without repentance, can actually make your body sick. In *Psalm 51:8 David says: "Make me hear joy and gladness, that the bones You have broken may rejoice"* Now David didn't have any broken bones, but He's talking about his bones being broken. He's using a figure of speech! We do the same thing today. Did you ever say, *"I was just crushed!"* Does that mean that somebody put you into a trash com-pactor? Doesn't it really mean that you were being squeezed in; that there was pressure on you; that you were terribly disappointed and hurt? What David was saying, in effect, was: "God, You are squeezing the life out of me. Make me hear joy and gladness that the bones You have broken may rejoice." You see, when we sin as Christians, God doesn't throw us out, He squeezes us in! God wouldn't let David go and God won't let us go when we sin, but He will and does put the pressure on. How long can a person have that kind of pressure on their life before it affects their body?

> *Proverbs 17:22 – "A merry heart does good, like a medicine, but a broken spirit dries up the bones."*

In the same way that JOY works like medicine, MISERY works like poison. The mind can make the body physically sick and when you read other Psalms it seems like David actually was physically ill because of a direct result of his sin.

1 Corinthians 11:30 Paul scolded the Corinthians for acting irreverently at the Lord's Table. He said: *"For this reason many are weak and sick among you, and many sleep."* He meant they were dead because of the sin that was in their life. Sin sickens the body! A merry heart, the joy of the Lord, is a wonderful medicine. The Bible says in *Nehemiah 8:10* *"The joy of the Lord is your strength."*

SIN DEFILES THE SPIRIT
In *Psalm 51:10* David says:, *"Create in me a clean heart, O God, and renew a steadfast spirit within me."* David had a sour spirit, a defiled spirit. Some of the most irritating people you will ever see are Christians who are out of joint spiritually. They get a sour spirit, and nothing will please them. You can tell when a person is backsliding. In church, they begin to get a critical spirit. When people are backsliding, they take their eyes off the Lord, and begin to put their eyes on the faults of others. A backslider is always that way; he always has a sour spirit, a vile spirit, finding fault in everybody else but himself.

In any church there is plenty for everybody to be critical about if that is what you are looking for. David had a critical spirit, a defiled spirit, and at this point in his life he realizes his sin and he wants to do something to get back right with God. And so, he humbles himself before God and begs God to cleanse his spirit and give him a love for the people, a right spirit of love and forgiveness, and steadfast spirit.

SIN DESTROYS YOUR TESTIMONY
In *Psalm 51:14* David says, *"Deliver me from the guilt of bloodshed, O God, the God of my salvation, and my tongue shall sing aloud of Your*

righteousness." Here's David, a man after God's own heart, who loves God, but has gotten into horrible, terrible sin. Not only does it defile his spirit, but it destroys his testimony! This is probably the worst thing about sin in the life of a Christian. David can't sing aloud of God's righteousness, he can't confess God before others because this sin is just eating him alive. *In Psalm 51:15 David says, "O Lord, open my lips, and my mouth shall show forth Your praise."* Here he begs God to open his lips, to please allow him, once again, to be a soul winner. Please let me tell others about Your praise. Please forgive me of my sin.

Many people never beg God for forgiveness of sin because in reality they don't think they have any sin. People will agree that all have sinned but in reality they just can't see their own sin. They haven't witnessed to anyone in years and they have the audacity to think they have no sin! A lady just the other day told me the only part of the song "Amazing Grace" that she didn't like was the part that said, "Amazing Grace how sweet the sound that saved a _wretch_ like me." She said, "I hate that part of the song" – "I'm not a wretch" – "I never have been a wretch" – "I've always been a good person" And whether we admit it or not that is the sentiment of many people. Until we see our sin and beg God for forgiveness of sin we will never be soul winners. Andrew Murray said there are two classes of Christians, soul winners and backsliders. Manley Beasley used to say, "You get right with God and you'll have to backslide to keep from winning souls."

WHAT ARE THE CONSEQUENCES OF SIN IN THE LIFE OF A CHRISTIAN?
1. Sin dirties the soul.
2. Sin dominates the mind.
3. Sin disgraces the Lord.
4. Sin depresses the heart.
5. Sin diseases the body.
6. Sin defiles the spirit.
7. Sin destroys your testimony.

Can a Christian sin? Yes! Can a Christian sin and not suffer? No! Remember the most miserable man on earth is not an unsaved man. The most miserable person on earth is a saved man (or woman) out of fellowship with God.

CLEANSING OF SIN IN THE LIFE OF A CHRISTIAN

I want to give us four steps that will show us how to bring the song back in our life, how to bring the joy back, how to get right with God.

CONFIDENCE

> *Psalm 51:1 – "Have mercy upon me, O God, according to Your loving kindness; according to the multitude of Your tender mercies, blot out my transgressions."*

Do you know what David knew? David knew for a multitude of sins, there were a multitude of mercies! David knew that God had not stopped loving him! He says *"According to Your loving kindness"*

God does not love us because we are valuable; we are valuable because He loves us. God does not love us because we are good.

> *Romans 5:8 – "God demonstrates <u>His own love toward us</u>, in that while we were still sinners. Christ died for us"*

<u>We need to always have the confidence, to know, that no matter what sin we have committed, God still loves us.</u> As a parent, a grandparent, or as an individual speaking to a child – NEVER tell a child when they are tempted to do wrong "Now, if you do that, God will not love you anymore." That is a LIE! There is nothing you can do to make God love you any more; there is nothing you can do to make Him love you any less. <u>*GOD LOVES YOU!*</u> Your sin may break His heart, but it will not break His love for you!

> *Romans 8:38-39 – "For I am persuaded that neither death nor life, nor angels nor principalities nor powers, nor things present nor things to come, nor height nor depth, nor any other created thing, shall be able to separate us from the love of God which is in Christ Jesus our Lord."* If we could only understand that God does love us, and *for a multitude of sins there is a multitude of mercies.*

BLESSED DOG - A man put the following ad in the Lost and Found section of the newspaper: "LOST DOG – Crippled in front paw, blind in left eye, mange on back and neck, tail missing. Recently neutered. Answers to the name of LUCKY." And he was a lucky dog. Do you know why he was lucky? In spite of all the stuff that was wrong with him, somebody loved him enough to want him. You know, we too are lucky dogs; better yet, we are BLESSED PEOPLE! God loves us out of sheer GRACE! God loves us with an *everlasting* LOVE! We need to always have the confidence that no matter what we have done – GOD LOVES US!

CONFESSION

> *Psalm 51:2-3 – "Wash me thoroughly from my iniquity and cleanse me from my sin. For I acknowledge my transgressions, and, my sin is always before me."*

Notice what David calls it, "MY SIN" - Not somebody else's but MINE! He is saying: "God, *I am* the sinner; God, *I am* the one that has sinned. I acknowledge my sin. *My sin*, my transgression." As the old spiritual goes, "Not my brother, not my sister, but it's me, O Lord, standing in the need of prayer." There is one thing that God will never accept for sin, and that is an alibi. **Jesus did not die for alibis, Jesus died for sin.**

WE MUST CONFESS OUR SINS – NOT JUST ADMIT OUR SINS

> *1 John 1:9 – "If we confess our sins, He is faithful and just to forgive us our sins and to cleanse us from all unrighteousness."*

To admit your sin is not to confess your sin in the Bible sense. The word CONFESS means "to say the same thing" - "to say the same thing that God is saying." God says, *"THIS IS WRONG – YOU HAVE DONE WRONG; YOU HAVE SINNED!!!"* And I say in return, *"Yes, Lord, I agree with you. I come over on your side, and I say about that sin what you say about that sin. God, I agree with you; I confess my sin."*

People have always wanted to make excuses for their sin. It began in the Garden of Eden. God said to Adam, *"Where are you? Have you done this?"* And Adam replies: "Well, Lord, it really wasn't my fault. It was the woman you gave me; it was her fault." And God spoke to Eve, and

Eve said, "Well, Lord, you know it really wasn't my fault. It was the fault of the serpent." Human nature always wants to say, "It's not me; it's somebody else." Our excuses abound!

> *Proverbs 28:13 – "He who covers his sins will not prosper, but whoever confesses and forsakes them will have mercy."*

Don't ever say to God, "O God, if I have sinned, please forgive me." The Bible says, "If we confess our sins!" NAME YOUR SIN! That's the only way you'll know that you're really forgiven. Just call it by name!

CLEANSING

> *Isaiah 1:18 – "Come now, and let us reason together, saith the Lord; though your sins be as scarlet, they shall be as white as snow; though they be red like crimson, they shall be as wool."*

> *John 1:9 – "If we confess our sins, He is faithful and just to forgive us our sins and to cleanse us from all unrighteousness"*

David sinned a horrible sin and he was cleansed of his sin. You and I may or may not ever commit such a sin as David committed but we too can be cleansed of OUR SIN. We don't have to carry the baggage of our sin around with us. God will and does cleanse us! Have you ever taken something to the cleaners to get a stain out and the stain was so bad that the cleaners could not remove it? Let me tell you – "There is no stain that the blood of Christ cannot remove – none!"

> *1 John 1:7 – The blood of Jesus Christ His Son cleanses us from all sin"*

> *Psalm 51:7 – "Purge me. . . and I shall be clean; wash me and I shall be whiter than snow."*

CONSECRATION

> *Psalm 51:12-15* David says *"Restore to me the joy of Your salvation and uphold me by Your generous Spirit. Then I will teach transgressors Your ways, and sinners shall be converted to You. Deliver me from the guilt of bloodshed, O God, the God of my salvation, and my tongue shall sing aloud of Your righteousness. O Lord open my lips, and my mouth shall show forth Your praise."*

David is saying – "Lord, put my feet on the right path, and God, I am going to get back to serving You." God doesn't just cleanse us, so we can sit around and be clean; He puts us back on the track of service. Do you know how David got into trouble in the first place? He was not doing what he should have been doing! The Bible says it was the time when kings went to war. David sent his army to war but He himself decided to stay home, to sit this one out. David got up from his afternoon nap and he looked from the rooftop and saw Bathsheba. The Bible says an idle mind is the devil's workshop! And that's the reason the sins of omission are greater than the sins of commission! Did you know that if you are doing what you ought to be doing, you can't be doing what you ought not to be doing?

REMEMBER THE FOUR STEPS OF RESTORATION:
1. Confidence in the love of God regardless of our sin
2. Confession of our sins to God
3. Cleansing from God
4. Consecration back to God – Get back to serving God

Don't get the idea that because you can be cleansed it makes no difference whether you sin. Just as surely as you put your hand on a hot stove and get burned, if you sin, you are bound to suffer! But thank God for His wonderful, marvelous, matchless grace that forgives and restores the sinning Christian.

CHAPTER 29

FORGIVENESS, WHO ME?

Matthew 18:21-35 — [21] Then Peter came to Him (Jesus) and said, "Lord, how often shall my brother sin against me, and I forgive him? Up to seven times?" [22]Jesus said to him, "I do not say to you, up to seven times, but up to seventy times seven. [23]Therefore the kingdom of heaven is like a certain king who wanted to settle accounts with his servants. [24]And when he had begun to settle accounts, one was brought to him who owed him 10,000 talents (10 million dollars). [25]But as he was not able to pay, his master commanded that he be sold, with his wife and children and all that he had, and that payment be made. [26]The servant therefore fell down before him, saying, "Master, have patience with me, and I will pay you all." [27]Then the master of that servant was moved with compassion, released him, and forgave him the debt. [28]But that servant went out and found one of his fellow servants who owed him 100 denarii (2 thousand dollars); and he laid hands on him and took him by the throat, saying, "Pay me what you owe!" [29]So his fellow servant fell down at his feet and begged him, saying; "Have patience with me, and I will pay you all." [30]And he would not, but went and threw him into prison till he should pay the debt. [31]So when his fellow servant saw what had been done, they were very grieved, and came and told their master all that had been done. [32]Then his master, after he had called him, said to him, "You wicked servant! I forgave you all that debt because you

begged me. ³³Should you not also have had compassion on your fellow servant, just as I had pity on you?" ³⁴And his master was angry and delivered him to the torturers until he should pay all that was due to him. ³⁵"So My heavenly Father also will do to you if each of you, from his heart, does not forgive his brother his trespasses."

"To forgive is to set a prisoner free, and to discover that the prisoner is you!"

To understand what God in Christ did for us, and then to refuse to forgive those who have wronged us is to be like the wicked, ungrateful servant of this text. Most people dealing with unforgiveness base their grudge, their offense, on what someone did to them or said to them. Forgiveness is the act of setting someone free who has wrong you. All of us, at one time or another, have been forgiven, or granted forgiveness. There is a temptation, however, to hold on to a grudge thus allowing bitterness to set in. The result of such bitterness is to become unforgiving. Unforgiveness is a bondage that stifles our ability to love and accept those that we know in our hearts most deserve our love. It is a bondage that chokes out the abundant life Christ, promised to those who would believe.

Forgiveness involves 3 elements:
1. Injury (what someone said or did to you)
2. Debt (resulting from the injury) - "He'll pay for this"
3. Cancellation of the debt

When we refuse to forgive others, there is a sense in which we hold them hostage. When a person is taken hostage on the international scene, the abductors usually want something. It may be money, weapons, or the release of prisoners. Their message is, "If you give us what we want, we will give you back what we have taken." There is always some type of condition; a ransom of some sort. When we refuse to forgive others for a wrong done to us, by them, we are saying the same thing. But instead of holding people hostage until we get our demands, we withhold love, acceptance, respect, service, kindness, patience, etc.

Matthew 18:21-35 describes quite a contrast of terms: Anger vs. Compassion, Forgiveness vs. Unforgiveness and Prison vs. Release.

Forgiveness reflects the highest human virtue, because it so clearly reflects the character of Christ. A person who forgives is a person who emulates godly character.

1. THE DEPTH OF FORGIVENESS: Matthew 18: 21-22

> *²¹Then Peter came to Him (Jesus) and said, "Lord, how often shall my brother sin against me, and I forgive him? Up to seven times?" ²²Jesus said to him, **"I do not say to you, up to seven times, but up to seventy times seven.***

Peter is trying to calculate things that don't seem to add up. How many times do I need to forgive somebody before I can make them pay what they owe me? Jesus has a different idea of the value of forgiveness. Jesus is about to teach Peter that he needs more than a calculator, he needs a change of thinking in his understanding of God's love and forgiveness.

21) Jewish tradition taught that we forgive three times. Peter doubled the number and added one for good measure. 22) Speaks of the immeasurable and unlimited terms of grace: 70 x 7 = 490 times. By the time we have forgiven a brother that many times, we are in the habit of forgiving. When we think of the depth of God's forgiveness, we realize that our forgiveness of others should be immeasurable.

2. THE DESCRIPTION OF FORGIVENESS: Matthew 18: 23-27

> *²³Therefore the <u>kingdom of heaven</u> is like a certain king who wanted to settle accounts with his servants. ²⁴And when he had begun to settle accounts, one was brought to him who owed him 10,000 talents ($10,000,000). ²⁵But as he was not able to pay, his master commanded that he be sold, with his wife and children and all that he had, and that payment be made. ²⁶The servant therefore fell down before him, saying, "Master, have patience with me, and I will pay you all." ²⁷Then the master of that servant was moved with compassion, released him, and forgave him the debt.*

NOTE: *"The kingdom of heaven" - Life in the kingdom; The kingdom life, The Christian life.*

"10,000 talents" - In the economy of that day, a man would have to work 20 years to earn one talent. In terms of buying power today, probably equivalent to our 10 million dollars. The talent was the highest known denomination of currency in the ancient Roman Empire and 10,000 was the highest number for which the Greek language had for a particular word. The amount was so enormous that it was on the borderline of what the ancient mind-set could have conceived. What is Jesus' point? The number is so vast, an uncountable amount; countless, incalculable, an un-payable debt. The un-payable debt represents the debt for sin that every person owes God. There is a song that says? **" I owed a debt I could not pay, He paid a debt He did not owe."**

SPECIAL NOTE: We can view our sin as 100 denarii ($2,000) sin and view the one who sinned against us as 10,000 talent ($10,000,000) sin. 100 denarii is about 3 month's wages. Contrasting the $2,000 debt compared to the $10,000,000 debt, as great as that is, is nothing compared to what we've been forgiven by Christ!

We do not truly grasp the gospel (good news) of Jesus Christ until we see that our sin against a holy God is a far greater injustice than anything that could be done to us. We must see ourselves in the shoes of the $10-million-dollar debt. The appreciation of a massive debt forgiven (our sin against a holy God) forms the bases and starting point for our forgiveness of one another's much smaller $2-thousand-dollar debt. Without understanding the depth of our sin against God and the riches of His forgiveness toward us, we will never be able to forgive others. In forgiveness, Jesus paid (absorbed) my debt (the debt that I was unable to pay). In the Greek culture a handwritten certificate of debt was nailed to the prisoner's cell door so that everyone knew the offense he had committed. He could not be released until the penalty for that offence had been paid. When a person was being crucified, similarly, the capital offence they had committed was written and nailed to the cross above their heads. They only way they could pay their debt was the giving of their life. We, like they, have all committed a capital offence. The Bible says, in Romans 3:23 and elsewhere, that we all have sinned, and the wages of sin is death. We owed the $10 million dollars, a debt that we could not pay. Christ took our place on the cross and thus paid our debt for us, freeing us from our penalty of sin. When we accept what He has done for us and receive Him into our lives as the Lord and Savior of our life, He forgives us and grants us eternal life in Heaven.

This story in Matthew ends with a somber warning.

> *Matthew 18:34-35 – ³⁴And his master was angry and delivered him to the torturers until he should pay all that was due to him. ³⁵"So My heavenly Father also will do to you if each of you, from his heart, does not forgive his brother his trespasses."*

Our Lord promises chastening (disciplining) until we are willing to forgive others.

3. **THE CONTRAST IN DEBT**
    Contrast your sin against the sins that others have committed against you. "The $2,000 debt could be carried in one pocket. The $10,000,000 debt would take an army of about 8,600 soldiers to carry. Each one would need to carry a sack of 60 lbs. in weight and would form, at a distance of a yard apart, a line 5 miles long." *Nothing that we have to forgive can ever faintly or remotely compare with what we have been forgiven.*

4. **FORGIVENESS FACTS**
    Forgiveness must be given (granted), not earned. Forgiveness is submitting in faith to truth, not to the flesh. Forgiven sinners forgive sin.

    1. Choose, by an act of your will to forgive, once and for all, the person who offended you.
    2. Release the person from the debt. Unlock the prison doors with the key of forgiveness.
    3. When you release the person from the debt owed to you, you actually free yourself from prison. You are releasing yourself from the prison doors of grudge, bitterness, unforgiveness, and bondage.

4. Once you have forgiven the offender, you are able to love and live the abundant life that Christ promised to those who would believe.

5. In most cases, the offender is not suffering. The offended goes through life, day by day, being hurt all over again with every remembrance of the wrong done to them. When you release the person who offended you, you are, in essence, releasing yourself from your own bondage.

5. REMEMBER

Remember that you are loved! Christ knows what has been done to offend you and He wants the best for you. When we obey Him, and forgive the offender, it doesn't mean that the offender goes free. It means that we go free.

Christ will never let a wrong go unpunished! The offender will get what is coming to them, either in this world or the next. So, let Christ handle the situation and free yourself from the bondage of unforgiveness!

CHAPTER 30

I CAN DO ALL THINGS THROUGH CHRIST WHO STRENGTHENS ME

Philippians 4:13

Philippians 4:13 – I can do all things through Christ who strengthens me.

Is this a true statement? Can we really do all things through Christ who strengthens us? Does God grant us super-human abilities to accomplish anything we can imagine or did the Apostle Paul have something else in mind when he gave us this verse? Let me give you four examples of things you cannot do.

1. With your nose pinched closed and your mouth closed tight, hum the tune to 'Jesus Loves Me.'

2. With your right hand out in front of you, and your elbow bent, rotate your arm in a clockwise direction. Now rotate your right foot on the floor in a clockwise direction. Now, reverse the direction of your hand only while keeping your foot going in a clockwise direction.

3. Sit in your chair with your arms folded across your chest and your back straight. Now stand up without leaning forward.

4. *Hebrews 11:6 – Without faith it is impossible to please God.* Please God without faith. Please God by complaining and always looking

around for things that are wrong. You can't do it and you're going to make yourself miserable trying to do it.

To get the jest of what Paul was saying here let's keep the scriptures in context. I think it's important for us to remember that when Paul wrote this letter he was in prison in Rome. And from his prison cell he tells us that he can do all things through Christ who gives him strength. What did he mean by that?

> *Philippians 4:1 – Therefore, my beloved and longed-for brethren, my joy and crown, stand fast in the Lord, beloved.*

How do we "stand fast in the Lord?" The way to stand fast or firm is to keep our eyes on Christ, to remember that this world (in its present form) is not our home. Focus our attention on the fact that Christ will bring everything under His control.

> *Philippians 4:2-3 – I implore Euodia and I implore Syntyche to be of the same mind in the Lord. And I urge you also, true companion, help these women who labored with me in the gospel, with Clement also, and the rest of my fellow workers, whose names are in the Book of Life.*

Notice that Paul did not warn the Philippian church of any doctrinal errors. They apparently had the truth of the gospel down. But he did address some relational problems. These two women had been workers for Christ in the church. Their broken relationship was no small matter because many had become believers through their efforts.

It is possible to believe in Christ, work hard for his kingdom, and yet have broken relationships with others who are committed to the same cause. But there is no excuse for remaining un-reconciled. There is no excuse for not working together in unity and harmony. If a church is to grow; the members must have a positive attitude, and everyone must do their part in the ministry.

How would you like for your name to be recorded in the Bible and the only thing recorded would be about how you couldn't get along with someone in the church.

> *Philippians 4:4 — Rejoice in the Lord always. Again, I say, "rejoice"!*

It seems strange that a man in prison would be telling a church to rejoice. But Paul's attitude teaches us an important lesson. Our outward circumstances do not have to reflect our inner attitudes. Paul was full of joy because he knew that no matter what happened to him, Jesus was with him. Several times in this letter, Paul urged the Philippians to be joyful. It's easy to get discouraged about unpleasant circumstances. We also get discouraged when we take unimportant events too seriously. If you haven't been joyful lately, you may be looking at life from the wrong perspective.

> *Philippians 4:5 — Let your gentleness be known to all men. The Lord is at hand.*

We are to be gentle (reasonable, fair minded, charitable) to those outside the church as well as to believers. This means we are not to seek revenge against those who treat us unfairly. Nor are we to be overly vocal about our personal rights or the things that bother us the most.

> *Philippians 4:6-7 – Be anxious for nothing, but in everything by prayer and supplication, with thanksgiving, let your requests be made known to God; and the peace of God, which surpasses all understanding, will guard your hearts and minds through Christ Jesus.*

Imagine never being "anxious" about anything! It seems like an impossibility. We have worries on the job. We have worries in our homes. We have worries in our schools. Paul's advice is to turn our worries into prayers. Do you want to worry less? Then pray more! Whenever you start to worry, stop and pray. God's peace is different from the world's peace!

> *John 14:27 – Peace I leave with you, My peace I give to*
> *you; not as the world gives do I give to you. Let not your*
> *heart be troubled, neither let it be afraid.*

True peace is not found in positive thinking, in absence of conflict, or in good feelings. It comes from knowing that God is in control. Our citizenship in Heaven is secured, our destiny is set, and we can have victory over sin. Let God's peace guard your heart against anxiety.

> *Philippians 4:8 – Finally, brethren, whatever things are*
> *true, whatever things are noble, whatever things are*
> *just, whatever things are pure, whatever things are*
> *lovely, whatever things are of good report, if there is*
> *any virtue and if there is anything praiseworthy – med-*
> *itate on these things.*

What we put into our minds determines what comes out in our words and actions. Paul tells us to program our minds with thoughts that are true, noble, right, just, pure, lovely, of good report, virtuous, and praiseworthy. Do you have problems with impure thoughts and daydreams? Examine what you are putting into your mind through television, internet, books, conversations, movies, and magazines. Replace harmful input with wholesome material. Above all, read God's Word and pray. Ask God to help you focus your mind on what is good and pure. It takes practice, but it can be done.

> *Philippians 4:9 – The things which you learned and*
> *received and heard and saw in me, these do, and the*
> *God of peace will be with you.*

It is not enough to hear or read the Word of God, or even to know it well. We must also put it into practice. How easy it is to listen to a sermon and forget what the preacher said. How easy it is to read the Bible and not think about how to live differently. Exposure to God's Word is not enough. It must lead to obedience. *James 1:22 – Be ye doers of the Word, and not hearers only, deceiving your own selves.*

> *Philippians 4:10-13 – But I rejoiced in the Lord greatly*
> *that now at last your care for me has flourished again;*
> *though you surely did care, but you lacked opportunity.*

> *Not that I speak in regard to need, for I have learned in whatever state I am, to be content; I know how to be abased, and I know how to abound. Everywhere and in all things, I have learned both to be full and to be hungry, both to abound and to suffer need. I can do all things through Christ who strengthens me.*

Are you content in any circumstances you face? Paul knew how to be content whether he had plenty or whether he was in need. The secret was drawing on Christ's power for strength. Do you have great needs or are you discontent because you don't have everything you want? If you always want more, ask God to remove that desire and teach you contentment in every circumstance. He will supply all your needs, but in a way that He knows is best for you.

Paul was content because he could see life from God's point of view. He focused on what he was supposed to do, not what he felt he should have. Paul had his priorities straight, and he was grateful for everything God had given him. Often the desire for more or better possessions is really a longing to fill an empty place in a person's life.

To what are you drawn when you feel empty inside? How can you find true contentment? The answer lies in your perspective, your priorities, and your source of power. So, Can We Really Do All Things? The power we receive, through the Holy Spirit when we receive Christ as our Lord and Savior, is sufficient to do His will and to face whatever comes our way when we are committed to do His will no matter come what may.

CHAPTER 31

THE TRANSFIGURATION

Matthew 17:1-13

Days before Jesus crucifixion there was a turning point in His ministry. He began to give less and less instructions to the multitudes and more instruction and training to his twelve disciples. What was the turning point? The transfiguration. A transformation. Transfigure comes from the Greek word metamorphoo from where we get the English word metamorphosis. When a tadpole turns into a frog or a caterpillar turns into a butterfly it goes through the process of metamorphosis; a complete change in appearance. A mysterious change in appearance came over Christ at His transfiguration. In like manner when we conform our lives spiritually and morally into the likeness of Christ we too undergo a change.

> *2 Corinthians 3:18a – But we all, with unveiled face, beholding as in a mirror the glory of the Lord, are being transformed into the image of Christ.*
>
> *Romans 12:1-2a – I beseech you therefore, brethren, by the mercies of God, that you present your bodies a living sacrifice, holy, acceptable to God, which is your reasonable service, and be not conformed to this world, but be transformed by the renewing of your mind.*

From the time of Jesus transfiguration, He was obsessed by the necessity of going to Jerusalem to die. There is no interpretation for the transfiguration, so we must look to the broader context. What was the transfiguration really all about? What lessons can we learn from the transfiguration? How can we apply these lessons to our life?

There is a logical connection to an event that happened six days prior to the transfiguration with the transfiguration itself. It happened in the region known as Caesarea Philippi.

> *Matthew 16:13-16, 21-23 – When Jesus came into the region of Caesarea Philippi, He asked His disciples, saying,* **"Who do men say that I, the Son of Man, am?"** *So, they said, "Some say John the Baptist, some Elijah, and others Jeremiah or one of the prophets." He said to them,* **"But who do you say that I am?"** *Simon Peter answered and said, "You are the Christ, the Son of the living God." From that time Jesus began to show to His disciples that He must go to Jerusalem and suffer many things from the elders and chief priests and scribes, and be killed, and be raised the third day. Then Peter took Him aside and began to rebuke Him, saying,* **"Far be it from You, Lord; this shall not happen to You!"** *But Jesus turned and said to Peter,* **"Get behind Me, Satan! You are an offense to Me, for you are not mindful of the things of God, but the things of men."**

The announcement of Jesus that He must go to Jerusalem to die and then be raised from the dead shocked the disciples beyond measure. For the next six days Peter and Jesus didn't speak to each other. Tensions were running high. Of the week that followed nothing is recorded. Jesus new that some new measure of convincing the disciples, of the necessity of the cross, was called for. This time instead of telling the disciples Himself, He would call in the big guns. He would pick three of the disciples, Peter, James, and John and lead them on top of a high mountain. Christ chose a mountain! A place for He, Peter, James, & John to be alone with the Father.

Lesson number one. If you want to befriend God, you must get alone with God. If you want to find intimacy with God and a renewed strength from God, you must get alone with God. On numerous occasions Jesus set the example by getting alone with the Father. If we want to have a transforming fellowship with God, we must not only get alone with

Him, but our hearts must ascend to Him. We must seek things above. *Revelation 4:1 says "Come Up Here"*

THE WITNESSES OF THE TRANSFIGURATION

He took with Him Peter, James, and John. He took three! A competent number to testify of what they saw. The Bible says, *"Out of the mouth of 2 or 3 witnesses every word shall be established."* Christ makes his appearance certain enough, but not too common. Not to all the people, but to His witnesses.

> *Acts 10:39-41 – And we are witnesses of all things which He did, both in the land of the Jews and in Jerusalem, whom they killed by hanging on a tree. Him God raised up on the third day, and showed Him openly, <u>not to all the people, but to witnesses</u> chosen before by God, even to us who ate and drank with Him after He arose from the dead.*

He took these three because they were the chief of His disciples. They were His favorites. Of all the disciples, we remember these three more than all the others. Peter, James, and John! Children's songs have been written about these three. They were the only disciples allowed into the house to see the resurrection of Jairus daughter. Christ, in His glory, prepared them to suffer with Him in this world knowing the glory of the next world. History tells us that Peter was crucified upside down after being forced to watch his wife's crucifixion. James had a sword run through him. John was exiled to an island as an old man to work in a rock quarry.

THE MANNER OF THE TRANSFIGURATION

He was transfigured before them. The substance of His body remained the same, but the appearance of it was greatly altered. He took on the glory that He had with the Father before the foundation of the world. His pre-incarnate glory!

> *John 1:14 And the Word became flesh and dwelt among us, and we beheld His glory, the glory as of the only begotten of the Father, full of grace and truth.*

> *John 17:5 And now, O Father, glorify Me together with Yourself, with the glory which I had with You before the world was.*

He took on the glory that will be His when He returns to earth as King of Kings and Lord of Lords.

> *Revelation 1:12-16 — Then I turned to see the voice that spoke with me, and having turned I saw seven golden lampstands, and in the midst of the seven lampstands* <u>One like the Son of Man,</u> *clothed with a garment down to the feet and girded about the chest with a golden band. His head and hair were white like wool, as white as snow, and His eyes like a flame of fire; His feet were like fine brass, as if refined in a furnace, and His voice as the sound of many waters; He had in His right hand seven stars, out of His mouth went a sharp two-edged sword, and* <u>His countenance was like the sun shining in its strength.</u>

The great truth is that God is light.

> *John 1:4-5 — In Him was life, and* <u>the life was the light of men.</u> *And the light shines in the darkness, and the darkness did not comprehend it.*

The great truth is that God dwells in light.

> *1 Timothy 6:16a — Christ, who alone has immortality,* <u>dwelling in unapproachable light.</u>

The great truth is that God covers Himself with light.

> *Psalm 104:1-2a — Bless the Lord, O my soul! O Lord my God, You are very great: You are clothed with honor and majesty,* <u>who cover Yourself with light as with a garment.</u>

On the first day of creation God said *let there be light and there was light.* But the sun wasn't created until the 4th day. In Heaven, the Bible says in Revelation that there will be no need of the sun for God will be its light. *God is light and in Him is no darkness at all.* Therefore, when Christ would appear in the form of God on top of the mountain, he appeared in light.

His Face did shine as the sun. The face is the principal part of the body. The part by which we are known. Such brightness was put on the face of Christ. The face that would later be slapped and spit upon. The face where blood would poor as great drops of sweat in the Garden of Gethsemane. The face where blood would run down from the crown of many thorns. It shone as the sun in all its brightness for He is the Son of righteousness, the light of the world! His face just suddenly, instantly broke out as it were from behind a dark cloud. His clothes became as white as light. All His body was altered, as His face was. Beams of light darting from every part of His body, coming through His clothes, made even His clothes white as light.

> Mark 9:3 – *His clothes became shining, exceedingly white, like snow, such as no launderer on earth can whiten them.*

HIS COMPANIONS AT THE TRANSFIGURATION
Gloried saints, Moses and Elijah, were at the transfiguration talking with Him; a resemblance of Christ's Kingdom made up of saints in heaven and saints on earth. We see then that Moses and Elijah, while not alive on earth anymore, never-the-less are still alive. Moses died and was buried and is therefore representative of those who have died in Jesus and will be resurrected with their new bodies at Christ's second coming. Elijah didn't die but was translated. He represents those who will be alive at the return of Christ and are caught up in the air to be with Christ forever. Moses and Elijah appeared to the three disciples. They saw them and heard them talk and they knew them to be Moses and Elijah. The Bible says that glorified saints will know one another in heaven. They talked with Christ!

THE GREAT PLEASURE AND SATISFACTION THAT THE DISCIPLES HAD AT THE TRANSFIGURATION
Peter, as usual, spoke for the rest. *"Lord, it is good for us to be here."* Though upon a high mountain, which was rough and unpleasant, bleak and cold, yet it is good to be here. The person who loves Christ and

loves to be with Him loves to go and tell Him so. *"Lord it is good for us to be here."*

Lesson number two. It is good to be where Christ is, wherever that may be. It is good and pleasant to hear Christ talk with Moses & Elijah; to see how all the institutions of the law and all the predictions of the prophets point to Christ and were fulfilled in Him. *"It is good to be here"*

They had a desire to stay there! *"Let us make here three tabernacles."* Peter thought this mountain was a fine spot of ground to build upon. He was for making tabernacles there as Moses in the wilderness made a tabernacle for the Shechinah glory of God. Here the authorities could not touch Jesus. Here He would be safe from the angry crowds. Here He would be safe from the beatings. Here, Jesus would be safe from the crucifixion! He wouldn't build a tabernacle for himself or his fellow disciples. He would build three tabernacles, one for Christ, one for Moses, and one for Elijah. He would be content to lie in the open air, on the cold ground, just to be close to Christ. Just to know that His master was safe was good enough for him.

> *Matthew 16:22 – "Far be it from You, Lord; this shall not happen to you!"*

THE VOICE FROM HEAVEN

There was a cloud! We often find in the Old Testament that a cloud was the visible token of God's presence. He came upon Mt. Sinai in a cloud. He came to Moses in a cloud. He took possession of the tabernacle in the wilderness in a cloud. It was a bright cloud! In the Old Testament, under the law, it was commonly a thick and dark cloud that God made his appearance in.

> *Exodus 19:16 – "He came down upon Mt. Sinai in a thick cloud."*

> *1 Kings 8:12 – "The Lord said He would dwell in the dark cloud."*

But now God appears in a bright cloud; a cloud of light, love, and liberty! The cloud overshadowed them! The cloud was intended as a protection to the disciples. To protect them from the light emanating from Christ lest they, like the apostle Paul be blinded by the light. There came a voice out of the cloud! It was the voice of God the Father! There was no thunder, no lightning, no trumpet blast as there was when the law was given to Moses, but only a voice. Moses and Elijah were witnesses, that in these last days God has spoken to us by His Son, in another way than he spoke to them formerly.

> *2 Peter 1:16b-18 – "We were eyewitnesses of His majesty. For He received from God the Father honor and glory when such a voice came to Him from the Excellent Glory: This is My beloved Son, in whom I am well pleased. And we heard this voice which came from heaven when we were with Him on the holy mountain."*

The Bible says that *"Faith comes by hearing."* The voice said, *"This is my beloved Son, in whom I am well pleased!"* These were the same words spoken at Christ baptism. This is the best news that has come to this earth since man sinned! *"This is my beloved Son, in whom I am well pleased!"* God was in Christ reconciling the world to Himself.

What God has spoken once, no twice, no doubt He expects us to sit up and take notice of it. It was spoken at His baptism because He was entering upon His temptation and the beginning of His public ministry. It was spoken at the transfiguration because He was entering His sufferings. He was on His way to the cross!

Lesson number 3. We must hear Him and believe Him! We must hear Him and be ruled by Him! We must hear Him and obey Him! God said, "Hear Him, hear my Son, listen to Him for He has the words of life!" This voice from heaven has made all the sayings of Christ as authentic as if they had been spoken out of a cloud. Moses said before He died *"A prophet will come after me, like unto me, Him shall you hear."* Deuteronomy 18:15 – see Acts 3:22

A cloud covered them! They were told not to look at Him but to hear Him! Their sight of His glory was soon intercepted by the cloud. Their business, likes ours, was and is to hear Him!

> *2 Corinthians 5:7 – "For we walk by faith, not by sight."*

231

Romans 10:17 – "Faith comes by hearing and hearing by the Word of God"

Moses and Elijah had been talking with Christ and the disciples probably wanted to know all that they said. But God said no! Hear Him, and that is enough! Don't be upset that Moses & Elijah stayed such a short time with you. Hear Christ and you will not want Moses & Elijah!

The voice frightened them, but Christ lifts them up in His tenderness and comforts them. Notice what Christ does. He touched them, the touch of Christ. He told them to get up. He told them not to be afraid. Notice that after God the Father had told them to listen to His Son that the sons first words were: *"Get Up, "Do not be Afraid!"* They get up, they open their eyes, they look around, Moses and Elijah were gone. The light radiating from Christ was gone, veiled until another time!

They had hoped that Christ would rule and reign as King of Kings and Lord of Lords. Jesus told them He would suffer many things, be crucified, and rise again on the third day. Peter rebuked Him just a few days ago for saying this. They hadn't spoken to each other for six days over this rift. Jesus had to convince them of the necessity of the cross! And so, He takes them to the top of a high mountain. God the Father says, *"Listen to My Son!"*

THEY CAME DOWN FROM THE MOUNTAIN
We must come down from the mountain! As great as worship is, as great as Bible study and fellowship is, we must come down from the mountain, even though it is *"Good to be Here."* Jesus said, *"The Harvest is plenteous, but the laborers are few. Pray that God will send laborers into the harvest."*

Notice when they came down that they talked with Christ. We must keep our line of communication open by confessed sin, repentance and forgiveness. Notice also that when they came down from the mountain that Christ came with them. We have a savior that will never leave us! Christ said, *"I will never leave you nor forsake you."* One day we will go to that mountain of God! Like Peter, we will say *"It is Good to be Here!"* But for now, there's work to be done and we must come down from the mountain and into the harvest field.

232

Lesson number 4. We must take up our cross and follow Christ! Wherever He Leads I'll go! Wherever He leads I'll go. I'll follow my Christ who loves me so. Wherever He leads I'll go!

CHAPTER 32

ARE YOU A BLESSED PERSON, ARE YOU A BLESSING TO OTHERS

In the Bible there are 544 uses of various forms of the word bless. To bless meant to fill with benefits either as an end in itself or to make the object blessed a source of further blessing for others; to fill others with benefits. Blessing can also mean to fill with honor and good words. Thus, we can bless God and bless others by our good words. In the Old Testament to be blessed by God was considered the essential ingredient of a successful and satisfying life. The word blessed occurs 50 times in the New Testament and means to be fortunate or happy. It is used most often with Jesus in His Sermon on the Mount on Beatitudes.

> *Matthew 5:3-11 – Blessed are the poor in spirit for theirs is the kingdom of heaven. Blessed are they that mourn for they shall be comforted. Blessed are the meek for they shall inherit the earth. Blessed are they which do hunger and thirst after righteousness for they shall be filled. Blessed are the merciful for they shall obtain mercy. Blessed are the pure in heart for they shall see God. Blessed are the peacemakers for they shall be called the children of God. Blessed are they which are persecuted for righteousness sake for theirs is the kingdom of heaven. Blessed are ye when men shall revile you and persecute you and shall say all manner of evil against you falsely for my sake. Rejoice and be exceedingly glad for great is your reward in*

234

heaven for so persecuted they the prophets which were before you.

Nowhere in the Beatitudes does Jesus speak of having a lot of money or a lot of things as a blessing. The blessing seems to come from knowing God and knowing that one day we will inherit the kingdom of heaven which always includes the New Heaven and the New Earth. As the scriptures say, "What does it really profit a man to gain the whole world and lose his own soul?"

Often when I am praying I ask God to bless me and that I will be a blessing to Him. What is it that I can give to God today that He doesn't already have? How can I bless Him? How can I fill Him with benefits? I can give Him my heart and life in total surrender. I can be kind to others. I can bless God by blessing others. *Jesus said if you give a cup of cold water to someone in my name, you are blessing not only the person; but you are also blessing God.* I can share God's good news with others.

What is the Good News that I can share with others?
We have always thought of the Gospel as good news. In fact, the Greek word evangelion, which is translated gospel, literally means 'good news'. Certainly, the fact that Jesus Christ died and rose again to give us salvation and victory over sin is good news. However, for many people in the world, the gospel will be extremely bad news! They will discover in the end that Jesus really is the standard of judgment for whether or not one receives salvation and enters into eternal life in heaven.

> *Jesus Himself said "I am the way, and the truth, and the life. No one comes to the Father except through me."* (John 14:6) The Apostle Paul testified of that day *"on that day, when, according to my gospel, God judges the secrets of men by Christ Jesus.* (Romans 2:16)

For those who reject Jesus, the gospel is very bad news because it describes who joins God in His eternal kingdom and who spends eternity in Hell.

How can we bless God today and throughout the year? Telling others, the good news of Jesus Christ, is certainly one way.

235

HOW ARE WE BLESSED BY GOD?

> *Romans 4:6-8 – Even as David also described the blessedness of the man, unto whom God imputes righteousness without works, saying, blessed are they whose iniquities are forgiven, and whose sins are covered. Blessed is the man to whom the Lord will not impute sin.*

> *Psalms 32:1-2 – Blessed is he whose transgression is forgiven, whose sin is covered. Blessed is the man unto whom the Lord imputes not iniquity, and, in whose spirit, there is no guile.*

The very fact that we are forgiven of sin and have a home waiting for us in heaven is a tremendous blessing of God. We receive this benefit not by working for it but by receiving it from God through His grace.

WHAT IS THIS BLESSEDNESS (THIS BENEFIT) THAT GOD SPEAKS OF?

> *Romans 5:1 – Therefore, being justified by faith, we have <u>Peace with God</u> through our Lord Jesus Christ. Acts 20:21 makes it clear that without repentance and faith in Christ there is no salvation. Luke 13:3 "Except you repent you shall all likewise perish"*

The blessing received from God is <u>Peace with God</u> through our repentance and faith in Christ. This is made possible because of God's love for us. His good news!

> *Romans 5:8 – But God commended (demonstrated) His love toward us, in that, while we were yet sinners, Christ died for us.* (In our place)

> *Romans 5:9 – Much more then, being now justified by his blood, we shall be <u>saved from wrath</u> through Him.*

Another tremendous blessing, we receive from God, pertains to this Peace with God. There is wrath coming from God and we will be spared the <u>Wrath of God</u>. What a blessing!

As we go through the year, let us be ever mindful that no matter what may happen to the economy, what may happen to our health or our health coverage, whatever may come our way, whether good or bad, that we are a very blessed people to have Peace with God. Jesus made that possible when He paid the sin debt at the cross. His blood cleanses us from past, present and even future sins. All of our sins were in fact future when Jesus gave Himself on the cross for us.

> *1 John 1:7,9 – If we walk in the light, as He is in the light, we have fellowship one with another, and the blood of Jesus Christ, His Son, cleanses us from all sin. If we confess our sins, He is faithful and just to forgive us our sins, and to cleanse us from all unrighteousness.*

1. First, be sure that you have a living relationship with God through the Lord Jesus Christ.

2. Second, pursue holiness. Holiness is what God wants from His people. Personal holiness is not keeping a long list of do's and don'ts. It is knowing the will of God and doing it. Daily submit to the Lordship of Jesus Christ. Daily find God's will and direction for your life. Discover God's will for each day. Obey what you discover. If we all will do this, we will be a very blessed people.

OBEDIENCE LEADS TO BLESSINGS

> *Acts 1:6-11 – When they therefore were come together, they asked of Him, saying, Lord, will you at this time restore again the kingdom to Israel? And He said unto them, "It is not for you to know the times or the seasons, which the Father has put in His own power. But you shall receive power, after the Holy Spirit is come upon you; and you shall be witnesses unto me both in Jerusalem, and in all Judea, and in Samaria, and unto the uttermost parts of the earth." And when He had spoken these words, while they beheld, He was taken up; and a cloud received Him out of their sight. And while they looked steadfastly toward heaven as He went up, behold, two men stood by them in white apparel; which also said, you men of Galilee, why do*

you stand gazing up into heaven? This same Jesus, who is taken up from you into heaven, shall so come in like manner as you have seen him go into heaven.

As we back up from the ascension to the resurrection let me point out two geographic points of interest.

Matthew 28:1-7 – At the end of the Sabbath, as it began to dawn toward the first day of the week, Mary Magdalene, and the other Mary, came to see his tomb. And, behold, there was a great earthquake; for the angel of the Lord descended from heaven, and came and rolled back the stone from the door; and sat upon it. His countenance was like lightning and his clothes were white as snow; And for fear of him the keepers did shake and became as dead men. And the angel answered and said unto the women; do not fear; for I know that you are seeking Jesus, who was crucified. He is not here; for He has risen, as He said. Come and see the place where the Lord lay. And go quickly and tell his disciples that He is risen from the dead; and, behold, He goes before you into Galilee; <u>there you shall see Him;</u> lo, I have told you.

YOU WILL SEE CHRIST WHEN YOU GO WHERE CHRIST IS AT

As an act of obedience, Christ told his disciples, through his angel, to meet him in Galilee. Now it is interesting to note that Galilee is some 90 miles from Jerusalem and they traveled primarily by foot in those days. But, did the disciples meet him in Galilee as the angel had instructed them?

Matthew 28: 16-20 – Then the eleven disciples went away into Galilee, into a mountain where Jesus had appointed them. And when they saw him, they worshipped him; but some doubted. And Jesus came and spoke unto them, saying, "All power is given unto me in heaven and in earth. Go ye therefore, and teach all nations, baptizing them in the name of the Father; and of the Son, and of the Holy Ghost; Teaching them to observe all things whatsoever I have commanded you;

> *and, lo, I am with you always, even unto the end of the world."*

Now I ask you, was this the end? Did Jesus ascend back to heaven at this point, from the top of a mountain in Galilee? The answer is no He did not. As a further act of obedience, He now tells them to meet him in Jerusalem, another 90-mile trek by foot!

> *Luke 24:46-51 – And He opened their understanding, that they might comprehend the Scriptures. Then He said to them, "Thus it is written, and thus it was necessary for the Christ to suffer and to rise from the dead the third day. And that repentance and remission of sins should be preached in His name to all nations, beginning at Jerusalem. And you are witnesses of these things. Behold, I send the Promise of My Father upon you; but tarry in the city of Jerusalem until you are endued with power from on high." <u>And He led them out as far as Bethany,</u> and <u>He lifted up His hands and blessed them.</u> Now it came to pass; while He blessed them, that He was parted from them and carried up into heaven.*

The point that I am making today is that total obedience, no matter what the cost, leads to blessings. Their obedience was tested in this manner. They were found ready and cheerful to obey their Lord in whatever command He might give them. If He asked them to walk 90 miles one way, meet Him on the top of a mountain, and then turn around and walk 90 miles back the other way, they were willing and ready to obey. What would we do if Jesus asked us to walk 90 miles and meet Him in a certain place and then turn around and walk 90 miles back the other way?

Many times, we want to be obedient in the larger things of life and we find the smaller things in life too menial a task for our character. However, Jesus said he who is greatest among you shall be your servant. Many times, we want to do great things for God when God can't even get us to do what He commanded us to do right before He left to go back to his home in heaven. What makes us think that God is going to bless us when we refuse to obey Him? Thank God that Christ is more faithful than we are, or we would never receive any blessings!

Exodus 24:7 – Then he took the Book of the Covenant and read in the hearing of the people. And they said, "All that the Lord has said we will do and be obedient."

2 Corinthians 2:9 – For to this end I also wrote that I might put you to the test, whether you are obedient in all things.

Philippians 2:1-8 – If there be therefore any consolation in Christ, if any comfort of love, if any fellowship of the Spirit, if any affection and compassion, fulfill ye my joy, that you be likeminded, having the same love, being of one accord, of one mind. Let nothing be done through strife or vainglory; but in lowliness of mind let each esteem others better than themselves. Do not merely look out for your own personal interests, but also for the interest of others. Let this mind be in you, which was also in Christ Jesus. Who, being in the form of God, thought it not robbery to be equal with God, but made himself of no reputation, and took upon Himself the form of a servant, and was made in the likeness of men. And being found in fashion as a man, He humbled himself, and became obedient unto death, even the death of the cross.

1 Peter 1:13-16 – Therefore, prepare your minds for action, keep sober in spirit, fix your hope completely on the grace to be brought to you at the revelation of Jesus Christ. As obedient children, do not be conformed to the former lusts, which were yours in your ignorance, but as He who called you is holy, you also be holy in all your conduct because it is written, be holy, for I am holy.

Hebrews: Forsake not the assembling of yourselves together as the manner of some is.

> *Malachi 3:10-12 — Bring ye all the tithes into the storehouse, that there may be meat in my house, and prove me now herewith, saith the Lord of hosts, if I will not open for you the windows of heaven, <u>and pour you out a blessing, that there shall not be room enough to receive it.</u> And I will rebuke the devourer for your sakes, and he shall not destroy the fruits of your ground; neither shall your vine cast her fruit before the time in the field, saith the Lord of hosts. <u>And all nations shall call you blessed; for you shall be a delightsome land, saith the Lord of hosts.</u>*

Do these scriptures really work? Are we blessed when we obey? When we put forth an effort to obey the great commandment, to love the Lord our God with all our heart mind and soul, and our neighbor as ourselves; when we put forth an effort to obey the great commission to go and tell others to repent and be reconciled with God; to reach out to a lost and dying world with the message of God's love and His salvation, will God bless us in our efforts? Will God bless us if we obey?

> *Acts 1:6a — Therefore, when they had <u>come together</u>. . .*

<u>They came together</u> at the appointed time to witness the ascension of our Lord Jesus Christ back to heaven. <u>They came together</u> as those that had consulted one another and agreed, as one, to obey their Lord. <u>They came together!</u>

> *Luke 24:50-51 — And He led them out as far as Bethany, and <u>He lifted up His hands and blessed them. Now it came to pass; while He blessed them,</u> that He was parted from them and carried up into heaven.*

Jesus went home! He now sits at the right hand of His Father interceding for His saints, for His brothers and sisters in Christ. <u>As He left He blessed them for their obedience.</u>

HOW DID HE BLESS THEM?

We sometimes have a very different idea of what a blessing is. When we receive something new or get some extra money in the mail we say "Boy, the Lord really blessed me." Did they go back to Jerusalem and say, "Boy I can't wait to see the new car the Lord blessed me with." No! What was the blessing? It was of the same type that Jacob blessed his sons with at his parting. It was the same type that Isaac blessed his son Jacob. You remember the story of how Jacob tricked his brother Esau out of the blessing. A blessing is not a blessing unless it is spoken. It is positive faith filled words about a person's future! <u>With our words we can either bless someone or curse them.</u>

> *James 3: 9-10 – With our tongue we bless our God and Father and with it we curse men, who have been made in the likeness of God. Out of the same mouth proceed blessing and cursing. My brothers and sisters in Christ, these things ought not be this way!*

> *Deuteronomy 30:19 – Today, I have given you the choice between life and death, <u>between blessing and curses</u>. I call on heaven and earth to witness the choice you make. Oh, that you would choose life, that you and your descendants might live!*

You may think there are times in your life when you are not blessed. You may think life is just too hard or you have too many problems. When you feel that way let me encourage you to remember the words to this great Hymn.

When upon life's billows you are tempest tossed, when you are discouraged, thinking all is lost, count your many blessings, name them one by one, and it will surprise you what the Lord hath done. Are you ever burdened with a load of care? Does the cross seem heavy you are called to bear? Count your many blessings, every doubt will fly, and you will be singing as the days go by. When you look at others with their lands and gold, think that Christ has promised you His wealth untold. Count your many blessings money cannot buy, your reward in heaven nor your home on high. So, amid the conflict, whether great or small, do not be discouraged; God is over all. Count your many blessings angels will attend, help and comfort give you to your journey's end. Count your blessings, name them one by one. Count your blessings, see what God hath done. Count your blessings, name them one by one. Count your many blessings, see what God hath done.

CHAPTER 33

PRONE TO WANDER

Luke 15:11-24

A re you at a point in your life when some of the following state-ments are true about you?

1. You can point to a time in your life when you were closer to God than you are now.
2. You know you should study your Bible and pray more, but you just don't have the desire.
3. You feel overwhelmed by the demands of work and family.
4. You feel guilty for thinking about money so much and God so little.
5. You find yourself repeating the same mistakes.
6. You wonder if your present problems are God's way of getting even with you.
7. You're filled with guilt over a past mistake and question whether God can ever forgive you.
8. You want to return to the kind of relationship you once enjoyed with God.

Most of us can remember a time when we felt closer to God than we do now. C.S. Lewis once said; "The road that most often leads a believer away from God is a gradual one, the gentle slope, the soft underfoot, without sudden turnings, without milestones, without signposts." We move away from God step by step, choice by choice, until one day we awaken in a distant country, far removed from the God we once knew.

Why is that?

A.W. Tozer once wrote: "Every farmer knows the hunger of the wilderness. That hunger which no modern farm machinery, no improved agricultural methods can quite destroy. No matter how well-prepared the soil, how well-kept the fences, how carefully painted the buildings, let the owner neglect for a while his prized and valued acres and they will revert again to the wilds and be swallowed by the jungle or the wasteland. The bias of nature is toward the wilderness, never toward the fruitful field." The same truth applies to our relationship with God. No matter how dramatic our conversion, no matter how sincere our intentions, no matter how saturated we are with doctrine, the bias of life pulls us away from God.

Many years ago, Jesus told a story about a son who allowed his *desire for material goods*, his *thirst for pleasure*, and his *drive for significance* to pull him away from his father. You know the story as "The Prodigal Son" and it's found in Luke chapter 15.

The son demanded his inheritance, departed from his father's home, and dissipated his wealth on wine and women. Only after experiencing a severe crisis did the son come to his senses and long to return to the security of his father's home. How would the father respond to his son's request for forgiveness? Could their relationship ever be the same again? Would the son suffer lasting consequences for his rebellion? What would keep the son from making the same mistake when he again grew tired of his father?

Although some use the prodigal son story to illustrate God's attitude toward non-Christians, I believe that the story best illustrates God's attitude toward those of us who have allowed our desire for: ***Money*** - ***Pleasure*** - and ***Ambition*** to slowly lure us away from our Father.

Using the prodigal son story as a backdrop, it is vitally important that we explore together the following:

1. How and why do we move away from God and enter the far country?
2. What is life really like in the far country?
3. How can we return to a vibrant relationship with our Heavenly Father?

While we may or may not have fallen into open rebellion against God, many of us have nevertheless grown cold in our faith and we wonder if we can ever reclaim the closeness to God that we once had.

Let me tell you about a man name Robert Robinson. Born in England during the 1700's, Robinson lost his father while just a boy. His mother, recognizing her inability to support her son, sent him to London to learn the barber trade. While there, Robinson became a Christian through George Whitefield's ministry and he dedicated his life to preaching the gospel. When he was only twenty-five, a prestigious Baptist church in Cambridge called Robinson to be its pastor. His fame spread rapidly, and his future seemed unlimited. But at the zenith of his ministry, Robinson fell into immorality and his star faded almost as quickly as it had appeared. Many years later, Robert Robinson was traveling by stagecoach and found himself seated next to a woman who was intently reading a passage from a book. The woman asked Robinson to read the passage and share his ideas about its meaning. Robinson read the first few lines. *"Come, Thou fount of every blessing, tune my heart to sing Thy grace. Streams of mercy, never ceasing, call for songs of loudest praise."*

Robinson looked away and quickly changed the subject. The woman, however, refused to let him off the hook and kept pressuring him for a response. Finally, Robinson broke down and replied, "Madam, I am the poor unhappy man who wrote that hymn many years ago, and I would give a thousand worlds if I had them to enjoy the feelings I had then." In that well-known hymn, Robert Robinson, either consciously or subconsciously, prophesied his own departure from the faith. *"Prone to wander, Lord, I feel it, Prone to leave the God I love; Here's my heart, O take and seal it; Seal it for thy courts above."*

Prone to wander. . .Prone to *leave* the God I love. Many of us have sung that song for so long that we're oblivious to its contradiction. Why would we ever desire to leave what we love? It doesn't make sense. Yet, the hymn writer says that we who genuinely love God also have a genuine desire to depart from Him.

We're prone to. . .
1. Fall into immoral relationships that destroy our families.
2. Go weeks and months at a time without talking to God.

3. Worship our possessions instead of our Heavenly Father.
4. Become obsessed with our jobs.
5. Renounce our entire belief system at the first hint of unjust suffering.

Why is that?

Why do we allow mundane attractions to so easily distract us from our pursuit of God and His Kingdom? Why, like the prodigal son, would we exchange our place of privilege in our Father's house for pig slop? The spirit of the "Prodigal Son," to some degree, can be found in all of us.

An Invisible Father

Robert Jeffress, the pastor at First Baptist Dallas, tells a story of when he was five years old. He says, "My father took me to the great State Fair of Texas, a fair with a midway so extraordinary that it was immortalized in the play and movie '*State Fair*'. As we were about to enter the midway, my dad left for the rest room, instructing me not to move. I stood there and waited for what seemed an eternity. But the appeal of the midway was too strong. The carnival music, the flashing lights, the screams of passengers on the roller coaster, lured me from my place of safety. Soon I was caught up in the crowd, far removed from my father. I'll never forget the terror of being surrounded by strangers and not knowing how to return to my Dad. Fortunately, a policeman found me and put me on the back of his three-wheel motorcycle to transport me to the Lost and Found area of the fair. We weaved through the midway crowd as I sat with my back against the officer, my feet dangling over the edge and my tears streaming down my face into the ice cream cone I was licking for comfort. As long as I live I will never forget how I felt when I spotted my dad frantically looking for me in the crowd. When his eyes connected with mine, he galloped toward the racing motorcycle. The policeman, oblivious to what was happening, didn't even notice when my dad reached out and grabbed me from the back of the motorcycle. Looking back on this frightening experience, my father recognized that he should never have left a five-year-old alone, even for a few moments. But who was responsible for my departure from my father? Certainly, I held the blame for disobeying my father's instructions and wandering away. Had a stranger kidnapped me, I would have suffered the consequences of my disobedience. But without the visible presence of my father to hold me in check, I couldn't resist the midway's attractions. Only the rare five-year-old could have resisted."

Our Heavenly Father has not abandoned His children! When Jesus left this earth, He left us with the Holy Spirit.

> John 14:16, 18 – "And I will ask the Father, and He will give you another Helper, that He may be with you forever. I will not leave you as orphans; I will come to you."

Nevertheless, the apostles enjoyed a spiritual advantage that we do not have. They saw, heard, and touched Jesus Christ, the physical manifestation of God. God hasn't shortchanged us in any way. He has given us His Holy Spirit to enlighten us, encourage us, and empower us to live obediently. Nevertheless, we find it easier to be lured away by the bells and whistles of the "midway" than to follow the quiet promptings of the invisible Spirit.

Perhaps you've wandered from God and you may wonder if you have any value with God. Are you still valuable to God? In his book *Meeting God at a Dead End*, Ron Mehl tells the story of Bob, a connoisseur of garage sales, who resides in Downey, California. One Saturday morning, Bob was at his last stop on his weekly tour of backyard boutiques when he noticed an old motorcycle in the owner's garage.

Bob asked the owner how much he would sell the bike for, but the owner tried to dissuade Bob from the purchase explaining that the motor was frozen and that restoring it would cost as much as a brand-new motorcycle. But Bob persisted, and the owner unloaded it for thirty-five dollars. A few days passed, and Bob finally found time to call the Harley Davidson Company to research the prices for new parts. Bob gave the sales person the bike's registration number and, after what seemed an interminable wait, the clerk returned to the phone. "Uh, sir. . .I'm going to have to call you back, okay? Could I get your full name, address, and phone number, please?" Bob gave the clerk the information but was concerned. Had his new-found treasure been involved in an accident, or worse, a crime? After a few days, Bob received a phone call from a man who introduced himself as an executive with Harley Davidson. The executive said, "Bob, I want you to do something for me. Take the seat off your bike and see if anything is written underneath. Would you do that for me, Bob?" Bob dutifully laid down the receiver, removed the seat from the bike, then returned to the phone as instructed. "Yes," Bob replied, "it does have something written there. It's engraved, and it says, THE KING." After a moment of silence, the executive said, "Bob, my boss has authorized me to offer you $300,000 for that motorcycle. How about it?" Bob was so startled he couldn't speak. "I'll have to think about it," he replied, and he hung up. The next day Bob received another phone call. Famed talk-show host and motorcycle enthusiast Jay Leno was on the other end of the line. "Bob," Jay said, "I've heard about your motorcycle and want to offer you $500,000 for it." You've probably guessed by now why everyone wanted that broken-down bucket of rust. The words 'THE KING' referred to the King of Rock and Roll himself, Elvis Presley. This motorcycle was worth an unbelievable amount of money, not because of its present condition, but because of the person who had once owned it.

Regardless of your present spiritual condition, the story of the prodigal son can remind you of your incredible value to God because you belong to Him! If you've repented of your sins, received Jesus Christ into your life, been born again by God's spirit; if you are a child of His that makes you <u>tremendously valuable</u> because of who you belong to.

No matter how far you've strayed, you have a loving Father who watches, waits, and works for your return. Today, if you've wandered from Him you can come home. You can come home to God. Take this truth home with you – ***<u>"No matter how far you may have drifted from God, He still loves you and longs for your return."</u>***

CHAPTER 34

THE BLUEPRINT FOR DESTRUCTION

How and why do we move away from God and enter the 'far country?' What is life really like in the 'far country?' How can we return to a vibrant relationship with our Heavenly Father?

Dr. Howard Hendricks tells of reading an article by General Douglas B. MacArthur, entitled "Requisites for Military Success." General MacArthur said that there were four ingredients necessary to win any battle; morale, strength, supply, and knowledge of the enemy. Of the last ingredient, MacArthur said, "The greater the knowledge of the enemy, the greater the potential for victory." This morning we are going to look at gaining knowledge of the enemy.

The apostle Paul expounded on the importance of understanding our enemy. In *Ephesians 6:12* he writes, *For, we do not wrestle against flesh and blood, but against principalities, against powers, against the rulers of the darkness of this age, against spiritual hosts of wickedness in the heavenly places.* There are two obvious, but important, truths in this passage.

1. **Living a God-Honoring life is difficult.**
   Paul refers to the spiritual life as a *"struggle."* The word translated 'struggle' refers to a wrestling match. When we think about a wrestling match, we think about those opponents on television such as Hulk Hogan against Gorgeous George or Python Pete. For all the romping, stomping, and chair throwing, no one ever seems to get seriously hurt. But in the apostle Paul's day, wrestling was serious

250

business. The 'struggle' Paul refers to here was a wrestling match in which the loser had his eyes gouged out and then was killed. It was a life-or-death battle.

Paul uses that imagery to describe the opposition we face in the Christian life. Is it any wonder that the Christian landscape is filled with believers who have fallen into immorality, materialism, and unbelief? <u>They lost the wrestling match!</u> Remember; the apostle Paul said that we wrestle. And when you wrestle there is always a winner and a loser.

2. **We don't wrestle against another person or against another Christian but against a demonic spiritual power.**
    We all tend to play the blame game. We want to lay our spiritual failures on the spouse who doesn't appreciate us, the parent who has abused us, the employer who underpays us, the friend who betrays us, or perhaps the church member who ignores us. But Paul says that our real battle in life is against the unseen forces of Satan himself. For this reason, Paul encourages us to put on the *"full armor of God, that you may be able to stand firm against the schemes (wiles) of the devil." Ephesians 6:11* You see, spiritual warfare demands that we use spiritual weapons and Paul spends the rest of Ephesians 6 describing the armor that is available to every Christian.

FOCUSING ON THE KEY WORD
The key word I want us to focus on this morning from this verse is <u>schemes or wiles</u>, the wiles of the devil. The Greek word used here is <u>methods.</u> If we are going to win the wrestling match, then we have got to have knowledge of the enemy. We have got to understand the enemies battle plan, his method of defeating us.

In 549 B.C., the Persian King Cyrus had one goal in life; to capture the influential city of Sardis in Asia Minor. Yet the king faced one formidable obstacle. Sardis was built on a fifteen-hundred-foot plateau surrounded by steep cliffs impossible to scale. You can understand then why the residents of Sardis didn't lie awake at night worrying about enemy invasions. All was secure!

251

Nevertheless, no one understood the intensity of Cyrus's resolve to conquer the city. The King offered a great reward to any of his soldiers who could figure out how to conquer the city. A soldier named Hyeroeades (don't ask me how to pronounce that) accepted the challenge. One day as Hyeroeades stood at the base of the plateau and observed the Sardian soldiers standing guard on top of the city wall, he saw one of the soldiers accidentally drop his helmet over the edge of the wall. He carefully observed the route the soldier took to descend the steep cliff, retrieve his helmet, and return to his place on the wall.

That night, while the city slept, Hyeroeades led a garrison of soldiers up the same cliff, over the wall, and into the unguarded city. The city of Sardis was defeated that night for two reasons.
1. The citizens overestimated their immunity from attack.
2. The citizens also underestimated their enemy's resolve to defeat them.

WHY DO WE EXPERIENCE DEFEAT IN OUR SPIRITUAL LIVES?
Many of us experience defeat for the exact same reasons that Sardis was defeated.
1. We overestimate our safety from Satan's attack on our lives.
2. We underestimate Satan's resolve to defeat us.

We think that because we're saved that we're immune to Satan's attacks on our lives. We've rightly heard it said that neither Satan nor his demons can possess a Christian and so we assume that we are safe from the enemy. We overestimate our safety from Satan and we underestimate his resolve to destroy us. Yet, God's word says just the opposite. The Bible tells us that it's the Christians, followers of Christ, that Satan is after! Paul warned the Christians at Corinth about the danger of spiritual complacency.

> *1 Corinthians 10:12 – Therefore let him who thinks he stands take heed lest he fall.*

When we see the word "therefore," we should always go back and read the preceding verses to find out what the word "therefore," is there for. Why did the apostle Paul say, "therefore, let him who thinks he stands take heed lest he fall?"

In 1 Corinthians 10:1-11, Paul had just recounted to them how God's chosen people had fallen away from God. Even though they had experienced God's supernatural deliverance from Egypt, His revelation to them at Mt. Sinai, and His supernatural provision for them in the wilderness, he states that <u>God was not well pleased with them.</u>

And why was God not pleased with them? They had mistakenly assumed that because God had blessed them in the past that they could live any way they pleased, and God would continue to bless them. And where do you suppose they got a thought like that? From the enemy of God; Satan.

Here is a list of some of the things they did that were displeasing to God. 1. Lusted after evil things (verse 6) 2. Became idolaters (verse 7) 3. The people sat down to eat and drink and rose up to play (verse 7) 4. Committed sexual immorality (verse 8) 5. Tempted God (verse 9) 6. Complained (verse 10).

How does Satan destroy a Christian's relationship with God? Subtly – very subtly. When Satan comes to you, he does not come in the form of a coiled snake. He does not approach with the roar of a lion. He does not come with the wail of a siren. He does not come waving a red flag. He does not come in a red suit with a pitch fork. Satan simply slides into your life. When he appears, he seems almost like a comfortable companion. There's nothing about him that you would dread. As the character Mephistopheles says in Shakespeare's 'Faust,' "The people do not know the devil is there even when he has them by the throat."

How does Satan slip into your life, grab you by the throat, and choke your love for God? What is his blueprint for your destruction?
1) The love of money
2) The love of pleasure
3) The love of ambition.

As we read and study the Bible we will understand that Satan only has three methods that he uses in this wrestling match. He uses **Money, Pleasure**, and **Ambition** to lure believers away from God. <u>That is his total battle plan!</u>

For Judas, he used money. "Those thirty pieces of silver, invested properly, could take care of my retirement." For David he used pleasure. "You need someone who will meet your needs and Bathsheba sure looks good." For Adam and Eve, he used ambition. "You can be like God." For Moses, he also used ambition. "You're forty years old and you've accomplished nothing, so you had better get this exodus thing going." For Solomon he used all three. "You can have it all, money, pleasure, and ambition."

Now, unless we think it is too simplistic to categorize Satan's battle plan under three headings, look at the warning from the apostle John.

> *1 John 2:15-16 – "Do not love the world, nor the things in the world. If anyone loves the world, the love of the Father is not in him. For all that is in the world, the lust of the flesh* **(pleasure)**, *and the lust of the eyes* **(money)** *and the boastful pride of life* **(ambition)**, *is not from the Father, but is from the world."*

In the New Testament, the word translated 'world' can mean 'that organized system headed by Satan which leaves God out and is a rival to Him.' Ephesians 2:2 says that Satan is the prince and power of the air according to the course of this world.

Satan has temporary control over the world system including Wall Street, Hollywood, and Washington D.C. and he can effectively employ the world system to lure Christians away from God. Specifically, Satan uses money (the lust of the eyes), pleasure (the lust of the flesh) and ambition (the boastful pride of life) to lead believers away from their Heavenly Father.

SATAN'S THREE-PART BLUEPRINT FOR OUR DESTRUCTION
Satan used all three of these methods when he tempted Jesus in the wilderness. Satan offered Jesus the kingdoms of the world (money), bread when He was hungry (pleasure) and he encouraged Jesus to bypass His Father's plan and reveal Himself as the Messiah (ambition).

When we look at the story of the prodigal son in Luke chapter 15 we find the same three temptations enticing the younger son to leave his father. He desired material goods (money), *"Father give me the share of the estate that falls to me."* He desired pleasure, *"He squandered his estate with loose (prodigal) living.* He desired ambition, He wanted to strike out and make a name for himself. He went on a journey into a far country. He left his Father.

We need to remember that we have an active opponent plotting our destruction. He wants to break up marriages. He wants our children to rebel against us. He wants us to gradually depart from God. He ultimately wants our premature death.

John 10:10 – "The thief comes to steal, kill and destroy."

I saw a video where a hunter, in Africa, shot a lion and was standing next to the lion with his arms raised up showing us his muscles. What he didn't see, as his gun lay at his feet, was another lion coming up from behind him ready to pounce and attack. He had spent hours hunting his prey not realizing that he, too, was being hunted. We're all hunting something. Some hunt for wealth (money). Some hunt for indulgence (pleasure). Some hunt for significance (ambition). But as we hunt these things, someone hunts us. We have an adversary who is stalking us and will not rest until he completely destroys us.

> *1 Peter 5:8 – "Be sober, be vigilant; because your adversary the devil, prowls about like a roaring lion seeking someone to devour."*

In and of themselves there is nothing wrong with money, pleasure, and ambition but they can trap us and bring us down and move us into a far country away from God. But Satan's ability to spiritually derail us would be severely limited if not for a third factor that makes us Prone to Wander. Remember the song: 'Come Thou Fount of every blessing' – 'Prone to wander Lord I feel it, prone to leave the God I love.'

Being honest with yourself, do you suffer from a powerful addiction? How many times have we resolved, "God, I will never do this again" only to find ourselves not only repeating the forbidden action but loving it? The apostle Paul vividly described the internal battle we all face.

> *Romans 7:18-23 – No matter which way I turn I can't make myself do right. I want to, but I can't. When I want*

> to do good, I don't; and when I try not to do wrong, I
> do it anyway. Now if I am doing what I don't want to,
> it is plain where the trouble is: sin still has me in its evil
> grasp. It seems to be a fact of life that when I want to
> do what is right, I inevitably do what is wrong. I love to
> do God's will so far as my new nature is concerned; but
> there is something else deep within me, in my lower
> nature, that is at war with my mind and wins the fight
> and makes me a slave to the sin that is still within me.

Satan actively seeks our destruction, but he wouldn't have much power over us if we didn't have cravings for sin – lusts.

> James 1:13-14 – Let no one say when he is tempted, I
> am being tempted by God; for God cannot be tempted
> by evil, and He Himself does not tempt anyone. But each
> one is tempted when he is carried away and enticed by
> his own lust.

The kind of craving James describes is a strong inward pull toward things outside of God's will for our lives. Our sin nature pulls us toward those things and entices us. _Enticed_ is a fishing term that means _"hooked."_ James employs a word picture of a fish so blinded by its desire for food that it snaps at the bait, not realizing that the bait contains a hook that will destroy it. Any good fisherman knows that you use different bait for different types of fish. In the same way, every Christian is enticed by different "bait," and Satan is a master fisherman who knows which bait will hook us; which bait will destroy us.

> Romans 6:11-12 – Likewise reckon ye also yourselves
> to be dead indeed unto sin, but alive unto God through
> Jesus Christ our Lord. Let no sin therefore reign in your
> mortal body, that ye should obey it in the lusts thereof.

I believe that Paul's words in Roman 6 mean that Christ has freed us from sins power in our lives. Once we become Christians, we have an incredible power to say no to sin. But we must act in a way consistent with that power. Although we are no longer slaves to our sin nature, we should never forget its presence within us.

James 1:13-14 – Let no one say when he is tempted, "I am being tempted by God;" for God cannot be tempted by evil, and He Himself does not tempt anyone. But each one is tempted when he is carried away and enticed by his own lust.

Enticed by his own lust! What is your lust? Remember that Satan uses three areas to pull us away from God. The love of money. The love of pleasure. The love of ambition. Which areas do you struggle with? Maybe you struggle with more than one. Maybe you struggle with all three.

We need to study ourselves so that we can identify those areas that make us vulnerable to temptation. Understanding the reality of our sin nature, and the resolve of our spiritual enemy, is the first line of defense against our defection from the faith.

The captain of the ship looked into the dark night and saw faint lights in the distance. Immediately he told his signalman to send a message. "Alter your course 10 degrees south." Promptly a return message was received. "Alter your course 10 degrees north." The captain was angered; his command had been ignored. So, he sent a second message. "Alter your course 10 degrees south, I am the captain!" Soon another message was received. "Alter your course 10 degrees north, I am seaman third class Jones." Immediately the captain sent a third message, knowing the fear it would evoke. "Alter your course 10 degrees south, I am a battleship!!" Then the replay came; "Alter your course 10 degrees north, I am a lighthouse."

We are the captain of our lives. We run our lives many times like we are a battleship, ruthlessly going through life in the pursuit of money, pleasure, and/or ambition, whatever makes you happy. What we don't realize is that we are on a collision course.

James 1:15 – The when lust hath conceived, it bringeth forth sin; and sin, when it is finished, bringeth forth death.

CHAPTER 35

THE LOVE OF PLEASURE

As Christians, we tend to go to one of two extremes in our attitude about pleasure. One of those extremes is denying ourselves the normal pleasures of everyday life. The other extreme is to love pleasure, pleasure, pleasure, and more pleasure.

Many times, we feel sick about our lack of self-control, our weight, our laziness, or our inconsistency in Bible study and prayer. We feel that we have failed God and our spiritual life is not what it should be. So, what do we do to get ourselves back on the right track with God? We deny ourselves! We cut out desserts, we quit watching television, we refuse to buy new clothes, and we trade our plans for Disney World for a mission trip to a third world country. This program lasts for maybe hours, days, or even months, and then we find ourselves back in the same condition as before. And, we feel so guilty! We feel so discouraged about our lack of self-control that we completely give up trying to live any kind of life that we feel is pleasing to God. Sometimes we feel like we're on a spiritual merry-go-round.

THERE HAS TO BE A BETTER WAY
One of the things that we need to understand about pleasure is that God designed us to enjoy and partake in good clean and morally pure pleasure. Some people feel like if you're a Christian you need to go around looking like you just ate a sour pickle. In one of my seminary classes, I used to walk in the room and tell a good clean joke and have everyone in the class laughing. It relaxed everyone and made them all feel better, especially on test day. That is, everyone except the professor who thought that it was wrong for Christians to laugh. However, before he passed away I went to see him, and he told me to keep laughing and

keep making others laugh. He said he was wrong and that laughter is a wonderful gift of joy that every Christian needs to enjoy. *"A merry heart does good like a medicine."* I appreciated him saying that and I have sought to make people laugh and hopefully feel better about themselves ever since then.

The old saying is more than true: "All work and no play makes Jack a dull boy." If we try and remove the element of relaxation and play from our lives then we cannot be all that God wants us to be either physically, mentally, or spiritually. The word JOY is mentioned approximately 165 times in the Bible. God wants us to be a joyful people. He designed us to be a joyful people. God is a joyful God. *Hebrews 12:2 For the JOY that was set before Him He endured the cross, despising the shame, and has sat down at the right hand of the throne of God.*

Hold on my child, JOY comes in the morning! It is JOY unspeakable and full of glory! We need to remember that God did not only endow us with a spirit, but also with a body and with that body comes the need for food, intimacy, exercise, play, and relaxation.

You might say: "But doesn't the Bible teach that we are created to work?" Yes, the Bible does teach this and there is a time for work, but the Bible also teaches that there is a time for pleasure and relaxation. God has wired each of us in such a way that we cannot work twelve hours a day, seven days a week, fifty-two weeks each year. God's Word says that pleasure and relaxation has a place in our lives.

THE DANGERS OF PLEASURE
However, God's Word also clearly sounds some warnings about pleasure.

> *Proverbs 21:17 – He who loves pleasure will become a poor man.*

> *Luke 8:14 – And the seed which fell among the thorns, these are the ones who have heard, and as they go on their way they are choked with worries and riches and pleasures of this life and bring no fruit to maturity.*

> *2 Timothy 3:2,4 – For men will be lovers of self, lovers of money, boastful, arrogant, revilers, disobedient to*

> *parents, ungrateful, unholy, unloving, unforgiving, slan-*
> *derers, without self-control, brutal, despisers of good,*
> *traitors, headstrong, haughty, <u>lovers of pleasure rather</u>*
> *<u>than lovers of God</u>.*

The above passages explain that pleasure, like money, is neither moral nor immoral in and of itself. But pleasure is wrong when it becomes your love and turns you away from God. Pleasure is wrong when it is in excess, when it becomes our life focus, and when it violates God's Word.

WHEN IT IS IN EXCESS

I love to play golf. I love to bowl. I love to work out at the gym. Last weekend we took a trip to Branson, Missouri. I love the shows, the restaurants, the shopping, the lake, the miniature golf, and the relaxation in Branson. There's not anything I've found that I do not love about Branson, Missouri. Is it wrong for me to love these things? Not really. What is wrong is when I have such a strong desire to enjoy all these things that I put them first in my life. When my desire to work, to make a difference with my life, to help other people, goes away, and my only desire is to enjoy myself, then I have become a lover of pleasure and not a lover of God.

When we took our anniversary trip to Hawaii a few years ago, we visited four different islands. By the time we had spent a week relaxing, I was going stir crazy. I was ready to help the bell boys take luggage to the rooms or anything I could get my hands on to get me back to work, back to making a difference with my life. As long as we keep pleasure in balance there is everything right and absolutely nothing wrong with it. We need pleasure. God designed us to enjoy pleasure, for a time.

Should a person work until the time they die? If you are able, then the answer is yes! You may not work on your vocation until you die but you need to find some work that is fulfilling in your life. You can volunteer in dozens of different areas. You can and should make a difference in your life as long as you are physically able to do so.

WHEN IT BECOMES OUR LIFE FOCUS

What is your life focus? What do you talk about most often? What do you think about most often? If someone were to give you a check for twenty thousand dollars, how would you spend it? Your answers to those questions reveal your priorities. If vacations, hobbies, recreational pursuits, sensuality, or comfort dominate your answers, then pleasure is probably your life-focus. If fact, pleasure may have become your idol! An idol is any person or thing we love more than God. And whatever we talk about, think about and spend our hard-earned money for, defines what we really love.

> *Colossians 3:1-2 — If then you were raised with Christ, seek those things which are above, where Christ is, sitting at the right hand of God. <u>Set your mind on things above, not on things on the earth.</u>*

WHEN IT VIOLATES GOD'S WORD
Sexual immorality, according to the Bible, God's Word, is wrong! It violates the Bible's teaching and hinders our relationship with God. Sexual immorality leads us away from God. No matter what the world may think or say, God's Word is still God's Word and God is still God!

However, there is a connection between sexual immorality and pleasure and if we are not careful we can easily fall into the snare that is so easily set for us. We have previously discussed how that Satan uses three methods, and only three methods, to lure us away from God; the love of money, the love of pleasure, and the love of ambition.

People who allow themselves to become lovers of pleasure, to put pleasure above everything else, often become entangled in sexual sin. We see that truth illustrated in the Prodigal son's life. Luke 15 tells us that the prodigal son spent all his money on "loose living." When we think of "loose living" we think of sexual immorality, but that isn't what the Greek word means in this verse.

From the Greek meaning we derive "wasteful and extravagant living." James has the same thought in mind when he writes in his epistle. *James 5:5 You have lived luxuriously on earth and led a life of wanton (wasteful) pleasure.* Tired of the discipline and restrictions imposed by a father, who had probably earned his wealth through hard labor, the prodigal son was ready to enjoy his wealth and live a life of extravagant wasteful pleasure, <u>a life filled with nothing but pleasure.</u> His lack of purpose, his desire for nothing but pleasure, not only led to his poverty but to his immorality as well.

> *Luke 15:30* (the older brother speaking) — *But when this son of yours came, <u>who has devoured your wealth with harlots;</u> you killed the fattened calf for him.*

We see the same relationship between pleasure and immorality in King David's life. Although King David was a man after God's own heart, the victor over Goliath and the most successful of Israel's kings, we mainly remember him for one thing; his one night of passion with the lady, Bathsheba. This mistake marked both him and his family forever. What caused such a great man to fall into adultery and murder? I believe that David had become a lover of pleasure. He had replaced his love for God with his love for pleasure. As king over Israel, he became accustomed to an easy life.

> *2 Samuel 11:1* — *It happened, in the spring of the year, at the time when kings go out to battle, that David sent Joab and his servants with him, and all Israel; and they destroyed the people of Ammon and besieged Rabbah. <u>But David remained at Jerusalem.</u>*

In those days, kings led their men into battle. But David chose to stay home. David knew he should have been with his men. He probably felt guilty for remaining in the palace. But he just couldn't make himself go. He was tired of lugging his heavy armor around the hot Palestinian desert. He had paid his dues as a young soldier; he could let someone else do the work. <u>After all, the king deserved some luxuries!</u>

> *2 Samuel 11:2-4* — *<u>Then it happened</u> one evening that David arose from his bed and walked on the roof of the king's house. And from the roof he saw a woman bathing, and the woman was very beautiful to behold. So, David sent and inquired about the woman. And someone said, "Is this not Bathsheba, the daughter of Eliam, the wife of Uriah the Hittite?" Then David sent messengers and took her, and she came to him and he lay with her, for she was cleansed from her impurity; and she returned to her house.*

David never had much self-discipline. We see David's inability to control his sensual appetite throughout his reign. When anointed king at the age of eighteen, David was a single man. By the time he actually assumed the throne, he had taken six wives in direct violation of God's law prohibiting multiple wives.

The scholar, F.B. Meyer sums up how David's desire for pleasure finally led to his downfall. "In direct violation of God's law, David took more concubines and wives; fostering in him a habit of sensual indulgence, which predisposed him to the evil invitation of that evening hour."

A strong relationship exists between our ability to curb our desire for pleasure and our ability to avoid immorality. Always remember, there are three methods that Satan uses for our destruction; the love of money, the love of pleasure, and the love of ambition. How are you doing in your life? Are you winning the battle? Is God winning the battle? Or, is Satan winning the battle?

CHAPTER 36

A PREREQUISITE FOR
ANSWERED PRAYER

The blueprint for a close relationship with God depends upon whether we <u>work</u> with God. God designed us to have a close, intimate, relationship with Him that comes from <u>working</u> with Him.

> *Genesis 1:26a, 2:8 – Then God said, let us make man in Our image, according to Our likeness. The Lord God planted a garden eastward in Eden, and there He put the man whom He had formed. What did God do next?*

> *Genesis 2:15 – Then the Lord God took the man and put him in the Garden of Eden to <u>tend and keep it.</u>*

> *John 5:20 – For the Father loves the Son and shows Him all things that He Himself does; and He will show Him greater <u>works</u> than these, that you may marvel.*

> *1 Corinthians 3:9 – For we are God's fellow <u>workers</u>; you are God's field, you are God's building.*

> *Colossians 1:29 – To this end I also <u>labor</u>, striving according to His working which works in me mightily.*

God prepared us to work before the foundation of the world. Work is a gift from God. If you don't believe that, just ask someone who is without work or looking for work. *Ecclesiastes 3: 12-13 I know that nothing is* better for them than to rejoice, and to do good in their lives, and also that every man should eat and drink and enjoy the good of all his _labor, it is the gift of God_.

> Ephesians 2:8-10 – *For by grace are you saved through faith; and that not of yourselves, it is the gift of God. Not of works, lest any should boast. For we are his workmanship, created in Christ Jesus unto _good works_, which God has before ordained that we should walk in them. We are not saved by works but we are saved to work!*

The Christian life only has fulfillment if you work with God.

> John 4:34 – *Jesus said to them, My food is to do the will of Him who sent Me, and to _finish His work._*

> John 9:4 – *_I must work the works_ of Him who sent Me while it is day; the night is coming when no one can work.*

During the last 24 hours on Jesus life on earth He made this statement.

> John 17:4 – *I have glorified You on earth. _I have finished the work which You have given Me to do._*

Jesus hadn't been to the cross yet. What work had He finished? He had finished the work of training His disciples to do the work!

You and I have an Assignment!
Inherit in the call to a relationship with God is the _requirement of work._ You can never have intimacy with God if you do not know what your work is!

> 1 Peter 4:10 – *As each one has received a gift, minister it to one another, as good stewards of the manifold grace of God.* We spend too much time trying to figure out what our gift is. If we pursue our assignment, God will equip us with our gift!

When you stand before God, He will especially inspect your work!

You will be judged based on the quality of your work in carrying out your assignments.

> *1 Corinthians 3:13-15 – Each one's <u>work</u> will become clear; for the day will declare it, because it will be revealed by fire; and the fire will test each one's <u>work</u>, of what sort it is. If anyone's <u>work</u> which he has built on it endures, he will receive a <u>reward.</u> If anyone's <u>work</u> is burned, he will suffer loss; but he himself will be saved, yet so as through fire.*

Your <u>reward</u> comes from your work!
Over and over in the New Testament, Jesus said; "<u>Great is your reward in Heaven.</u>" He wants to reward us for work well done. At least 24 times the Bible pictures God rewarding work.

> *Matthew 16:27 – For the Son of Man will come in the glory of His Father with His angels, and then <u>He will reward each according to his works</u>.*

> *Ecclesiastes 12:14 – For God will bring <u>every work into judgment</u>, including every secret thing, whether good or evil.*

Whatever else it is that you pray about, you had better make sure you are praying for your assignment.

Therefore, you must identify your assignment. First, pray for a right relationship with God.

> *Psalm 66:18 – If I regard <u>iniquity</u> in my heart, the Lord will not hear.*

> *Isaiah 59:1-2 – Listen now! The Lord isn't too weak to save you, and He isn't getting deaf! He can hear you when you call! But the trouble is that your <u>sins</u> have cut you off from God. Because of sin He has turned His face away from you and will not listen anymore.*

1 John 1:5-9 – This is the message which we have heard from Him and declare to you, that God is <u>light</u> and in Him is <u>no darkness</u> at all. If we say that we have fellowship with Him, and walk in darkness, we lie and do not practice the truth. But if we walk in the light, as He is in the light, we have fellowship with one another and the blood of Jesus Christ, His Son, cleanses us from all sin. If we say that we have no <u>sin</u>, we deceive ourselves, and the truth is not in us. If <u>we confess our sins</u>, He is faithful and just to forgive us our sins and to cleanse us from all unrighteousness.

A Prerequisite to Answered Prayer

James 5:16 – The effective, fervent prayer of a <u>righteous person</u> avails much.

1. What kind of person gets God's attention in prayer? A righteous person! If we are living in sin and enjoying it, if we are keeping it there, finding that it feels good, if we're regarding, nurturing, patting that little sin along, God does not hear us when we pray! The only prayer that He will hear is a prayer of repentance!

2. Second, always pray for those within your family. An intimate relationship with God begins in the family. If your family is falling apart, so is your relationship with God.

3. Third, write down and pray for those who are in your circle of influence; neighbors, co-workers, and people you come in contact with.

Identify what it is that you do that makes a difference in other people's lives, especially as it relates to the spiritual .

John 6:29 – This is the <u>work of God, that you believe in Him</u> whom He sent.

Colossians 1:27b-29 – <u>Christ in you</u>, the hope of glory. Him we preach, warning every man and teaching every man in all wisdom, that we may present every man perfect in Christ Jesus.

So, to speak, you may be the only Jesus that someone ever sees. I must obey God and share the love of Christ with those within my circle of influence. If it is to be, it's up to me!

Order Your Quiet Time

Rearrange your day to include a time alone with God. Meet God at a regular place and time each day. Begin with a short prayer acknowledging your relationship with Christ, and your dependence on Him. Spend time reading God's word. Highlight or underline areas where God is speaking with you. Align your life with God's will. Remember, the purpose of prayer is not to conform God to our will but to conform us to His will.

Pray in Authority for your Assignment.

Jesus connects authority and power in prayer to <u>working with Him</u>.

> *John 14:12-14 – Most assuredly, I say to you, he who believes in Me, the works that I do, he will do also; and greater works than these he will do, because I go to My Father. And whatever you ask in My name, that I will do, that the Father may be glorified in the Son. If you ask anything in My name, I will do it.*

You have Carte Blanche as long as you're working with God on <u>your assignment</u>. Authority in Christ primarily relates to your assignment. God has granted you the authority to ask what is necessary for the work of God to come about in your life and in the lives of those you are assigned to pray for. One of the gauges to see if you're on track is whether or not you are being <u>rewarded.</u>

> *Matthew 6:6 – But you, when you pray, go into your room and when you have shut your door, pray to your Father who is in the secret place and your Father who sees in secret will<u> reward you openly.</u>*

If you want more authority in prayer, be faithful in what God has assigned you.

Authority is increasingly granted.

> *Luke 19:17 – And He said to him, well done, good servant; because you were faithful in a very little, have authority over ten cities.* If you are faithful in a little, He will give you <u>more</u>.

Working with God draws you much closer to God.
Working with God creates an atmosphere where you can understand His purposes, His mind, and His heart more clearly. For example; the longer you live with your spouse, the more you understand each other.

> *Isaiah 42:9 – Behold, the former things have come to pass, and new things I declare; before they spring forth I tell you of them.*

> *John 16:13 – When He, the Spirit of truth, has come, He will guide you into all truth; for He will not speak on His own authority, but whatever He hears He will speak, and He will tell you things to come.*

If you don't do your assignment, what else is God going to talk to you about? Be a friend of God, get close to Him. Spend time in prayer. Read and study your Bible. Respond to God's word by listening, obeying, and following Him. Get involved in the lives of others. **<u>Do your assignment!</u>**

CHAPTER 37

AN ATTITUDE OF GRATITUDE

1 Thessalonians 5:16-18 – Rejoice always, pray without ceasing, <u>in everything give thanks</u>; for this is the will of God in Christ Jesus for you.

W hy is it that we must set aside one day a year to be thankful? Shouldn't we be thankful every day? Sometimes we spend so much time griping and complaining that we don't have time to be thankful. Maybe we should start a new custom. We should set aside one day a year to gripe and complain and call it "Grumbling Day". Then we could spend the next 364 days being thankful.

Few things affect a person's life more dramatically than developing an attitude of gratitude. An attitude of gratitude is a biblical principle. There are 138 verses in the Bible dealing with "thanksgiving" alone. Many more talk about rejoicing, happiness, and joy. Paul told the Colossian Christians "<u>in all you do</u> give thanks to God."

How did the Day of Thanksgiving originate in America?
When the New England colonies were first planted, the early settlers endured many hardships and difficulties. The winters were hard, and the crops were poor. Even with the help of the Indians more than half of the original settlers died the first year. They went to the Lord frequently in prayer and fasting laying all their problems upon the Lord. Constantly thinking about their problems kept them discouraged and made them think of returning to their homeland even with all its religious perse-cutions. When one of the leaders proposed another day of prayer and fasting, one of the settlers spoke up and said: "I think that we have brooded long enough over our difficulties, and it is high time that we

270

consider how good God has been to us. After all, the colony is growing strong, the fields are increasing in harvest, the rivers are stocked with fish; and above all, our wives and children are healthy, and we now possess that which we have come to this land for, full religious and civil liberty." He then proposed that in place of the day of prayer and fasting over their problems, they put in its place a day of Thanksgiving, with prayer of thanks, and a wonderful meal together. As a result, in 1621, the Pilgrims observed the first Thanksgiving Day. Lincoln acknowledged it nationally in 1863; and, in 1941, Congress passed into law that the 4th Thursday of every November be officially recognized as Thanksgiving Day.

I like the words of William Law: "Would you know who is the greatest saint in the world? It is not he who prays, or fast most; it is not he who gives most; nor, is it he who is most imminent for temperance, chastity or justice. Rather, the greatest saint in the world is the one who is always thankful to God, who wills everything that God wills, who receives everything as an instance of God's goodness and has a heart always ready to praise God for it!"

While prayers, petitions, and fasting over our concerns certainly has its place and is very important; it is also extremely important to our lives that we learn to be thankful and look for things on a daily basis to be thankful for.

Why is it important to develop an attitude of gratitude?
1. A heart of gratitude doesn't have room for anything else
2. It's impossible to be thankful and anxious at the same time
3. Your outlook determines your outcome

1. **A heart of gratitude doesn't have room for anything else.**
   Someone wisely said, "The Most destructive acid in the world is found in a sour disposition." Someone else said, "**Whine** is made from sour grapes." In *Ephesians 4:31* the Bible makes a list of these "sour grapes" The list includes *bitterness, wrath, anger, clamor, speaking evil,* and *malice*. The Bible commands us to get rid of those things. But how? One way is to develop an attitude of gratitude.

271

Ephesians 4:32 says: Be kind to one another, tender-hearted, forgiving one another, even as God in Christ forgave you.

A person cannot be kind, tenderhearted, and forgiving and at the same time be full of bitterness, wrath, anger, clamor, malice with speaking evil. A person whose heart is filled with thanksgiving will have no room for such things as anger, bitterness, and grumbling. *Song: Thank you Lord for saving my soul, thank you Lord for making me whole, thank you Lord for giving to me, Thy great salvation so rich and free.*

2. **It's impossible to be thankful and anxious at the same time.**
    We all go through our times of distress, heartache, depression, and oppression. None of us are exempt from the hardships of life. The economy can affect us, illnesses, disease, losing someone we love, wars, natural disasters, and famines can all take their toll on us. Added to this stress are the everyday concerns of raising children, school, marriages, personal finances, growing old (when our health seems to fail us almost on a daily basis.)

Martin Luther lived from 1483–1546 and began the Protestant Reformation by nailing his 95 theses to the door of the Wittenberg Church. That document contained an attack on papal abuses and the sale of indulgences by church officials. Luther's crime was affirming the gospel. Luther preached the doctrine of justification by faith – the teaching that Christ's own righteousness is imputed to those who believe, and on that ground alone, they are accepted by God. As this teaching spread, thousands upon thousands of Christians were martyred, a large percentage of them being burned at the stake for their belief in Christ. Do you think they might have been a little bit anxious during this period of time?

Martin Luther claimed that the greatest preacher he ever knew was a tame little robin. Each evening, Luther would place crumbs on his windowsill. The robin would hop on the sill and eat as much as he needed. From there the little bird would fly to a little tree close by, lift up his voice to God, sing songs of gratitude, tuck his head under his wings, and go to sleep. The robin would not worry about tomorrow until the next day. Oh, to be like that robin, Grateful, Thankful, Worry-free.

> *Psalm 95:1-2 – O Come, let us sing to the Lord! Let us shout joyfully to the Rock of our salvation. Let us come before His presence with thanksgiving; let us shout joyfully to Him with psalms.*

> *Psalm 96:1-4 – O, sing to the Lord a new song! Sing to the Lord, all the earth. Sing to the Lord, bless His name; Proclaim the good news of His salvation from day to day. Declare His glory among the nations, His wonders among all peoples. For the Lord is great and greatly to be praised.*

> *Psalm 100 – Make a joyful noise to the Lord, all you lands! Serve the Lord with gladness; Come before His presence with singing. Know ye that the Lord, He is God; It is He who has made us, and not we ourselves; We are His people and the sheep of His pasture. Enter into His gates with thanksgiving, and into His courts with praise. Be thankful to Him and bless His name. For the Lord is good; His mercy is everlasting, And His truth endures to all generations.*

Do you know one main ingredient in heaven? Of all the things we will be doing in heaven - one main thing that we're going to be doing is singing, praising and thanking God. Over and over in the Bible and even in the Book of Revelation we see joyful Christians singing, giving praise and thanksgiving.

3. **Your outlook determines your outcome.**
   Over the California desert fly two birds; the vulture and the hummingbird. The vulture looks for dead, rotten, decaying meat. The vulture thrives on what has passed. The hummingbird looks for the tiny blossoms of the cactus flower. The hummingbird thrives on what is living and growing. And you know what? Each bird finds what it's looking for. What are you looking for? There's an old saying: If you're looking for trouble you'll find it on every corner. A better question is; what are you finding?

<u>What you're finding is what you're looking for!</u> Are you looking for the past? Are you wallowing in self-pity, or are you looking, through faith, toward the future? Are you thankful to a God who can forgive, heal, cleanse, wipe away every tear and give you a hope and a future? Or do you just hang onto your past?

> *Jeremiah 29:11 – I know the plans that I have for you, declares the Lord, plans to prosper you and not to harm you, plans to give you hope and a future.*

Jesus said: *"A person reaps what he sows"* When we are looking for things to be thankful for; that is what we find. When we are looking for things to complain about; that is what we find.

> *Jesus said in John 10:10: "The thief comes to steal, kill and destroy. I am come that they might have life and that they might have it more abundantly."*

One of the keys to this abundant life Jesus wants us to enjoy is in an <u>attitude of gratitude;</u> a life that has learned how to be thankful no matter what the situation is. That's what the apostle Paul meant when he said: *"I can do all things through Christ who strengthens me."*

> *Ephesians 5:20 – Give thanks always <u>for all things</u> to God the Father in the name of our Lord Jesus Christ.*
>
> *Colossians 3:17 – And <u>whatever you do in word or deed, do all</u> in the name of the Lord Jesus, <u>giving thanks</u> to God the Father through Him.*
>
> *Hebrews 13:15 Therefore by Him (Jesus) let us continually offer the sacrifice of praise to God, that is, <u>the fruit of our lips, giving thanks to His name.</u>*

How do I develop such an attitude when things don't seem to be going right in my life? When my troubles, my worries, my illnesses, my pains, my emotions seem to overwhelm me, how do I live this abundant worry-free life; a life of gratefulness and thankfulness? And we don't need to make light of this because our pains, our emotions, are a very real part of our lives! <u>You develop it as you grow in your faith, and as you grow in faith; faith develops you.</u>

> *Hebrews 11:6 says "Without faith it is impossible to please God. He who comes to God must believe that He is and that He is a <u>rewarder</u> of them that diligently seek Him.*

Do you want to be rewarded by God? Then you must diligently seek Him. And you begin seeking Him by learning to be thankful. And not only thankful to God but you must learn to be thankful for others and let others know that you appreciate them and are thankful for them. It comes down to a "Heart Condition" - A Heart Attitude!

In Luke 17:11-19 we read the account when Jesus cleansed 10 lepers and only one returned to give thanks. *Now it happened as He went to Jerusalem that He passed through the midst of Samaria and Galilee. Then, as He entered a certain village, there met Him ten men who were lepers, who stood afar off. And they lifted up their voices and said, "Jesus, Master, have mercy on us!" So, when He saw them, He said to them, "Go, show yourselves to the priests." And so, it was that as they went, they were cleansed. And one of them, when he saw that he was healed, returned, and with a loud voice glorified God, and fell down on his face at His feet, giving Him thanks. And he was a Samaritan. So, Jesus answered and said, "Were there not ten cleansed? But where are the nine? Were there not any found who returned to give glory to God except this foreigner?" And He said to him, "Arise, go your way. Your faith has made you well."*

Why is it that Christ healed 10 men that day but only one was thankful? Is it possible to receive God's grace, His cleansing in your life, and not be thankful for it? The other nine might have had an attitude something like this; well you might have healed me but now what am I going to do? I had a home among the lepers, people brought us food. What am I going to do now? Where am I going to live? Where am I going to find a job? Will my family take me back or have they gone on with their lives? **If you're looking for things to complain about you'll find it on every corner. But if you're looking for blessings, things to be thankful for, you'll find those as well!** Even though this man had had one of the most dreaded diseases in the world, he praised God and returned to give thanks. He looked ahead to a new life, a new year, new relationships. He looked ahead to where God lives. He looked ahead by faith! You see, I believe this man was thankful for his cure of leprosy because he was thankful in his leprosy. This man had learned the secret found in 1 Thessalonians 5:16-18.

> *1 Thessalonians 5:16-18 – Rejoice always! Pray without ceasing. In everything give thanks; for this is the will of God in Christ Jesus concerning you.*

Can we really give thanks in <u>all things?</u> Daniel was captured by a foreign enemy when he was a teenager. He was taken from his homeland and never saw his parents or his brothers or sisters again; never even heard from them again. But the Bible says he went to his room three times a day and gave thanks to God. David rose at midnight to thank God for His word. Paul gave thanks to God even though he was literally whipped 5 times within an inch of his life. *<u>This was the same type of scourging Jesus went through before His crucifixion.</u>* He was stoned and left for dead. And right before the ship he was on was about to go down he gave thanks to God for the meal he was about to eat.

Can we do the same thing as the saints in the Bible did? Can we <u>choose</u> to be kind, tenderhearted, forgiving, thankful and gracious or will we <u>choose</u> to live with worry? Will we <u>choose</u> to live with negative thoughts? Will we <u>choose</u> to live as a vulture looking for dead, rotten, decaying things or will we <u>choose</u> to live as a hummingbird thriving on what is living and growing and good and positive about life? Remember, every bird finds what it's looking for! Be thankful every day of your lives.

> *1 Chronicles 16:34 – Oh, give thanks to the Lord, for He is good! For His mercy endures forever.*
>
> *1 Chronicles 16:8 – Oh, give thanks to the Lord! Call upon His name; Make known His deeds among the peoples!*

Why should we give thanks to the Lord? We should give thanks:
1. Because God is good and kind and loving
2. Because a thankful heart increases and matures our faith in the Lord
3. For answered prayer

4. For all that God has given us
5. To let others know how wonderful God is
6. For our salvation
7. For our victory in Christ
8. For Jesus who is coming again to rescue this world - Do you know that mankind has brought sin into this world? Do you know that Satan has ruled this world? But thanks be to God who is coming to rescue this world!

How should we give thanks to the Lord? We should give thanks:
1. By living in Christ and believing in Christ. *John 11:26 "And whoever lives and believes in Me, shall never die. Do you believe this?"*
2. By confession of sin and reconciling with God.
3. By receiving the gift of love, the gift of eternal life, that God is offering us in His Son Jesus Christ.
4. By singing: *Psalm 147:7 "Sing out your thanks to the Lord; sing praise to our God."*
5. By honoring and obeying Him with our lives.
6. By coming together on Sundays to worship the Lord together
7. By giving of our tithes and offerings
8. By reading His word daily
9. By telling others the way of salvation through Christ alone

When should we give thanks to the Lord?

Psalm 92:2 – "It is good to proclaim your unfailing love in the morning, your faithfulness in the evening"

Luke 9:16 – "Jesus took the five loaves and two fish, looked up toward heaven, and asked God's blessing on the food.

Colossians 3:15 – "Always be thankful"

1 Thess. 5:18 – "No matter what happens, always be thankful, for this is God's will for you who belong to Christ Jesus"

A lack of Thanksgiving puts a barrier between us and God
When we're not thankful, when we allow thankfulness to fade with time, it can be very detrimental to our lives. A fading memory, procrastination, forgetting what God has done for us and what others have done for us can lead to bitterness in our lives, discontent, lack of faith and even depression.

What we should do!
Look for ways to say thank you to God and thank you to others. Reach out during this season of thanksgiving to help others who are less fortunate than yourself and who need a helping hand.

Remember the words of our Lord when He said: "**It is more blessed to give than to receive.**"

How often do we think about giving thanks, not only to God, but to each other? Do we take time to give thanks?

A wife works hard all day on a job outside the home. Men, does the thought ever cross our mind to say thank you to our wives for all they do? Do we show our thanks by helping around the house? Do we show our thanks by cherishing and loving our wives as Christ loves the church and gave Himself for the church?

A wife works hard all day in the home cleaning, washing, preparing meals. Do we come home like an old bear sometimes saying: "Where's Dinner?!," or do we thank and appreciate them. And ladies; do you thank you husbands for all they do for you? How often do we thank our parents or our children or those who love us? How often do we thank the store clerk for helping us or the waiter or waitress for serving us?

Think about how often in a day someone does something for you, no matter how small. How often do you stop to say thanks? Think about how often God helps you in a day. Think about how much God has given you; whether great or small. How often do we say thank you Lord?

The Practical Benefits of Thanksgiving in My Life
1.   Keeps my focus on God and the positive things about life
2.   Honors God
3.   Acknowledges God's influence in my life

4. Keeps my problems in their proper perspective
5. Encourages those around me
6. Trains my children how to view life and be thankful
7. Prepares me for success in human relationships
8. Creates an atmosphere where God can work in my life
9. Opens opportunities for relationships and intimacy with God and others
10. Properly honors and acknowledges the sources of blessing in my life and encourages them to continue blessing me

Give thanks! Give to God! Give to others! And you will be blessed by God beyond measure.

CHAPTER 38

THE TRUTH ABOUT HELL

S tudies show that over 90% of people in the world believe in a "heaven" while less than 50% believe in an eternal hell. Hell is not a popular topic of discussion these days. Very seldom will you ever find a preacher that will preach on the subject of hell. We live, as if hell were not real. We share Christ with others, as if Heaven were all there is. God loves you and wants you to go to Heaven, is what we tell them. Most of the time we never even mention that Hell exists. But, according to the Bible and according to Jesus Himself, Hell is a very real place.

In Revelation 9:1-12 we see that Jesus gives the key to the abyss (bottomless pit, Hell) to Satan. Satan opens up Hell and demons swarm the earth. This is called the fifth trumpet judgment, also known as the first woe judgment. These demons torment everyone on the earth that are not spiritually saved (born again as Jesus said in John 3). The torment will be unbearable. People will desire death but will not be allowed to die.

> *Revelation 9:6 – In those days men will seek death and will not find it; they will desire to die, and death will flee from them.*

> *Revelation 9:1-2 – Then the fifth angel sounded; and I saw a star fallen from heaven to the earth. To him was given the key to the bottomless pit. And he opened the bottomless pit, and smoke arose out of the pit like the smoke of a great furnace. So, the sun and the air were darkened because of the smoke of the pit.*

This is not a star in the sense that we think of the stars in the heavens. When we think of a movie star or a star athlete this is that kind of star. This is a star angel. The one angel that God created more beautiful than all the others. And it is in the past tense. *I saw a star fallen from heaven*

> *Isaiah 14:12-15 – How you have <u>fallen</u> from heaven, <u>O star of the morning</u>, son of the dawn! You have been cut down to the earth, you who have weakened the nations! But you said in your heart, I will ascend to heaven; I will raise my throne above the <u>stars of God</u>, and I will sit on the mount of assembly in the recesses of the north. I will ascend above the heights of the clouds; I will make myself like the Most High. Nevertheless, you will be thrust down to Sheol, to the recesses of the pit.*

> *Luke 10:18 – And He (Jesus) said to them, I saw Satan fall like lightning from heaven.*

> *Revelation 9:1b – to him was given the key to the bottomless pit* - Satan was given the key to the bottomless pit by the one who had the key. This pit is often referred to in scripture as the abyss.

> *Revelation 1:18 says: I (Jesus) am He who lives, and was dead, and behold, I am alive forevermore, Amen. <u>And I have the keys of Hades and of Death.</u>*

While the demons that are the most wicked, vile, and depraved of all the fallen angels are kept in the bottomless pit (the abyss), Satan has always had access to God's presence where he constantly accuses believers such as he did in Job's day.

Picture what the world would be like if we were to open the doors of all the prisons on earth and set free the world's most vicious and violent criminals upon this earth.

Something worse than that will happen in the future when Satan is permitted to open the bottomless pit and summon to his aid the most heinous and diabolical fiends in the universe to act as his agents in bringing mankind to his knees. (But remember God is in control. God is allowing this to happen.)

> *Revelation 9:2 – And he opened the bottomless pit, and smoke arose out of the pit like the smoke of a great furnace. So, the sun and the air were darkened because of the smoke of the pit.*

When the pit is opened smoke rises out of the pit like the smoke of a great furnace so that the sun is darkened all over the world as this smoke moves around the entire circumference of the earth.

> *Revelation 9:3a, 7-12 – Then out of the smoke locusts came upon the earth. The shape of the locusts was like horses prepared for battle. On their heads were crowns of something like gold, and their faces were like the faces of men. They had hair like women's hair, and their teeth were like lion's teeth. And they had breast-plates like breastplates of iron, and the sound of their wings was like the sound of chariots with many horses running into battle. They had tails like scorpions, and there were stings in their tails. Their power was to hurt men five months. And they had as king over them the angel of the bottomless pit, whose name in Hebrew is Abaddon, but in Greek he has the name Apollyon. One woe is past. Behold, still two more woes are coming after these things.*

Now remember that these demons have been in the bottomless pit ever since the first rebellion in heaven when Satan was kicked out. Many Bible scholars believe that these demons (fallen angels) were those who tried to co-habitat with women to produce giants upon the earth as recorded in the book of Genesis chapter 6. They were wicked, vile, and despicable and God put them into a bottomless pit.

WHAT IS THE PURPOSE OF THESE DEMONS RELEASED UPON THE EARTH?

> *Revelation 9:3 – Then out of the smoke locusts came upon the earth. And to them was given power, as the scorpions of the earth have power.*

These were not ordinary locusts that can wreak havoc on crops. They covered the earth <u>like locusts,</u> but they were very different. They were eerie.

> *Revelation 9:7-11 – The shape of the locusts was like horses prepared for battle. On their heads were crowns of something like gold, and their faces were like the faces of men. They had hair like women's hair, and their teeth were like lion's teeth. And they had breastplates like breastplates of iron, and the sound of their wings was like the sound of chariots with many horses running into battle. They had tails like scorpions, and there were stings in their tails. Their power was to hurt men five months. And they had as king over them the angel of the bottomless pit, whose name in Hebrew is Abaddon, but in Greek he has the name Apollyon.*

The Hebrew word Abaddon and the Greek term Apollyon both signify "destruction." However, this should not be understood as annihilation. The word means "to lose," and is a preposition indicating movement away. The idea is that the destruction caused by Satan, and sin, is, in effect, the loss of all meaningful existence and is due to being loosed forever from God.

> *Revelation 9:4 – They were commanded not to harm the grass of the earth, or any green thing, or any tree, but only those men <u>who do not have the seal of God on their foreheads.</u>*

Prior to this, Revelation tells us that the green grass was burned up on the earth; referring to food crops. Enough time has elapsed for the green grass that was burned up to begin growing again. In God's grace He was providing for man's needs so they would not starve to death.

They were to hurt every person who did not have the seal of God on their foreheads. And who were these? The 144,000 and all other's that had placed their faith in Christ as their Savior and Lord.

> *Revelation 9:5-6 – And they were not given authority to kill them, but to torment them for five months. Their torment was like the torment of a scorpion when it strikes a man. In those days men will seek death and will not find it; they will desire to die; and death will flee from them.*

Only one species of scorpion in North America and about 20 others worldwide have venom potent enough to be dangerous to human beings. But here in the Tribulation these demons all have power to hurt human beings.

The venom of a scorpion can cause severe pain and swelling at the site of the sting. Numbness, frothing at the mouth, respiratory difficulties, muscle twitching, and convulsions result from the sting of a normal poisonous scorpion.

Who gave these demons authority to do anything? Satan you may say? Wrong! It was God who gave Satan the key to the bottomless pit. It was God who gave these demons the authority to do anything. Remember, as in the days of Job, that Satan nor his demons can do anything without the permission of God.

God did not give them authority to kill people. He did give them authority to torment people so as to roll and scream in unbearable pain for five months.

In the days when Rome ruled the world the Roman soldiers were trained to ignore pain. If they cried out in pain during battle they were considered cowards and not worthy of their position but when one of them was hit by a scorpion it is said you could hear their screams all the way back to Rome.

The pain will be so intense that they will seek death only to find that there is no escape from this agony. All attempts at suicide, whether by gunshot, poison, drowning, or leaping from tall buildings will fail. They will not be allowed to die.

All the time they are in this pain they will hear the voices of the 144,000 Evangelists and other Christians pleading with them and telling them of God's love and grace and how to be saved, how to repent, how to receive Jesus Christ as their Lord and Savior.

What is God telling them here? **This is what HELL is like!** There is unbelievable pain and torment forever and ever in Hell and you cannot die. Never, ever! Listen to my servants, my witnesses, as they tell you how to avoid hell and be save, in Heaven, forevermore. Repent and receive the gospel before it is too late! God is showing them His mercy. He takes no pleasure in anyone going to Hell and will do whatever He can to get our attention to keep us from going there.

But the question begs to be asked; "Why couldn't they die?" In some commentaries it suggests that the reason they couldn't die was probably because Satan has the key to Hell and will not allow his followers to leave the earth scene where the battle of light and darkness is being waged. But this is terribly wrong!

The Bible is its own best commentary. When we understand the grace of God then we begin to understand what 2 Peter 3:9 means.

> *2 Peter 3:9 – The Lord is not slack concerning His promise, as some men count slackness; but is longsuffering toward us, not willing that any should perish, but that all should come to repentance.*

Satan is not in control here is Revelation 9. God is! God is giving them a taste of hell while He is trying to convince them to repent and receive Jesus Christ. It's stated in Revelation 9:20-21 that they did not repent. But the aim was that they would repent!

> *Revelation 9:20-21 – But the rest of mankind; who were not killed by these plagues, did not repent of the works of their hands, that they should not worship demons, and idols of gold, silver, brass, stone, and wood, which can neither see nor hear nor walk. And they did not*

repent of their murders or their sorceries or their sexual immorality or their thefts.

In *Genesis 18:25* the Bible says: *"Shall not the judge of all the earth do right?"*

This can be a great comfort to those of us with loved ones who have passed into eternity and we are not sure of the destination of their souls. God is a sovereign judge of righteousness, full of grace and mercy to all who call upon Him. It is His very grace that offers a "way" for all to escape the judgment of His wrath and it is by that grace that we are saved. It is grace that saves us, and it is grace in which we must stand when we go through the double grief of the death of an unsaved loved one. We must remember that we cannot make this choice for anyone else, and if they went into eternity without Christ, that is their choice in spite of the offer of grace.

WHAT IS HELL?
Hell, like heaven, is not only a state of existence, but a literal and very real place. It is a place where the unrighteous will experience the never-ending eternal wrath of God. They will endure emotional, mental and physical torment, consciously suffering from shame, regret, and contempt.

The Bible continually warns of a place called hell. There are over 162 references in the New Testament alone which warns of hell. And over 70 of these references were uttered by the Lord Jesus Christ!

Jesus Christ gives a frightening picture of hell.

> *Luke 16: 22-28 – And the rich man also died and was buried; And in hell he lifted up his eyes, being in torments, and saw Abraham far off and Lazarus in his bosom. And cried and said, father Abraham, have mercy on me, and send Lazarus, that he made dip the tip of his finger in water, and cool my tongue; for I am tormented in this flame. But Abraham said, son, remember that you in your lifetime received good things , and likewise Lazarus evil things; but now he is comforted, and you are tormented. And besides all this*

between us and you there is a great Gulf fixed; so, they which would pass from here to you cannot; neither can they pass to us, that would come from there. Then he said I pray you therefore, father, that you would send him to my father's house: for I have 5 brothers ; that he may testify to them, less they also come to this place of torment.

Hell is described as a bottomless pit.

Luke 8:31 – And they besought Him that He would not command them to go out into the bottomless pit.

Revelation 9:1 – And the fifth angel sounded, and I saw a star fall from heaven unto the earth; and to him was given the key to the bottomless pit.

Revelation 20:1-3 – And I saw an angel come down from heaven, having the key of the bottomless pit and a great chain was in his hand. And he laid hold on the dragon, that old serpent, which is the Devil, and Satan, and bound him a thousand years. And He cast him into the bottomless pit and shut him up, and set a seal upon him, that he should deceive the nations no more, till the thousand years should be fulfilled and after that he must be loosed a little season.

Hell is also described as a Lake of Fire, burning with sulfur, where the inhabitants will be tormented day and night forever and ever.

Luke 16:24 – "I am tormented in this flame!"

Matthew 13:42 – "And shall cast them into a furnace of fire; there shall be wailing and gnashing of teeth.

Matthew 25:41 – "Depart from Me, you cursed, into everlasting fire!"

Revelation 20:15 – "And whosoever was not found written in the book of life was cast into the lake of fire!"

Revelation 20:10 — And the devil that deceived them was cast into the Lake of Fire and brimstone, where the beast and the false prophet are, and shall be tormented day and night; forever and ever.

In Hell, there will be weeping and gnashing of teeth, indicating intense grief and anger.

Mark 9:48 — Where their worm dieth not and the fire is not quenched.

God takes no pleasure in the death of the wicked but desires them to turn from their wicked ways so that they can live.

Ezekiel 33:11 — Say unto them, as I live, saith the Lord God, I have no pleasure in the death of the wicked; but that the wicked turn from his way and live; turn ye, turn ye from your evil ways; for why will ye die, O house of Israel.

But God will not force us into submission. If we choose to reject Him, He has little choice but to give us what we want — to live apart from Him. Some people simply don't understand this. They view the Lake of Fire as a person being annihilated. It doesn't make sense, they say, that a person could withstand a Lake of Fire and live through it. If a human being were cast into a lake of burning lava, they would be instantly consumed. However, the lake of fire is both a physical and a spiritual realm. It is not simply a human body being cast into the Lake of Fire; it is a human body, soul and spirit. A spiritual body cannot be consumed by a physical fire. It seems from understanding Revelation 20:13 and Acts 24:15 that the unsaved are resurrected with a body prepared for eternity just as the save are. These unsaved bodies are prepared for an eternal fire.

Revelation 20:13 — The sea gave up the dead who were in it, and Death and Hades delivered up the dead who were in them. And they were judged, each one according to his works.

> *Acts 24:15 – I have hope in God, which they themselves also accept, that there will be a resurrection of the dead, both of the just and the unjust.*

Another objection of those who believe the unsaved are simply dead is that it would be unjust for God to punish unbelievers in Hell for eternity for a finite amount of sin. How could it be fair for God to punish a person, who lived a sinful life for say 70 years, for all eternity? How could a God of love do that? How could He be so unfair? The answer is this – our sin bears an eternal consequence because it is ultimately against an eternal God. When King David committed the sin of adultery and murder he stated the following:

> *Psalm 51:4 – Against Thee and Thee only have I sinned and done this evil in Thy sight. . .*

David had sinned against Bathsheba and Uriah, her husband, so why did he claim to have only sinned against God? David understood that all sin is ultimately against God. God is an eternal and infinite Being. He had no beginning and He has no end. He is the Alpha and the Omega. As a result, all sin is worthy of an eternal punishment.

An earthly example of this would be comparing attacking your neighbor and attacking the President of the United States. Yes, both are crimes, but attacking the President would result in far greater consequences. How much more does attacking a Holy and infinity God warrant a terrible consequence? And that's what we do when we sin! We attack God! God says: "I love you, follow Me" and in the face of God we say: "I don't want to have anything to do with You or your Son!"

Some annihilationist cannot see how we could possibly be happy in Heaven if we knew that some of our loved ones were suffering an eternity of torment in Hell. The truth is, there will be sadness, crying, and sorrow in Heaven. But this sadness will not last.

> *Revelation 21:1-4 – And God shall wipe away all tears from their eyes and there shall be no more death, neither sorrow, nor crying, neither shall there be any more pain for the former things are passed away.*

It is hard to understand this, but we will not remain saddened by the lack of our loved one's presence in Heaven. I'm not sure how God will accomplish this, but I believe God's word is true and I believe God will wipe away all tears with an eternal cloth. We will never sorrow or cry anymore and there will be no pain. We will no longer have the desire to cry. Miraculously, somehow, all of this pain and sorrow will be lifted from our hearts.

Your focus should not be on how you can enjoy Heaven, without all of your loved ones there, but rather how you can point your loved ones to faith in Christ so that they will be in Heaven with you. The eternal existence of Hell is the very reason why God sent Jesus Christ to pay the penalty for our sins on the cross! Being "extinguished" after death is no fate to dread, but **an eternity in Hell should scare the Hell out of us!** Jesus' death was an infinite death, paying our infinite sin debt so that we would not have to pay for our own sins, in Hell, for all eternity.

> *2 Corinthians 5:21 – For God has made Him (Jesus) to be sin for us. Jesus knew no sin before this. He did this so that we might be made righteous (in right standing) before God in Christ.*

He did this so that we would not have to go to Hell!

CHAPTER 39

WHAT IS HEAVEN LIKE?

Is Death our Enemy or our Benefactor?

> *Philippians 1:21-23 – For to me, to live is Christ and to die is gain. If I am to go on living in this body, this will mean fruitful labor for me. Yet what shall I choose? I do not know! I am torn between the two: I desire to depart and be with Christ, which is better by far . . ."*

Just what is everlasting life? Just what is it that you get? What is everlasting life like? Why did the apostle Paul say that Heaven was 'Better by Far'? Well, for one reason, he had been there and seen it himself.

> *2 Corinthians 12:2-4 – I know a man in Christ who fourteen years ago was caught up to the third heaven. Whether it was in the body or out of the body I do not know, God knows. And I know that this man was caught up to paradise. He heard inexpressible things, things that man is not permitted to tell.*

> *1 Corinthians 2:9 – Eye has not seen, nor ear heard, neither has it entered into the heart of man, the things which God has prepared for them that love Him.*

> *2 Timothy 4:6-8 – For I am now ready to be offered, and the time of my departure is at hand. I have fought a good fight, I have finished my course, I have kept the faith; Henceforth there is laid up for me a crown of righteousness, which the Lord, the righteous judge,*

*shall give me at that day; and not to me only, but unto
all them also that love his appearing.*

What are some of the benefits we will enjoy in Heaven?
1. We will enjoy eternal life in the immediate presence of God.
2. All that diminishes the quality of life on earth is banished from heaven.
3. The heights of joy we have experienced on earth are eclipsed in heaven.
4. We will be "saved to sin no more." In heaven Jesus will remove our sinful nature, completely making us new creations.
5. No more will we be subject to temptations from the world, the flesh, and the devil.
6. Knowledge is not limited in Heaven.
7. Limitations of the body do not exist in heaven. In John 20:19,26 we find Jesus walking through walls and locked doors to reach the disciples. Our bodies will be like His. We will be able to travel anywhere instantly.
8. Everything that would enrich our lives is available to us in heaven.
9. Reunion with loved ones and the formation of new relationships make heaven a wonderful place of fellowship. We will sit down and eat and touch and hug each other's necks. Jesus sat down and ate with his disciples in his resurrected body.
10. Heaven's music will far surpass earth's finest achievements.
11. There will be full satisfaction for every holy and wholesome longing and aspiration.

If you want a glimpse of what Heaven looks like, the glory and majesty of it, you only have to turn to Revelation chapters 21 and 22 and read them.

> *Revelation 21:12-21a (NAS) – It had a great and high
> wall, with twelve gates, and at the gates twelve angels;
> and names were written on them, which are the names
> of the twelve tribes of the sons of Israel. There were
> three gates on the east and three gates on the north and
> three gates on the south and three gates on the west.
> And the wall of the city had twelve foundation stones,
> and on them were the twelve names of the twelve apos-
> tles of the Lamb. The one who spoke with me had a gold*

*measuring rod to measure the city, and its gates and its
wall. The city is laid out as a square, and its length is
as great as it's width; and he measured the city with
the rod, fifteen hundred miles; its length and width and
height are equal. And he measured its wall, seventy-two
yards, according to human measurements, which
are also angelic measurements. The material of the
wall was jasper; and the city was pure gold, like clear
glass. The foundation stones of the city wall were
adorned with every kind of precious stone. The first
foundation stone was jasper; the second, sapphire;
the third, chalcedony; the fourth, emerald; the fifth,
sardonyx; the sixth sardius; the seventh, chrysolite; the
eighth, beryl; the ninth topaz, the tenth, chrysoprase;
the eleventh, jacinth; the twelfth, amethyst. And the
twelve gates were twelve pearls; each one of the gates
was a single pearl.*

We will live in this New Jerusalem (city of peace). More important than
anything is the fact that we will be with Jesus forever. From His throne
flows the River of Life. It will be perfect, clear as crystal. And we will see
Him face to face. We shall worship Him and be His people and He will be
our God. When we see Christ face to face, His presence will dominate
heaven the same way the sun dominates the hot summer sky. If heaven
had streets of gold, precious gems, and angels singing overhead but no
Jesus then we wouldn't even notice those other things. Because just as
the sun illuminates the summer sky, so the glory of Christ illuminates
all of heaven. As you read Revelation 21-22 there seems to be a sense
of excitement coming from Jesus himself. You can sense that He longs
to share heaven with us. When you get to heaven, He will smile, put His
arms around you, and say, "All this I have prepared for you because I
love you. Enjoy my fellowship!

That the city had a great high wall indicates that it is not floating in
space. It comes down and sits upon the earth. It has specific dimen-
sions. It can be entered and left through any of its twelve gates. There
are three gates each on the north, south, east and west walls. At those
gates twelve angels are stationed at all times. The gates have names
written on them which are the names of the twelve tribes of the sons
of Israel (Jacob). This signifies God's covenant relationship with Israel

for all eternity. The massive wall of the city was anchored by twelve foundation stones. On these stones were the twelve names of the twelve apostles of the Lamb. This signifies God's covenant relationship with the church for all eternity.

At the top of each gate was the name of one of the tribes of Israel; at the bottom of each gate was the name of one of the apostles. This city is laid out as a square or better yet a cube. Its length, width, and height are equal in distance. It is fifteen hundred miles long, fifteen hundred miles wide, and fifteen hundred miles high. If it was placed inside the United States it would extend from the tip of Florida up the east coast to Maine, across the lower part of Canada till you are even with Denver, Colorado, then down equal with the Gulf of Mexico and back across to the tip of Florida.

The city is roughly 250 million square miles; the approximate size of the moon. Could all the people that have ever lived on the earth fit in an area this size? Today, there are approximately 7 billion people on the earth. How many billion could you put in this area and still have plenty of elbow room? It has been estimated that you could put 30 times the current population of the earth in such a space. That's 180 billion people! But will there be that many people there?

Dr. Henry Morris is a renowned scholar. He has his PHD in science and hydraulics and is head of the Institute for Creation Research in San Diego, California. In his book, 'The Revelation Record', Dr. Morris has calculated that there have been 40 billion people on earth from the time of Adam and Eve till our present day. He says that if you take that 40 billion and add another 20 billion to account for all those who have lost children prior to birth, and to abortions, and then add another 40 billion to account for all those that will be born during the future 1,000-year reign of Christ on this earth, you come up with 100 billion people that could possibly live in this city that is coming down from God.

If you assume that 20% of them are saved, that is 20 billion people who will live here. Now if you take this city and use 75% of it for the Throne of God and of the Lamb, other areas for public buildings, parks, and recreational areas and use only 25% of it for living quarters, how much room does each person get for their mansion? The answer: 75 acres on each side of the cube. Folks that is 75 acres to the east, west, north, south, and up. That's a total of 375 acres. Assuming that 40% of the people are saved, 40 billion, you would have to cut your property down to only 187.5 acres. That's 187.5 more acres than I currently have!

> *1 Corinthians 2:9 – Eye has not seen, nor ear heard, nor have entered into the heart of man the things which God has prepared for those who love Him.*

The angel then measured the thickness of this huge wall; 72 yards thick. But even though it is that thick, you can see right through it. It is transparent. The city itself was pure gold, like clear glass. The foundation stones of the city wall were adorned with every kind of precious stone. The first foundation stone was jasper, best identified as a diamond. The second was sapphire; a brilliant blue stone. The third, chalcedony; a sky-blue stone with colored stripes. The fourth, emerald; a bright green stone (the greenest of all green stones). The fifth, sardonyx; a blood red stone with white stripes. The sixth, sardius; a stone with various shades of red. The seventh, chrysolite; a transparent gold or yellow-hued stone. The eighth, beryl; a stone found in various colors, including shades of green, yellow, and blue. The ninth, topaz; a transparent yellow-greenish stone. The tenth, chrysoprase; a gold tinted green stone. The eleventh, jacinth; a blue or violet colored stone. And the twelfth, amethyst; a purple stone.

As God dwells in this city, the light from His glory will shine through these stones producing a brilliant rainbow of colors. Can you imagine such a sight? These colors will not only be seen inside the city but remember that this 72-yard thick wall is also transparent as God's glory and beauty shine in and through and around all the world.

Then, there are twelve gates which are made out of pearls. Pearls were highly prized and of great value in John's day. But these pearls are like no pearl ever produced by an oyster because each one of the gates is a single gigantic pearl nearly 1,500 miles high. All the other precious gems mentioned in the beauty of this city are metals or stones, but the pearl is a gem formed within an oyster; the only gem formed by living flesh. When an oyster gets a parasite in it, a foreign matter, or a wound that hurts it, the oyster slowly builds a protective barrier for himself around what has hurt him. This barrier becomes known as a pearl. The pearl, we might say, is the answer of the oyster to that which has injured it.

The great pearls in this heavenly city are God's answer to what has hurt Him! All the sin of mankind, that cost his Son His life on the cross, is represented in these pearls! Every time we go through those gates of pearl we will be reminded of the price that Christ paid for our entrance into the heavenly city. Thank of the size of those gates! Think of the supernatural pearls from which they are made!

What gigantic suffering is symbolized by those pearls! Those pearls will hang eternally at the access to the city, reminding us forever of the One who hung upon a cross and whose answer to those who injured Him was to invite them to share His home, all because He loves them.

> *Revelation 21:22 – But I saw no temple in it for the Lord God Almighty and the Lamb are its temple.*

We worship God in Heaven, but we do not go inside a building to worship. What a thought! Every day, when we wake up the weather is perfect, a beautiful, glorious, spring day with no hay fever, no sinus problems, no headaches, and no pain. And then we go worship God on an absolutely glorious, beautiful morning. All gathered outside to worship.

> *Revelation 21:1-3 – Now I saw a new heaven and a new earth, for the first heaven and the first earth had passed away. Also, there was no more sea. Then I, John, saw the holy city, New Jerusalem, coming down from God out of heaven, prepared as a bride adorned for her husband. And I heard a great voice out of heaven saying, Behold, the tabernacle of God is with men, and he will dwell with them, and they shall be his people, and God himself shall be with them, and be their God.*

In the end, after the 1,000-year reign of Christ on the earth, we become the host of God. God no longer host us in His heaven, but He comes to live here on earth with us. And we live with Him right here on this earth. But this earth will be so different from what it is now that we won't even recognize it as the same earth. It is a new earth! I believe there will be a lot more land than we have today, and all the land will be gathered together into one place. The ocean will still exist, but it will no longer separate us from one another. It will be absolutely magnificent in its beauty. We can't even begin to imagine! We always say that we are going to live forever with God in heaven but that's not what the Bible teaches. The Bible teaches that we are going to live forever with God here on this earth. And what will it be like? **Paradise – A Beautiful Park Area!**

The idea that we live forever with God in heaven comes from Greek mythology. The Greeks believed that everything material was evil and thus we cannot live with God on this earth because God would never live in a material world where things were evil. With this belief they said that Jesus did not come here in a physical body because everything physical and material is evil, and God is not evil, therefore, Christ was here in Spirit only and not body. But, on this new earth, there will be no evil. Sin will be banished forever. The sin nature will be banished forever.

> *Revelation 21:23 – The city had no need of the sun or of the moon to shine in it, for the glory of God illuminated it. The Lamb is its light.*

This has led some to believe that there is no sun or moon to shine on this new earth. With this thinking then I suppose there are no stars either. That's not what God's word says! Remember, God made a new heaven and a new earth. He restored the glory of the sun, the moon, the stars, and the atmosphere. The Bible says there is no need of the sun to shine on this heavenly city for the glory of God illuminates this city. The rest of the earth is still going to need the sun. What kind of earth could exist without the sun?

Remember that in God's creation, before He created the sun, light shone and illuminated the earth. In Genesis the very first thing that God created was light. *And God said: let there be light and there was light.* But God did not create the sun until the fourth day.

Throughout history, people all over the world have worshipped the sun. Ancient civilizations worshipped the sun god. Why did God wait until the fourth day to create the sun? To show people that although He created it for us, He doesn't need it. We are not to worship what God created but we are to worship the creator. We are to enjoy what God created.

> *Revelation 22:3-5 – And there shall be no more curse, but the throne of God and of the Lamb shall be in it, and His servants shall serve Him. They shall see His face, and His name shall be on their foreheads. There shall be no night there; they need no lamp nor light of the sun, for the Lord God gives them their light. And they shall reign forever and ever.*

The Bible teaches that God will rule and reign forever and that we will rule and reign with Him; we will serve Him. What will we be like?

> *1 John 3:2 – Dear friends, now we are children of God and what we will be has not yet been made known. But we know that when He appears, we shall be like Him.*
> John tells us that we will be like Jesus.

What will that be like?

1. **We will no longer sin.** *Philippians 1:6 He who has begun a good work in you will complete it until the day of Jesus Christ.* In heaven, Jesus will remove our sinful nature completely, making us new creations.

2. **We will not be subject to the laws of physics.** In John 20:19,26 we see Jesus in these verses walking through walls and locked doors to reach the disciples. Elsewhere in the Bible we read about angels that appear and disappear. We will be able to travel anywhere instantly. We will be able to go in and out of the gates of heaven and move about the earth and even through the entire universe. To Lord will give us assignments and we will go in and come out and rule and reign with Him and serve Him.

3. **We will still eat and touch.** We will be able to walk through solid objects and still be able to touch and eat like Jesus did after His resurrection. In 1 Corinthians 15:50 Paul tells us that flesh and blood cannot inherit the kingdom of heaven, so eating will be done for pleasure and not of necessity. Revelation 22:2 tells us that there will be a tree of life that bears twelve different kinds of fruit each month. Some think that there may be a feast each month when this tree blooms. There will be a time of great fellowship as we gather

around to share a meal together. What a novel idea, dinner on the ground as we sit next to this beautiful river that flows from the throne of God.

> *Revelation 22:1 – And he showed me a pure river of water of life, clear as crystal, proceeding from the throne of God and of the Lamb.*

There is a throne there. The throne of God the Father and the Lamb. Can't you see it! We all gather at the river to praise and worship God. Shall we gather at the river where bright angel feet have trod. Gather with the saints at the river that flows by the throne of God. Yes, we'll gather at the river, the beautiful, the beautiful river. Gather with the saints at the river that flows by the throne of God.

4. **God will wipe away our tears.**

> *Revelation 21:4 – And God will wipe away every tear from their eyes; there shall be no more death, nor sorrow, nor crying. There shall be no more pain, for the former things have passed away.*

God will wipe away every tear from their eyes. From whose eyes? From the redeemed; from those who are in their glorified bodies whose salvation is complete. They have undergone regeneration, justification, sanctification, and glorification.

This is personal to each and every one of us. God does not simply wave his hand and wipe away all tears, but He wipes away every tear. Don't you have the feeling that Jesus is personal to you? He is your personal Lord and Savior. Every one of us feel this personal relationship with Him. He doesn't say that we are just one of his many sheep. The Lord is My Shepherd. I shall not want! He is My Lord! Don't you feel the same way?

The indication is God comes here to personally be with us. He walks up to me, He walks up to you, and gently wipes away every tear. I will never die again, nor will I ever experience another day of sorrow. Not only does He wipe away every tear, but I will never cry again! I will never again experience a day of pain, sorrow, or depression!

5. **We will never be sick again.** Revelation 22:3 tells us there will no longer be any curse. Revelation 21:4 tells us tells us there will no longer be any death, nor mourning, nor crying, nor pain, for the old order of things has passed away.

6. **We will recognize each other.** In Matthew 17:3 Moses and Elijah appear and talk with Jesus. Peter recognizes both of them even though they both lived hundreds of years before him. In heaven we will know, not only our loved ones, but everyone else that is there. Somehow, by some miracle of God, we will just know everyone!

7. **We will have deeper relationships.** Matthew 22:30 tells us that there will be no marriage in heaven. The reason is that relationships will be much deeper than anything on earth. Relationships will be pure and free of doubt, jealousy and gossip. Some people say: "Well, I don't want to give up my spouse. I don't want to give up intimate relationships. Remember that it is God that gave us our intimate lives. He is the one who created marriage. He is the one who created sex. If we've enjoyed what God has given us here on earth, can't we believe that God has something a million times better for us in heaven; something that we will enjoy even more?

Face to face with Christ my Savior, face to face what will it be, when with rapture I behold Him, Jesus Christ who died for me. Only faintly now I see Him, with the darkling veil between. But a blessed day is coming when His glory shall be seen. What rejoicing in His presence, when are banished grief and pain, when the crooked ways are straightened, and the dark things shall be plain. Face to face O blissful moment, face to face to see and know, face to face with my Redeemer, Jesus Christ who loves me so.

HOW DO WE GET TO HEAVEN?

Is there a roadmap? Are there directions? Is there a road we must travel? Does everyone go to heaven?

Jesus said these very words: *John 14:6 I am the way, the truth, and the life: no one comes unto the Father except through me.* What do these words mean that we must go through Jesus to get into heaven? Many in this world would disagree with this statement. But these are the very words of Jesus himself.

1. The Bible says we've all sinned

   Romans 3:23 – For all have sinned and fall short of the glory of God.

2. The Bible says the wages (end result of sin) is death and separation from God for all eternity

   Romans 6:23 – The wages of sin is death, but the gift of God is eternal life.

3. The Bible says that sin must be punished. It must be dealt with. Sin cannot exist in heaven. Would heaven be heaven if you had all the sin, all the heartache, all the sickness, all the pain, all the wars, all the death that we have on earth? But God loves us so much that He does not wish to punish us for any of our sins, so, instead, He used a substitute. He punished his only begotten Son, Jesus Christ, for our sins.

   Romans 5:8 – But God demonstrates his love for us in that while we were yet sinners Christ died for us.

4. It is not enough for us to only know these three things. We must do something with the knowledge we have. We must respond in some way to this message of love.

   Romans 10: 8-10, 13 – But what does it say? The word is near you, even in your mouth and in your heart: that is, the word of faith, which we preach. That if you shall confess with your mouth that Jesus is Lord and shall believe in your heart that God has raised him from the dead, you shall be saved. For with the heart man believes unto righteousness; and with the mouth con-fession is made unto salvation. For whosoever shall call upon the name of the Lord shall be saved.

Revelation 3:20 – Behold I stand at the door and knock; if anyone hears my voice and opens the door I will come into their life.

Will you open the door of your heart to Christ? Will you ask him to come in and be your Lord and Savior? Will you repent of your sin and give your heart and life to Him? The choice of heaven belongs to each and every one of us. Christ will never knock the door down. He says that he will knock on the door of your heart and if you will graciously open your heart to him, He will gladly come into your life. But the choice is yours. I encourage you today to choose heaven, to choose life! Invite Christ into your life.

Dear Lord, Father in Heaven:

I know that I am a sinner! I've done things in my life that I shouldn't. I've thought things that are not pure and wholesome. I didn't do many of the good things that I should have done! I'm willing to turn from my sins and I ask you to please forgive me and save me. I believe that you died on the cross for my sins. I believe that you rose from the grave and are alive today! I give my heart and my life to you this day! Please come into my heart, into my life, and give me a new heart, a new life with you. If you'll receive me Jesus, today I receive you into my heart and life.

Please help me Lord to serve you all my life. In your name Jesus I pray and ask all these things.

Amen

Chapter 40

Are We Close to the End?

O ur generation has more powerful reasons for believing that Jesus can come in our lifetime than any generation before us! Even though there are several signs of the end in existence today, we cannot state categorically that Christ will come in our lifetime. However, the time for Christ to return and set up His kingdom appears to be drawing near.

The 'time of the end' refers to the days just before the beginning of the Tribulation, up to and including the Second Coming of Christ. Terms for the 'end times' are: The Latter Days / The Last Times / The Latter Years / The Time of the End.

In most cases the terms for the 'last days' or 'end times' refer to a period of 7 to 10 years or so. It cannot be pinpointed any more accurately because we are not certain how much time elapses between the Rapture (which ends the church age) and the beginning of the Tribulation (begun by the signing of the covenant between the Anti-Christ and Israel.)

The rapture will occur first, followed by the signing of the peace treaty with Israel. How much time elapses between the rapture and the tribulation is not certain but probably one to three years. The signing of the peace treaty begins the tribulation.

> *Daniel 9:20-23 – Now while I was speaking, praying and confessing my sin and the sin of my people Israel, and presenting my supplication before the Lord my God for the holy mountain of my God, yes, while I*

was speaking in prayer, the man Gabriel, whom I had seen in the vision at the beginning, being caused to fly swiftly, reached me about the time of the evening offering. And he informed me, and talked with me, and said, "O Daniel, I have now come forth to give you skill to understand. At the beginning of your supplications the command went out, and I have come to tell you, for you are greatly beloved; therefore, consider the matter, and understand the vision.

Daniel 9:27 – <u>Then he shall confirm a covenant with many for one week</u>; but in the middle of the week he shall bring an end to sacrifice and offering. And on the wing of abominations shall be one who makes desolate, even until the consummation, which is determined, is poured out on the desolate.

In this instance, one week stands for seven years; a week of years instead of a week of days.

The 'last days' or 'end times' refer to any point just prior to the rapture all the way to the Glorious appearing. *Titus 2:13 Looking for the blessed hope and <u>glorious appearing</u> of our great God and Savior Jesus Christ.* If we are in the period of time just prior to the rapture then we are living in the 'last days.' Date setters, however, are to be avoided, ignored and rebuked as false teachers.

Matthew 24:36 (Jesus speaking) – "But of that day and hour knoweth no man, no, not the angels of heaven, but my Father only."

Christ did say, however, that we could know the general time of his coming. *Matthew 24:33 (Jesus speaking) "So, likewise ye, when ye shall see all these things, know that it is near, even at the doors."* You've probably heard the expression, "This is the sign of the times." But is this the "time of the signs?"

One of the signs to look for is the Russian invasion. Ezekiel 38-39 says that Russia and her Arab allies will go down to destroy the nation of Israel but will be destroyed supernaturally by God. No one knows for sure if this invasion will happen right before or right after the rapture. If we see it happen, we can be sure that the rapture is not far behind.

TWO SIGNS BY THE PROPHET DANIEL

> *Daniel 12:4 – "But thou, O Daniel, shut up the words, and seal the book, even to the times of the end; many shall run to and fro, and knowledge shall be increased."*

Daniel was told to seal the book for now. A time would come when <u>knowledge will be increased, and people will run to and fro upon the face of the earth.</u>

In 1914 the average speed of cars and trucks was 15 to 20 mph. Today rockets and satellites average 24,000 mph. It is unbelievable how much knowledge has increased over the past 100 years. Why are knowledge and speed mentioned together? Because, with knowledge comes speed. So, our Lord was saying that when this happens, the book will be re-opened, and people will begin to understand prophecy again.

Should we take prophecy literally? Test the case in Matthew 24.

> *Matthew 24:1-2 – Then Jesus went out and departed from the temple, and His disciples came up to show Him the buildings of the temple. And Jesus said to them, "Do you not see all these things? Assuredly, I say to you, <u>not one stone shall be left here upon another, that shall not be thrown down."</u>*

Our Lord's prophecy was fulfilled in 70 A.D. The Roman army, under command of Titus, destroyed the city of Jerusalem. After fire had burned the city and the temple was destroyed, large amounts of gold had melted and flowed into the crevices of the blocks of the temple. They took the temple apart, stone by stone, to get to the gold. <u>Not one stone was left upon another.</u>

> *Matthew 24:3-8 – Now as He sat on the Mount of Olives, the disciples came to Him privately, saying, "Tell us, when will these things be? And what will be*

*the sign of Your coming, and of the end of the age?"
And Jesus answered and said to them: Take heed that
no one deceives you. For many will come in My name,
saying, I am the Christ, and will deceive many. And you
will hear of wars and rumors of wars. See that you are
not troubled; for all these things must come to pass,
but the end is not yet. For nation will rise against
nation, and kingdom against kingdom. And there will
be famines, pestilences, and earthquakes in various
places. All these are the beginning of sorrows. (The
New American Standard Bible says it like this: "But all
these things are merely the beginning of birth pangs.")*

1. **The first sign: The Sign of Deception:**
    For many will come in My name, saying, I am the Christ, and will
    deceive many. The times just before the return of our Lord will be
    filled with deception as will the times during the seven-year tribula-
    tion period. You can count on it. Jesus Christ predicted it. At least six
    times in His Olivet discourse our Lord warned His disciples against
    false teachers and deceivers.

    A well-known saying is appropriate here: "Future events cast their
    shadow before them." So, if worldwide deception will be prevalent
    during the seven-year tribulation period, you can rest assured that
    it will be on the increase just before the tribulation starts.

    *Matthew 24:4-5 – Take heed that no one deceives you
    for many will come in My name, saying, I am the Christ,
    and will deceive many.*

    *Matthew 24:11 – Then many false prophets will rise up
    and deceive many.*

    *Matthew. 24:23 – Then if anyone says to you, Look,
    here is the Christ! Or There! Do not believe it.*

    *Matthew 24:24 – For false christ's and false prophets
    will rise and show great signs and wonders to deceive,
    if possible, even the very elect.*

> *Matthew 24:26 – Therefore, if they say to you, 'Look,*
> *He is in the desert! Do not go out; or 'Look, He is in the*
> *inner rooms!' Do not believe it!*

Of course, there have always been false teachers, for that is Satan's way of distorting the truths of God. Jesus called Satan a "deceiver" and a "liar" declaring that he had been a liar from the very beginning. That is why we have so many cults, religions, and other –*isms* that claim a Christian basis, or a religious basis, for their beliefs. If Satan cannot get people to disbelieve or rebel against God altogether, he will get them to believe some false doctrine to lead them astray. There is nothing new about that. But who can deny that everywhere we look today, we find deception growing stronger and more prevalent?

Dr. M.R. DeHaan, a popular Bible teacher in the fifties and sixties, wrote: Never before in all history have there been such divisions in Christendom. There are today over 350 denominations, sects and cults in Protestantism in America alone. All of these claim that they are right and that all others are necessarily wrong. He then added, "It has been said that a new cult springs up at least once a month in the United States, and that no matter how fantastic and fanciful its teaching may be, or how wild its claims, there are always those who are willing to be deceived. And that was written over fifty years ago! Think of what he would say today with all the occult and spiritualist activities that multiply each day. In the last 50 years at least 1,100 false messiahs have come from every corner of the world in all shapes and sizes.

The apostle John, in the book of Revelation, warned several times against false teachings, false religion, and even an official false prophet who leads people astray by the millions upon millions during the Tribulation. The greatest time of deception the world will ever face is the seven-year Tribulation, when the contest between God and Satan for the souls of men will reach its greatest heights.

There are at least 6 ways to recognize a False Prophet.

1. Know your Bible

Jesus said, "The truth shall make your free" The Bible is the truth of God, so the better you know the Scriptures, the better prepared you will be to withstand false prophets.

2. Test the spirits

   1 John 4:1 – Beloved, do not believe every spirit, but test the spirits, whether they are of God; because many false prophets have gone out into the world. That is why you need to study your Bible regularly, so that you can test any new teaching by the Scriptures.

3. Seek God's guidance in your life.

   Proverbs 3:6 – In all your ways acknowledge Him, and He will direct your paths. If you are willing to be led by God, He will guide you to the truth.

4. Avoid immorality! Nothing clouds the mind like lust and sin.

   1 Corinthians 6:18 – Flee sexual immorality. Every sin that a man does is outside the body, but he who commits sexual immorality sins against his own body.

5. Share your faith with others. As you witness to others about your faith, you strengthen your own convictions.

   James 1:22 – But be doers of the word, and not hearers only, deceiving yourselves.

6. Walk in the spirit

   Ephesians 5:17-21 – [17] Therefore do not be unwise but understand what the will of the Lord is. And do not be drunk with wine, in which is dissipation; but be filled with the Spirit, speaking to one another in psalms and hymns and spiritual songs, singing and making melody in your heart to the Lord, giving thanks always for all things, to God the Father, in the name of our Lord Jesus Christ, submitting to one another in the fear of God.

As the Holy Spirit fills and uses your life, He will make you sensitive to both truth and error. Remember this, false teachers are endowed with a natural charisma, which at first makes them seem tremendously spiritual and insightful. But by following the steps just mentioned, the Holy Spirit within you will witness to your spirit about whether a teacher is dispensing truth or error. Since God authored the Bible, He will never inspire His true prophets to teach anything contrary to His written word.

2. The second sign. The sign of wars and rumors of wars.

> *Matthew 24:6-7a – You will hear of wars and rumors of wars. See that you are not troubled; for all these things must come to pass, but the end is not yet. <u>For nation will rise against nation</u>, and <u>kingdom against kingdom.</u>*

Did you know that there have been approximately fifteen thousand wars in recorded human history? The twentieth century has been far bloodier than any century before it. As a matter of fact, more people have died in wars during the past hundred years than in all the centuries before it. A military strategist said that we now have the ability to annihilate the earth with weapons of war 17 times.

World War I was supposed to be the war to end all wars and then came World War II followed by the Korean war, the Vietnam war, the Gulf war, the Iraqi war, and the Afghanistan war just to name a few. In the last 100 years there have been 389 major military conflicts and now the war against terrorism. The world is not through with war! World War III is coming and will commence shortly after the tribulation begins.

How did Jesus say that we are to respond to these wars and rumors of wars? <u>He said: "See that you are not troubled."</u> And why shouldn't we be troubled? All these things must come to pass, but the end is not yet. Obviously, wars are not "the sign" of the end! The fact is; however, Christ did inject the subject of war into His answer to His disciple's question "What will be the sign of Your coming, and of the end of the age?" This can only mean that "the sign" had to be a special kind of war.

Matthew 24:7 – "For nation will rise against nation, and kingdom against kingdom. And there will be famines, pestilences, and earthquakes in various places. All these are the beginning of sorrows.

In these verses Jesus used two Hebrew idioms that His Jewish friends would have recognized. The first, based on 2 Chronicles 15:1-7 and Isaiah 19:1-2, is *"nation will rise against nation, and kingdom against kingdom."* He was speaking of a war started by two nations. Each nation would soon be joined by the surrounding kingdoms until all the nations involved in the prophet's vision are included.

In Matthew 24 Jesus has the world in mind. He is saying, *"When you see a war started by two single nations that is soon joined by the kingdoms of the world, followed by unprecedented famines, pestilence, and multiple earthquakes at the same time, you have the sign!*

That is exactly what occurred in June 1914 when the Archduke of Austria, Prince Francis Ferdinand, was shot by a Serbian zealot. Serbia is the land of Eastern Yugoslavia. Croatia is the land of western Yugoslavia and even today U.N. forces are stationed there to keep peace between the two. One month later Austria declared war on Serbia, followed shortly by the other kingdoms of the world, until all but seven nations officially joined the conflict (and even the seven "neutral" countries sent mercenaries).

The war, World War I, involved more men in uniform (estimates total 53 million, 13 million of whom were killed) than all the troops in all the wars before it. If this was all that happened between 1914-1918 it would not be sufficient to fulfill all of Jesus prophecy. In the war Jesus referred to, He said that war would be followed by famines and pestilences.

In 1918 a flu epidemic spread throughout Europe, Canada, and the United States and took more lives than were lost on the battlefields. Much of the disease was caused by malnutrition and famine as a result of the war. In fact, because of this acute lack of food due to the First World War, farmers were exempted from military service in World War II.

So, you had the special kind of war, followed by famine which caused pestilence. Pestilence means any contagious or infectious disease that is fatal or very harmful, especially an epidemic of such disease. Today half the world goes to bed hungry every night and there are pestilences of unprecedented proportions all over the world.

Jesus also said that after this special kind of war, multiple earthquakes would begin happening in enormous proportions all over the world. The only known multiple earthquakes have been recorded since World War I. In the 14th century there were 137 earthquakes, 15th century 174, 16th century 253, 17th century 381, 18th century 640, 19th century 2,119, and in the 20th century there were over 5,000 earthquakes.

On May 31, 1935 the most devastating earthquake in all history was recorded at the time in west Pakistan. That record has been broken many times since then. Major earthquakes have occurred since World War I in such various places as Kansu Province, China, Tokyo, Japan, Persia, India, Peru, Taiwan, Southern California and many other places as well. The only known multiple earthquakes in history have been recorded since World War I. During the Turkish earthquakes, similar reports came in from Africa, South America, South Carolina, and Southern California. During a prolonged quake in Helena, Montana, there were similar reports coming in from New York and Honduras.

In 2004 alone more than 300,000 people were killed in earthquakes, 87,000 of those alone were killed in Pakistan. And over 100,000 were killed in earthquakes that caused great tsunamis. The 7.0 magnitude earthquake that struck the nation of Haiti on January 12, 2010 killed hundreds of thousands of people and left an estimated 1 million with nowhere to live. It may surprise you to know that at 7.0, that quake doesn't make the list of the 10 largest earthquakes of the past century. Then there was the devastating earthquake on March 11, 2011 in Japan that killed thousands and devastated coastal communities in northeastern Japan even leaving the nuclear power plants in jeopardy of exploding.

One seismologist at the Scripps Research Center in La Jolla, California, said, "It is almost as though the earth's plates are gyrating in anticipation of the world's greatest earthquake. In the book of Revelation, the Lord tells us that the greatest earthquakes to ever hit this planet will occur during the tribulation. Whether the La Jolla seismologist was describing the earthquake in Revelation 6, 11, or 16, is yet to be determined.

> *Revelation 6:12-17 – I looked when He opened the sixth seal, and behold, there was a <u>great earthquake</u>; and the sun became black as sackcloth of hair, and the moon became like blood. And the stars of heaven fell to the earth, as a fig tree drops its late figs when it is shaken by a mighty wind. Then the sky receded as a scroll when it is rolled up, and every mountain and island was moved out of its place. And the kings of the earth, the great men, the rich men, the commanders, the mighty men, every slave and every free man, hid themselves in the caves and in the rocks of the mountains, and said to the mountains and rocks, "Fall on us and hide us from the face of Him who sits on the throne and from the wrath of the Lamb! For the great day of His wrath has come, and who is able to stand?"*

> *Revelation 16:17-21 – Then the seventh angel poured out his bowl into the air, and a loud voice came out of the temple of heaven, from the throne, saying, "It is done!"* [18] *And there were noises and thundering's and lightnings; <u>and there was a great earthquake, such a mighty and great earthquake as had not occurred since men were on the earth.</u> Now the great city was divided into three parts, and the cities of the nations fell. And great Babylon was remembered before God, to give her the cup of the wine of the fierceness of His wrath. Then every island fled away, and the mountains were not found. And great hail from heaven fell upon men, each hailstone about the weight of a talent. Men blasphemed*

God because of the plague of the hail, since that plague was exceedingly great.

When all four parts of this "sign" are considered together, I believe it is reasonable to conclude that this earth has already witnessed the beginning of the end. The closer we get to the coming of Christ, the more of an increase we will see in earthquakes. On September 11, 2001 while the Twin Towers were being attacked, an earthquake was occurring in California. Since that time there have been numerous earthquakes around the world. If you'll look at the weather section of any major newspaper you will notice that there is hardly a day that goes by that there is not an earthquake someplace on earth.

The mistake many people make in rejecting World War I and its subsequent events as the fulfillment of 'the sign', mentioned in Matthew 24:3, is they claim that another war, World War II, came just 22 years later. Jesus, however, did not say the first sign would user in the end. He said the four parts of the one sign are the beginning of sorrows.

> *Matthew 24:8 – All these are the beginning of sorrows. (The New American Standard Bible says it like this: "But all these things are merely the beginning of birth pangs."*

The term, 'beginning of sorrows or birth pangs', was used by four of the Hebrew prophets to describe a woman in labor and the pain Israel will endure at the end of the age. A woman's first birth pain does not mean her baby will be born immediately. In fact, she may have thirty, forty, or fifty birth pains, some of which are days apart before giving birth.

World War I did not signal that we should look for the immediate coming of Christ or 'the end of the age.' It signaled that we should look for more birth pains. Many other signs or birth pains have arisen during the last 100 years since that 'Great War.' Today the 'birth pains' are very intense and may even be in the last phase. If so, 'the end' may be rapidly approaching. In fact, it may be as Jesus said: "Near, even at the doors" (Matthew 24:33).

3. Israel, once again, becomes a nation

Has it ever seemed strange to you that almost every night on the evening news the eyes of the world focus on a little country of five million people in the Middle East, Israel? Only recently has China, a nation of 1.2 billion people, gained recognition on the international news airwaves. Seldom does Mexico City, one of the largest population centers in the world, draw international attention. Singapore is similarly out of the news, despite the fact that if you drew a 2,000-mile circle around the island, you would encompass 50 percent of the world's population.

Why do these enormous centers of world population regularly stay out of the news when hardly a week goes by when we don't see Israel and Jerusalem in the headlines? It is not really a beautiful place. It's crowded, smelly, and extremely noisy. It has been built and destroyed and rebuilt more than any other city. It is not famous for any great river that flows through it. It does not have a harbor to connect it to the great shipping routes of the world. It is many miles from any airport. At one point it is only nine miles wide. It is not the headquarters of any world government body. It is not the headquarters of any world banking institution. Yet it remains at the center of world attention.

This fascination with Israel is not accidental. It was predicted long ago, and many ancient prophecies are unfolding before our eyes. Dr. John Wolvoord, the dean of all living prophecy experts, says the prophecies about Jerusalem make it clear that the Holy City will be in the center of world events in the end time. The conflict between Israel and the Palestinian Arabs will focus more and more attention on Jerusalem. In all of these situations, Jerusalem is the city to watch as the city of Prophetic destiny prepares to act out her final role. It seems that the stage and the actors are ready for the final drama, in which Jerusalem will be the key.

The regathering of five million Jews back to the Holy Land and their becoming a nation in our generation is the infallible sign of the approach of the end times. It is a miracle today that the Jews exist at all! They were driven out of Israel by the Romans in 135 A.D. The Roman government even issued a decree that any Jews found in Palestine could be killed on sight. They were scattered throughout eastern Europe, Spain, and eventually America. Why have they survived when the mighty Hittites,

Assyrians and Babylonians have vanished from the face of the earth? They have survived because of God's promise!

It is almost impossible to exaggerate the importance of our Lord's Olivet discourse found in Matthew 24. It's not only the most important prophecy of future events, but it provides an outline of the future to which you can relate to the book of Revelation. It is like a clothesline from which you can hang all of prophecy. And it was given to us not by one of God's prophets but by the Lord Jesus Christ Himself.

In Matthew 24:5-28 you see what's happening in Revelation chapter 6 – 19. The entire tribulation period is located here. But before that period begins, Jesus gives us some signs to look for. In Matthew 24:32-35 Jesus gives His disciples the main SIGN to look for before the tribulation begins, and in the following verses of this chapter I believe Jesus speaks of the rapture of the church before the tribulation and exhorts us to be doing God's work when the rapture takes place.

> *Matthew 24:32-33 – Now learn this parable from the fig tree: When its branch has already become tender and puts forth leaves, you know that summer is near. So, you also, when you see all these things, know that it is near – even at the doors!*

Do you think Jesus was giving His disciples a lesson in agriculture here? Do you think, that they thought, that He was talking about a literal fig tree? Most conservative scholars believe that Jesus was telling them: <u>When Israel once again becomes a nation that is the major sign that you are looking for.</u>

Remember that Jesus was talking to Hebrew men. Men that were raised with the teaching of the Old Testament and they would understand that Jesus was referring to Israel when He spoke of the fig tree, for many times in the Old Testament God referred to Israel as His fig tree.

> *Joel 1:7 – He has laid waste My vine and ruined My fig tree.*

> *Hosea 9:10 – I found Israel like grapes in the wilderness; I saw your fathers as the first fruits on the fig tree.*

But you might say, when Jesus said this to them; Israel was a nation. Sure, they were under the occupation of Rome, and were still allowed to exist and function under their Mosaic and Levitical laws, but they were not a free and independent nation. As a matter of fact, Herod was in the process of rebuilding Solomon's Temple and it was more gorgeous than it was during the days of Solomon. It was said that when the sun came up in the morning you had to turn your head from the Temple because of the blinding light that emanated from the beautiful limestone structure on the Temple. But this would all change rather quickly.

> *Matthew 24:1-3 – Then Jesus went out and departed from the temple, and His disciples came up to show Him the buildings of the temple. And Jesus said to them, "Do you not see all these things? Assuredly, I say to you, not one stone shall be left here upon another, that shall not be thrown down." Now as He sat on the Mount of Olives, the disciples came to Him privately, saying, tell us, when will these things be? And what will be the sign of Your coming, and of the end of the age?*

Now Mark 13 tells us that the disciples who came to Jesus privately and asked these three questions where Peter, Andrew, James and John. And we are forever indebted to these four men for asking the questions because Jesus gives us the outline for the future with His answer.

Now, I believe, unbeknownst to these disciples, they had asked the questions in the correct order. They may have thought they were asking one question, but Jesus gives them the answer to all three.
1. When will the temple be destroyed?
2. What will be the sign of the rapture?
3. What will be the sign of the 1,000 years (millennial) reign of your kingdoms beginning?

Now listen to their question.
1. In response to Jesus telling them the Temple would be destroyed: "When will these things be (the Temple being destroyed?)
2. What will be the sign of Your coming (Rapture?)
3. What will be the sign of the end of the age? (Millennial reign of Christ on earth?)

Now there have been, over the centuries, 1,000 of books written and years of sermons preached on this subject. There are 1,845 verses in the Old Testament concerning Christ second coming. There are 318 verses in the New Testament. One out of every 30 verses in the New Testament speak of Christ second coming and for every verse that speaks of Christ first coming there are 8 verses that speak of His second coming. Now we may not take it that serious that Jesus is coming again but He is coming! And when He comes it will be quickly. In the twinkling of an eye we, the saved born-again followers of Christ, shall all see him.

JESUS ANSWERS THEIR QUESTIONS

1. **When will the temple be destroyed?**

    Matthew 24:2 – "Do you not see all these things? Assuredly, I say to you, not one stone shall be left here upon another, that shall not be thrown down."

About 40 years after Jesus left this earth, this prophecy came true. When the Jews revolted in the year 66 A.D., the Romans, under the command of Titus, came into Jerusalem in the year A.D. 70 A.D. and completely destroyed the Jewish temple and the city of Jerusalem. Fires raged throughout the city and in the temple area itself. After the flames burned themselves out, the soldiers saw that large amounts of gold had melted and flowed into the crevices of the blocks of the temple. In order to recover the precious metal, the Romans had to take the buildings apart, stone by stone.

And so, Jesus' prophecy was literally fulfilled; not one stone was left upon another. Some of those stones were later used to erect the wall we see standing today near the edge of the temple mount. Every time you see pictures of the Wailing Wall in Jerusalem, you see the pinpoint accuracy of Jesus' prediction. You can see the wall today at www.thewall.org. And that gives us a big hint about how to interpret the rest of Jesus Olivet discourse; Literally!

2. **The last Jewish stronghold.**
    In A.D. 90, in the fortress built by Herod the Great called Masada, there were 137 Jewish Zealots (rebels) that held off the Roman army for over a year. But finally, the Romans took the Jewish captives,

those that they already had, and made them build ramps that you can still see to this day up to the walls of Masada. The night before the Romans began to scale the walls of Masada these Jews wrote out their decision. It is recorded history, you can read it even today. "We will rather die in dignity than be taken as slaves and watch our wives be raped and our children taken off and separated from us". This is what they wrote. So here is what they did.

There were 10 men that were chosen, and these 10 men drew straws. Now all the men got their wives and their children together with them in family groups. The families all laid down on their backs side by side in family groups. The men then proceeded to kill their wives and their children. Then every man laid down beside their dead wives and their children and these ten men went around to all the men and killed every man lying down by his wife. Then these ten men laid down beside their wives and the man who had drawn the short straw went around and took the lives of the other nine men. Then he laid down beside his wife and took his own life.

3. **Israel's last stand.**
   The Bar Kokhba revolt, led by a man named Shimon Bar Kokhba, between 132 and 135 A.D. was also suppressed, Jericho and Bethlehem were destroyed, and the Jews were barred from Jerusalem. The Roman Emperor Hadrian was determined to wipe out the identity of Israel-Judah-Judea. Therefore, he took the name Palastina and imposed it on all the Land of Israel. In the year A.D. 135, Israel was finally driven out of the land God had originally promised to Abraham. After the rebellion of Bar Kokhba – the Roman government even issued a decree that any Jews found in Palastina could be killed on sight. They renamed the city of Jerusalem Aelia Capitolina and a decree was made that no one would ever again mention the word Jerusalem, or their life would be taken. The Romans killed 10,000 of thousands of Jewish people during this time and sold many more into slavery. Those that survived were scattered throughout Eastern Europe, Spain, the Americas and to the uttermost parts of the earth. For the next nineteen hundred years the Jews ceased to be a nation. They had been tortured, raped, murdered, put into slavery and were scattered all over the face of the earth. They were, as a nation, no more!

4. Can the Bones Live Again?

In the Old Testament God showed the prophet Ezekiel the bones of the Hebrew nation and asked him if they could live. The godly prophet could only reply, O Lord God, only You know."

> *Ezekiel 37:1-11, 21-23 – The hand of the Lord came upon me and brought me out in the Spirit of the Lord and set me down in the midst of the valley; and it was full of bones. Then He caused me to pass by them all around, and behold, there were very many in the open valley; and indeed, they were very dry. And He said to me, Son of man, can these bones live? So, I answered, O Lord God, You know. Again, He said to me, Prophesy to these bones, and say to them, O dry bones, hear the word of the Lord! Thus, says the Lord God to these bones: Surely, I will cause breath to enter into you, and you shall live. I will put sinews on you and bring flesh upon you, cover you with skin and put breath in you; and you shall live. Then you shall know that I am the Lord. So, I prophesied as I was commanded; and as I prophesied, there was a noise, and suddenly a rattling; and the bones came together, bone to bone. Indeed, as I looked, the sinews and the flesh came upon them, and the skin covered them over; but there was no breath in them. Also, He said to me, Prophesy to the breath, prophesy, son of man, and say to the breath, thus says the Lord God: "Come from the four winds, O breath, and breathe on these slain, that they may live." So, I prophesied as He commanded me, and breath came into them, and they lived, and stood upon their feet, an exceedingly great army. Then He said to me, Son of man, these bones are the whole house of Israel. They indeed say, our bones are dry, our hope is lost, and we ourselves are cut off!*
>
> *Then say to them: Thus, says the Lord God: Surely, I will take the children of Israel from among the nations, wherever they have gone, and will gather them from every side and bring them into their own land. And I will make them one nation in the land, on the mountains*

of Israel; and one king shall be king over them all; they shall no longer be two nations, nor shall they ever be divided into two kingdoms again. They shall not defile themselves anymore with their idols, nor with their detestable things, nor with any of their transgressions; but I will deliver them from all their dwelling places in which they have sinned and will cleanse them. Then they shall be My people, and I will be their God.

5. **What is the main sign, the main event, that tells us when the end times are getting near?**

   Matthew 24:32-35 – Now learn this parable from the fig tree: When its branch has already become tender and puts forth leaves, you know that summer is near. So, you also, when you see all these things, know that it is near-at the doors! Assuredly, I say to you, this generation will by no means pass away till all these things take place. Heaven and earth will pass away, but My words will by no means pass away.

So, you also, when you see all these things, know that it is near, even at the doors! A question, of *Matthew 24:34*, always arises as to what Jesus meant when He *said, "this generation will by no means pass away till all these things take place".*

When Jesus made the prediction, in Matthew 24:1-2 of the temple being destroyed, there were still people alive at that time that did live to see the temple destroyed so part of His prophecy referred to the generation of people that were living at that time. But in a greater sense, all the future predictions that Jesus mentioned in Matthew 24 certainly did not come true during that generations lifetime. So, what exactly is a generation and what did Jesus mean.

In keeping with the context of Matthew 24:32-35, a common sense of Jesus meaning would mean that the Jewish people would still exist at His second coming or when they once again became a nation.

> *Genesis 15:12-16 – Now when the sun was going down, a deep sleep fell upon Abram; and behold, horror and great darkness fell upon him. Then He said to Abram: "Know certainly that your descendants will be strangers in a land that is not theirs, and will serve them, and they will afflict them <u>four hundred years</u>. And also, the nation whom they serve I will judge; afterward they shall come out with great possessions. Now as for you, you shall go to your fathers in peace; you shall be buried at a good old age. But in the <u>fourth generation</u> they shall return here, for the iniquity of the Amorites is not yet complete.*

God said to Abraham that after 400 years He would deliver Israel, . . .*in the fourth generation.* . . A generation in the Bible is normally 40 years. However, here a generation is 100 years (4 x 100 = 400). Both 100 years and 40 years are a generation in the Bible. However, the average of these two, 70 years, is on occasion also found in the Bible as well as 80 years.

> *Psalm 90:10a – The days of our lives are seventy years; and if by reason of strength they are eighty years. . .*

A generation can also be understood as the age of a man when his first child is born but in Abraham's case he was 100 years when his first child was born. There has been much discussion over the years as to the meaning of Matthew 24:34 *(this generation will by no means pass away till all these things take place)*. However, if Jesus was talking about the generation of people that would be alive after Israel once again became a nation then we could be getting very close to the return of Christ.

That could mean either of the following dates.
1948 plus 40 = 1988 (and we know he didn't return at that time)
1948 plus 70 = 2018
1948 plus 80 = 2028
1948 plus 100 = 2048

These are all speculations. But remember that it could simply mean that the Jewish people would still be around when He returns.

Matthew 24:36 – But of that day and hour no one knows, not even the angels of heaven, but My Father only. However, there is a certain surety of it happening!

Matthew 24:35 – Heaven and earth will pass away, but My words will by no means pass away.

Jesus, in essence, was saying: Heaven and earth would pass away before the truth of my words would ever pass away.

Do you know him today? Do not turn him away, Jesus, oh Jesus, without Him how lost I would be.

Believe on the Lord Jesus Christ with all your heart, mind, and soul and you will be saved.

LIFE LESSONS FROM THE BOOK OF JAMES

C ount it all joy when you fall into various trials. Trials produce patience which we all need more of.

Ask in faith. If you don't ask in faith then don't expect to get what you asked for.

When we are tempted to do wrong, that temptation comes from our own lust. When you follow through with your lust it becomes sin which brings death.

Don't err from doing right.

Be swift to hear, slow to speak, slow to anger. Listen closely when people are speaking to you. Don't let your mind wander. In doing so, you show others that you care about their needs.

Give careful thought in what to say before you speak. Don't explode. Count to 10 or maybe 100.

Don't just listen to the Bible, the preacher, the Bible teacher. Be doers of the word of God and not just hearers. If you don't put into practice what the word of God says, you are just deceiving yourself. You are not accomplishing anything towards self-improvement or Godly causes.

We must take care of those who are in need.

Love your neighbor as yourself. Go out of your way to do something good for your neighbor.

Don't consider some people more important than others. Remember, God loves everyone and died for everyone.

Faith without works is not faith at all. Get to work! Do the work of God! Yes, it takes time out of your life. You have to visit others, disciple others, take food to others, share Christ with others and this takes a commitment on your part.

Just believing there is a God will not get you into heaven. Even Satan believes this.

We are saved by the grace of God through faith. However, if we really have faith it will be followed by obeying the word of God. This proves that we have faith.

If you are a Bible teacher, take it very seriously. God will hold you accountable.

Be careful what you say. Your tongue can do great things, or it can destroy many things. What you say can build someone up or tear someone down. God will hold you accountable.

When there is envy and strife going on then there is confusion and evil work going on.

Where do wars come from? They come from your own lusts! You always want more and more. Some people don't even mind killing to get what they want.

Many times, when we ask God for something, we don't get it. At times we don't ask in faith. At other times we ask with wrong motives. Consider the will of God before you ask. You have got to take a stand for right and for God. If you try to straddle the fence and be part of the sin that is around you and love God at the same time, it won't work. Either take a stand for God or you are God's enemy.

Submit yourself to God's will for your life. Draw near to God and He will draw near to you. Resist the devil and he will leave you alone.

Don't be double minded. Stop being hands on involved with sin. Change your heart. Change your attitude. Take a stand for God.

Don't speak evil about each other in the church or behind each other's backs. We are here to love, pray for, and care about each other.

Don't boast about what you are going to do or accomplish in life. Yes, make plans. But always consider God's will in your life and your business.

There is a sin of omission. When we know we ought to do a good thing and we don't do it, then that is sin.

If you are an employer then you are commanded to treat your employees fairly and with respect. You should create an atmosphere where people enjoy coming to work.

Be patient. The Lord Jesus Christ is coming back again. Everything in the Bible is true. Be confident in the Lord and in His teachings.

Don't swear. Don't even say I promise by heaven or on a stack of Bibles, etc. Just say yes or no and be truthful in all you do.

If you are sick; pray. If you are happy; hum or sing praise songs in your heart.

If you are sick you can call the preacher or other leaders of the church. They will come put olive oil on you and pray for you; if you want them to. By doing this it has the effect of strengthening your faith and it is the faith heals the sick.

If we've messed up then we need to confess our faults to each other and ask for forgiveness. Then we can pray together and for each other and our fellowship will be healed. Don't let things fester.

James closes with a two-fold message:

1. If a Christian has messed up by getting away from God's word and His teaching, then, as God leads you, you should go to that person and get him or her back on the right track. By doing this you may

be saving the persons life and God will forgive a multitude of your sins also.

2. If someone is not saved then you should go and share Christ's salvation plan with them. When they receive Christ, you have taken part in saving that soul from eternal separation from God. God does the saving but isn't it great that we get to take part in it. God even says He will hide a multitude of your own personal sins if you will share Christ with others.

These are some of the highlights of the book of James. Study it again for yourself. Find verses that are particularly meaningful to you and memorize them. Above all else, be doers of the word and work of God and not hearers only.

God bless you all,
Ray

CPSIA information can be obtained
at www.ICGtesting.com
Printed in the USA
FFHW010207220619
53139590-58787FF